This book is about the spiritual power
that you can bring into
bar and bat mitzvah

This book was read by

D1117964

_____

Name of parents, grandparents, child, relatives, friend

To prepare for the bar/bat mitzvah ceremony of

_____

Child's name

_____

Date

_____

Torah portion

_____

Name of synagogue and community

This book was a gift from

_____

Putting God on the Guest List is written for:

- Parents of young people who are about to become bar or bat mitzvah, who are looking for inspiration and meaning in their upcoming *simcha.*

- A young man or woman who is preparing to become bar or bat mitzvah, who wants to find some deeper meaning beyond learning Torah and *haftarah.*

- Grandparents of young people who are about to become bar or bat mitzvah, who want to reclaim that ceremony's sense of holy purpose or reacquaint themselves with the customs and meanings of these sacred moments.

- An adult who is becoming an adult bar or bat mitzvah—to see how these meanings might become reflected in his or her own life.

- Professionals and lay leaders in the Jewish community—rabbis, cantors, educators, tutors, and synagogue leaders—who want to reinvigorate bar/bat mitzvah within their own synagogues.

- Non-Jewish friends and family members, who will be attending a bar or bat mitzvah ceremony and want to understand its historical and theological meaning.

Other Jewish Lights Books by Jeffrey K. Salkin

The Modern Men's Torah Commentary
New Insights from Jewish Men on the 54 Weekly Torah Portions
(Edited by Jeffrey K. Salkin)

Text Messages
A Torah Commentary for Teens
(Edited by Jeffrey K. Salkin; available Spring 2012)

A Dream of Zion
American Jews Reflect on Why Israel Matters to Them
(Edited by Jeffrey K. Salkin)

For Kids—Putting God on Your Guest List, **2nd Ed.**
How to Claim the Spiritual Meaning of
Your Bar or Bat Mitzvah

The Bar/Bat Mitzvah Memory Book, **2nd Ed.**
An Album for Treasuring the Spiritual Celebration
(with Nina Salkin)

Being God's Partner
How to Find the Hidden Link
Between Spirituality and Your Work

Putting God on the Guest List

3rd Edition
Revised
Updated
Expanded

How to Reclaim the Spiritual Meaning of Your Child's Bar or Bat Mitzvah

~~~~~~

Rabbi Jeffrey K. Salkin

Foreword by Rabbi Sandy Eisenberg Sasso
Introduction by Rabbi William H. Lebeau

JEWISH LIGHTS Publishing
Woodstock, Vermont

Putting God on the Guest List, 3rd Edition:
How to Reclaim the Spiritual Meaning of Your Child's Bar or Bat Mitzvah

2012 Third Edition, Quality Paperback, Fourth Printing

The Library of Congress has catalogued the second edition as follows:
Salkin, Jeffrey K., 1954–
Putting God on the guest list : how to reclaim the spiritual meaning of your child's bar or bat mitzvah / Jeffrey K. Salkin ; new foreword by Sandy Eisenberg Sasso ; new introduction by William H. Lebeau. — Expanded, updated, rev.
        p.   cm.
Includes bibliographical references
ISBN-13: 978-1-879045-58-3 (hardcover)
ISBN-10: 1-879045-58-3 (hardcover)
ISBN-13: 978-1-879045-59-0 (quality pbk.)
ISBN-10: 1-879045-59-1 (quality pbk.)
1. Bar mitzvah—Handbooks, manuals, etc. 2. Bat mitzvah—Handbooks, manuals, etc. 3. Jewish way of life—Handbooks, manuals, etc. 4. Jewish youth—Religious life—Handbooks, manuals, etc. 5. Commandments (Judaism)—Handbooks, manuals, etc.
I. Title
BM707.2.S25   1996
296.4'424—dc20   96-27836

Third Edition
ISBN-13: 978-1-58023-260-9 (hardcover)
ISBN-10: 1-58023-260-4 (hardcover)

ISBN-13: 978-1-58023-222-7 (quality pbk.)
ISBN-10: 1-58023-222-1 (quality pbk.)

Third Edition
10 9 8 7 6 5 4

Manufactured in the United States of America

Cover art: Robert Lipnick

Published by Jewish Lights Publishing
A Division of LongHill Partners, Inc.
Sunset Farm Offices, Route 4, P.O. Box 237
Woodstock, VT 05091
Tel: (802) 457-4000   Fax: (802) 457-4004
www.jewishlights.com

To our children—
Sam, Rachel, Alex and Gabe

Contents

Contents

Acknowledgments

This third edition of *Putting God on the Guest List* represents ongoing conversations that I have had over the past decade regarding the American Jewish institution of bar and bat mitzvah, the most popular ceremony in American Judaism. It is also the least understood, the most distorted, and the most sanctifiable. I have often said that if American Jews could just get bar/bat mitzvah "right," this act—and this act alone—could redeem our community. I remain hopeful that we may, indeed, be successful.

Over the past thirteen years, I have visited countless communities, both in the United States and abroad, and have spoken about the spiritual potential that is present in bar and bat mitzvah. In each community that I visited, I have been inspired by the stories of both adults and children who have tried to make bar/bat mitzvah more meaningful and more passionate. I am grateful to all of them for what they have shared with me. I continue to be in awe of the rabbis, cantors, and Jewish educators who truly labor in the "trenches" of American Jewish life—often not in ideal conditions—and yet remain stubbornly committed to excellence in Jewish education. Many of them are doing amazing things with bar/bat mitzvah education; they are the genuine heroes of American Judaism.

As to this book itself: Joel Hoffman of Hebrew Union College–Jewish Institute of Religion (New York) made both the Hebrew texts and his copyrighted translations of the prayers available, with the exception of "Avodah," which is my own translation.

My publisher, Stuart M. Matlins of Jewish Lights Publishing, has helped guide and sustain this project, adding innumerable comments and suggestions, always thinking creatively and lovingly. I have grown immeasurably through my partnership with him.

Finally, to the One God Who sustains us and teaches us, and to Whom our prayers must ultimately turn. You have blessed me with strength and with purpose. You have kept my spirits alive, even in the midst of frustrations and struggle. To You, Eternal One, I am grateful.

Foreword

Most of bar and bat mitzvah preparation focuses on synagogue skills, Hebrew language, and chanting, while most parents of b'nai mitzvah focus on party planning, invitations, and guest lists. Adults worry about whether they can afford their friends, and youngsters worry about whether they can get through the Torah reading without a glaring error.

Intellectual challenge and skill acquisition are important. Uncertain that they can accomplish anything well in the adult world, as they move through the ever-changing, ambivalent time of puberty, b'nai mitzvah take great personal pride in displaying Hebrew competence and liturgical leadership. Celebration among family and friends is not a luxury. In a world of increasing fragmentation and mobility, the need for moments of binding is critical to communal connectedness.

And yet, bar and bat mitzvah is more than simply a graduation, an affirmation of intellect, and an excuse for a party. It is the confirmation of character development, a window to the sacred. We need ever more opportunities to help our children learn the difference between being smart and being wise. As they begin to put on deodorant, as their voices change and they menstruate or have wet dreams for the first time, it is not enough to teach our children how to make a blessing. We must also teach them how to *be* a blessing. They need to know God, not just from the prayer book, but from life, to see God in acts of kindness and in pursuit of peace. As their teachers and parents, we want them to bring God into the world by being fair, honorable, considerate. As they develop physically and mentally, we need to help them develop spiritually and to exercise their soul.

Bar and bat mitzvah is too often a time for unwrapping presents when it should be a time for unwrapping the gifts of the spirit which created the art and literature, the heroic deeds and moral teachings of our people.

The first two editions of *Putting God on the Guest List* have helped a new generation of families do just that. Children and parents in my congregation have used this book as part of their b'nai mitzvah seminars. Through the windows of these heartfelt words, they have seen a new dimension to this sacred life cycle ceremony.

I have worked with b'nai mitzvah for many years. They worry about whether they are too tall for thirteen or too short to see over the pulpit. Jeffrey Salkin encourages them to measure themselves by the breadth of their wisdom and the expanse of their heart.

While the bar mitzvah has for centuries been a rite of passage for men, the opportunity for young women to become b'not mitzvah, which began in 1922, has not only enriched women's personal lives but Jewish communal life as well. Studies in adolescence find that girls emerge from their teenage years with a poor self-image and much less confidence in their abilities than boys. Bat mitzvah is a door to self-esteem. It says that girls count, that their voice and experience are integral parts of a sacred community. As adolescent girls and increasing numbers of adult women ascend the *bimah* to become b'not mitzvah, they are building a home and a memory for future generations.

When my own daughter became a bat mitzvah, I spoke these words to her:

"There was a time when women were told what they could *not* be. Then there came a time when women were told what they *needed* to be, if they wanted success. But I want you to know: There is nothing as a woman you cannot be, and there are two things you need to be—true to yourself and responsible to your community."

WHAT I WISH FOR MY DAUGHTER,
I WISH FOR ALL OUR CHILDREN.
I wish for you to be a
person of character
strong but not tough,
gentle but not weak.

I wish for you to be
righteous but not self-righteous
honest but not unforgiving.

Wherever you journey, may your steps be firm
and may you walk in just paths
and not be afraid.

Whenever you speak, may your words
be words of wisdom and friendship.

May your hands build
and your heart preserve what is good
and beautiful in our world.

May the voices of the generations of our people
move through you
and may the God of our ancestors
be your God as well.

May you know that there is a people,
a rich heritage, to which you belong
and from that sacred place
you are connected to all who dwell on the earth.

May the stories of our people
be upon your heart
and the grace of the Torah rhythm
dance in your soul.

Putting God on the Guest List is Rabbi Jeffrey Salkin's invitation to all families, to link the sacred act of "going up" to the Torah with the sacred process of "growing up" in faithfulness to God and community.

Rabbi Sandy Eisenberg Sasso
Congregation Beth-El Zedeck
Indianapolis, Indiana

Introduction

In this valuable book, Rabbi Jeffrey Salkin urgently invites parents, children becoming bar or bat mitzvah, and the entire Jewish community to recapture the spiritual meaning of one of the most critical moments for determining a Jewish child's connection to our tradition and to God.

Each family approaches the guest list for its bar or bat mitzvah with care, for it is clear that the nature of the event will be influenced by those who attend. We carefully plan accommodations for our guests. With sensitivity we tend to travel arrangements and special dietary requirements. And yet, the most important element of all may be taken for granted or neglected. Have we remembered to extend an invitation to God? Have we planned the bar and bat mitzvah in a way that God's comfort and dignity will be assured throughout our services and celebration?

Despite tales of crass bar or bat mitzvah celebrations, I have found that most often the religious and social celebrations of this moment of transition in Jewish life have succeeded in bringing the young man or woman into serious contact with God, perhaps for the first time. As a congregational rabbi, I enjoyed the privilege of standing on the *bimah* as more than eleven hundred thirteen-year-olds were called to the Torah to establish their independent connection to God, the Torah, and the Jewish people. I also taught many of these young people in our community's Hebrew High School programs. Four years after their bar or bat mitzvah, I would ask them to write a statement describing the times in their lives when they felt closest to God. So many responded to my question with powerfully affirming statements about their bar or bat mitzvah. They described how reading from the Torah, chanting and standing before the Ark on that day created a moment with God that continued to touch them.

The feelings of these young men and women were also recounted by many older adults whom I encountered when they came to my synagogue seeking a fuller Jewish identity. In discussing what had sustained their connection to Judaism, they said they had never forgotten the feelings of comfort and closeness with God they had experienced on that special day of youthful spirituality.

I believe that we, as parents and educators, can learn to deepen the meaning of bar and bat mitzvah for our children and our families. We can capture the spiritual, religious awakenings set in the ritual of our tradition and enhanced by the sacred setting of the sanctuary. Rabbi Salkin's book takes this challenge seriously. He offers us a wise and insightful presentation that suggests how the young Jewish child becoming a man or woman can encounter God in transition from dependence to emerging adulthood. Rabbi Salkin also explains why the tears we cry when a bar or bat mitzvah reaches out to touch the Torah for the first time, not only reflect our joy, but also measure our anxiety. We rejoice in our realization that the years of Jewish continuity in our family will not end with us. But we worry about the influences in today's Jewish life that threaten the link just formed between past and future generations by the young Jew standing before us.

The author speaks with candor, yet offers encouragement to the many children and their parents who face the difficulties of the changing Jewish family. The tensions of divorce and remarriage, intermarriage, conversion, and grandparents of different faiths jeopardize the pursuit of spirituality at a bar or bat mitzvah. The full and open discussion of these issues in *Putting God on the Guest List*, however, gives us hope that even these concerns can be addressed. God can be invited and afforded a place of dignity, even in the midst of crisis. God's Presence can help the child transcend his or her adversity with a new measure of comfort and confidence.

The greatest anxiety experienced at every bar or bat mitzvah today is our concern about the celebrant's Jewish future. We celebrate the child's newly acquired adult privilege of freedom to choose. We express our thankfulness to God for the freedom granted Jews in today's society. Yet how fearful we are, for the freedoms are so vast and society so accepting, that Jews are tempted to embrace the array of alternative choices to Judaism.

It is a dilemma, not unlike the moment in the Garden of Eden when God watches with anxiety as Adam and Eve reach out to take the fruit of the forbidden tree of the knowledge of good and evil. The narrative describes God's ambivalence about these first children becoming something more than children. God points out the tree of knowledge of good and evil and urges Adam and Eve to protect their childlike innocence by not exercising their freedom to choose. "And the Lord God commanded ... Of every tree of the garden you may freely eat; but of the tree of the knowledge of good and evil you shall not eat of it; for in the day you eat thereof you [your innocence] shall surely die." The Wisdom of God anticipates the anguish Adam and Eve, and their descendants, will encounter once they discover their power to freely choose and influence their own destiny.

Still, the act of eating from the tree should not be viewed as the failure of the occupants of Eden. When they reach out to the tree, God does not prevent them from eating. The story's most important lesson is that God will not stand in the way of our choices, for only by exercising choice can we become fully human, with the potential to reflect the image of God. Only by choosing between alternatives can our faith in God and the Jewish tradition be considered as true commitment to God.

The story of the Garden of Eden has yet another dimension. There is a second tree planted in the midst of the garden called the *Eitz Hachayim*—the tree of life. It was not forbidden to Adam and Eve. They had the opportunity to taste of that tree as well and "eat and live forever," or at least learn from this tree how to contribute to the world in a way that their presence on earth would have everlasting value. The tree of life would have provided a balance for their newly acquired knowledge of good and evil. God would have welcomed their eating its fruit. Regrettably, they did not choose to taste it.

Today at the moment of bar and bat mitzvah the young Jew is offered a similar lesson. He or she is called before the Torah, which in Jewish tradition is also called *Eitz Chayim*. The reader points to a word and in effect offers the young person the opportunity to taste of the tree of life. The critical moment comes when the child decides to touch the Torah. The words of the Torah are brought, symbolically, to his or her mouth to be devoured as food for thought and instruction. Finally the bar or bat mitzvah grasps the Torah itself as a sign of recognition that this tree—God's Tree of Life—offers the source of guidance for a full, productive, moral life.

Rabbi Salkin stimulates us to imagine the full possibilities for the next bar and bat mitzvah, in our personal families or in the larger family of the Jewish community. He makes it clear that without God's Presence, this moment in Jewish life will lose its promise.

A distinguished Reform rabbi, Rabbi Salkin once again demonstrates how vital it is for Jews of every segment of our community to share ideas. Since the publication of the first edition of *Putting God on the Guest List*, his book has offered guidance to all Jews, no matter what their affiliation. I know that it has been used in synagogues throughout my Conservative movement as required reading in many pre-bar/bat mitzvah classes. It has also been used as a guide by countless numbers of families seeking sanctity for their moment of *simcha* shared with their children. This book will continue to be an invaluable resource for many years to come. Rabbi Salkin's religious passion and concern for the future of the Jewish people is evident in every chapter. Above all his love for God, and his confidence that God and religious experience can be found in Jewish rituals and celebrations like bar and bat mitzvah, will inspire the Jewish community to treasure this sacred experience even more.

Rabbi William H. Lebeau, *Vice Chancellor,*
The Jewish Theological Seminary of America

Preface to the Third Edition

Whenever I go to Israel, I remember that there are two ways of traveling to holy places: You can go as a tourist—or, you can go as a pilgrim. Some say that the difference is irrelevant because, no matter what, the traveler still gets there. I disagree. The intention and the level of consciousness with which you go to a holy place makes all the difference in the world.

But what is the difference between traveling as a tourist and traveling as a pilgrim? A *tour* to Israel is prompted by a brochure or an advertisement. A *pilgrimage* to Israel (or to any place) is prompted by a sacred text or an ancient tradition.

Also, a tourist goes when the time is convenient. A pilgrim goes when the time is right.

Just as we can go to sacred places as either pilgrims or tourists, we can also find ourselves at sacred *times* as either pilgrims or tourists. Too many Jewish parents make the journey to bar and bat mitzvah as tourists—with a casual air, looking, watching and observing, but not really participating or being touched spiritually. For this, they must approach bar and bat mitzvah as people who are making a sacred journey that is potentially filled with great meaning.

Thirteen years ago, I wrote *Putting God on the Guest List* for parents who wanted to approach Jewish life as pilgrims, not as tourists. I wanted to restore *sanctity* and *sanity* to American Jews' celebration of bar and bat mitzvah. Judging from the reaction to the book, *Putting God on the Guest List* has helped some Jews cultivate a deeper sense of purpose and of spirituality, a deeper ability to hear how Torah can speak to us and to our lives. Of that, I am proud.

This third edition of *Putting God on the Guest List* reflects what I have learned in recent years about bar and bat mitzvah. My lessons have come from Jewish adolescents and parents and grandparents; from rabbis, cantors, educators, and lay leaders; and from my own struggle with this challenging—and potentially rewarding—life passage.

If American Jewish culture is to change from within, it must create a Judaism with depth, purpose, holiness, and community. Only this way can bar and bat mitzvah be radically transformed. Asking probing, challenging questions about bar and bat mitzvah will help American Jews to clarify their values, create new paths to an authentic, satisfying spirituality, and forge new meanings for Judaism and the Jewish community.

In a story by the Israeli author Shmuel Yosef Agnon, some children are playing in a field. They uncover a structure that they think must have once been a castle, or perhaps a church. When they look more closely, they realize that it must have been an ancient synagogue. They want to enter, but even the most skilled locksmiths could not open the door of that ancient synagogue. And then, the door swings open by itself. Everything was still in place, ready for sacred use once again.

Bar and bat mitzvah can be the way in which we uncover that ancient synagogue that is within our souls. We will not need locksmiths to open the door. If we put in the time, effort, and love, the door will open, almost by magic, all by itself.

Why This Book Was Born

Moses ascends Mount Sinai to receive the tablets of the covenant. "Adonai said to Moses, 'Come up to me on the mountain *veyeheh sham*, and *be there*'" (Exodus 24:12).

Menachem Mendl of Kotsk, a great Chasidic teacher, asked, "If Moses had come up the mountain, why did God also have to tell him to '*be there*'?" Because, the Chasid answered, it is possible to expend great effort in climbing a mountain, but still not *be there*. Not everyone who is there is *there*. Sometimes they're somewhere else.

Bar and bat mitzvah is a sacred mountain in Jewish time. We climb this particular mountain because it brings us closer to God, closer to Judaism, closer to our people, closer to ourselves. And what modern Jews need, more than ever, is a way to really *be* there at the summit of this holy mountain.

You started walking a Jewish path decades ago. Now your children are starting to walk the same path. It is a path up a sacred mountain, a mountain very similar to Sinai, yet very much our own. Parents want to appreciate the full richness of the bar and bat mitzvah experience; they want their children to also experience it fully. They know that bar and bat mitzvah marks the passage from Jewish childhood to the beginnings of Jewish maturity. And they seek Jewish tools that will help them and their child make that sacred journey.

Bar and bat mitzvah is among the most popular of American Jewish rituals. Yet, few understand its history and deeper theological implications. It is more than a glitzy theme party, more than a moment of ethnic nostalgia. It is a glorious moment in the life of the family, the synagogue, and the Jewish people. And yet, over the years bar and bat mitzvah has too often become a banal event, a confused event, a ridiculed event, an event that sometimes lacks meaning because we are not sure what it *should* mean, because we have not learned how to *be* at the mountain.

Traditionally, bar and bat mitzvah occurred as part of the natural rhythm of a family's life. This is still true for committed, involved

Jewish families. By "committed" and "involved," which I am using in a nondenominational way, I mean those Jews who care about Judaism, who seek Jewish meanings, who care about Jewish traditions, who live by the Jewish calendar. Such Jews are Reform, Conservative, Reconstructionist, and Orthodox. Not accidentally, such involvement and commitment reduces the amount of a family's bar and bat mitzvah-related stress. They see the bar and bat mitzvah ceremony as part of the natural Jewish rhythm of their lives.

Once a relatively peripheral ceremony in Judaism, bar and bat mitzvah has now moved to center stage of the consciousness of American Jews. It is the primary reason Jews even join synagogues. Parents say they want to give their children a "Jewish education," but their implicit (and often explicit) goal is for their child to complete her or his bat or bar mitzvah ceremony, and then play hooky from any further Jewish education. In virtually every Jewish community, there are even "bar mitzvah factories" where children can receive "quickie" bar mitzvah ceremonies—no synagogue membership required.

Some families engage private tutors to prepare their children for a bar or bat mitzvah ceremony—complete with a rabbi or cantor that they have hired just for the ceremony, which is sometimes held in their backyard, living room, or country club. True, the ceremony winds up being personal and warm. But that warmth is only temporary. Because the ceremony occurs outside the structure of a synagogue or a *havurah*—outside the structure of an organic worshipping community that would give the ceremony any ongoing meaning—the experience winds up lacking Jewish communal "velcro." It just doesn't stick.

The American Jewish focus on bar and bat mitzvah is too often counterproductive. We define our goals too narrowly. The mechanics of managing the celebration—designing invitations, arranging the catering, dealing with relatives—consumes too much of our energy. So, too, does the goal of prowess in Hebrew, the demand that everything sound letter-perfect. It turns too many young people into expert lip-synchers of Torah and haftarah.

From the educational standpoint, the "bar mitzvah centrism" of American Judaism forces educators and lay leaders alike to focus too much on basic Hebrew skills, which means guaranteeing that children are (at most) capable of not embarrassing themselves on the *bimah* on their day of bar or bat mitzvah. Is it any wonder, then, why bar mitzvah (and to a much lesser extent, bat mitzvah) is so often the painful subject of American Jewish fiction and popular culture?

To most American Jews, bar and bat mitzvah is a product and a performance that leads to a party. It must become more of a process, part of an ongoing sense of becoming more Jewish, not only for the child but also for the family. Even more important is that we must recapture the long-lost sense of coherence between bar and bat mitzvah and the other moments of our Jewish lives. Inner meaning, spirituality, and such venerable Jewish values as study, justice, giving, sanctity, and moderation in consumption can become more real as a result of bar and bat mitzvah. We should focus not only on reading the Torah, but also on hearing the Torah as uniquely addressed to us, in our time, in our place.

The bar and bat mitzvah ceremony presents a challenge to today's scattered, sometimes fractured families. Guests and family members are often not clear about the meaning of the service and how to participate in it. The family of the bar or bat mitzvah child is often caught in the ethics of celebration—and in the highly subjective matter of "good taste." Bar and bat mitzvah ostentation has become a morally debilitating part of the American Jewish landscape, though many families have rebelled admirably against the culture of glitz. Their experiences prove that this trend can be reversed, that the celebration can be kept in perspective, that the sense of spirituality that is inherent in the ceremony can be reclaimed.

Judaism's teachings on contemporary moral issues encapsulate Torah's goal—to shape us into better human beings, and to bring a deep, powerful message to the world. What wisdom does Judaism offer our young people as they enter maturity? And how do we keep them learning from this wisdom? It is precisely for this reason that Jewish life after bar and bat mitzvah presents a major challenge. About half of all post-bar and -bat mitzvah youths end their Jewish education soon after the service. This disastrously affects the future Jewish identity of the child. Our young people lose access to Jewish wisdom on such primary issues as self-esteem and sexuality and interpersonal and social ethics when they—and the world— need it most.

Much of what happens in connection with bar and bat mitzvah is spiritual sleepwalking. Or, to put it in terms that Menachem Mendl, the Chasidic teacher, would have understood—some people just aren't there. That lack of spiritual presence is not unique to Jews. My Christian colleagues describe how many of their parishioners have lost or forgotten the meaning of first communion or confirmation. They speak of how these celebrations, too, have become secularized and distorted.

Several years ago in Paris, for instance, my wife and I eavesdropped on a baptism at the cathedral in Montmartre. As the priest recited the ancient words, the grandparents' faces were beaming. But the father had his hands shoved nervously into his pockets. His eyes were wandering across the stained glass. He wanted, it seemed, to be anywhere but there. He had forgotten the meaning of the moment.

Parents and their children acutely feel the social pressures that surround bar and bat mitzvah. But they want to feel the spiritual promise of the event, the pull of the divine, and the knowledge that they are participating in an event that has meaning both in the ancient past and in the very immediate present. They want to know that the steep incline before them is their family's own version of Sinai, the summit where, in every generation, Jews meet God, individually and as a people.

They want to know that bar and bat mitzvah can be a path to that summit. And they want to know how to get there.

This book can be their guide.

At the end of each chapter, we've suggested some questions for you to consider. Our hope is that by addressing these questions, you will be able to truly "put God on the guest list," and that the words in this book will move from paper to reality.

CHAPTER

1

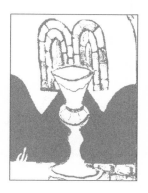

Beyond "Today I Am a Man"

When I became bar mitzvah, my grandfather, Eleazar of Amsterdam, of blessed memory, came to me one night in a vision and gave me another soul in exchange for mine. Ever since then, I have been a different person.

—SHALOM OF BELZ, HASIDIC MASTER

Beyond "Today I Am a Man"

Let's get it correct, right from the beginning. The way we view bar and bat mitzvah begins with the language that we use to describe it. Bar and bat mitzvah is not a thing to be owned: "My son *had* his bar mitzvah last month." It is not an object to be acquired: "I *got* my bat mitzvah last week!" It is not an event: "Jonathan's bar mitzvah was a huge success." It is not a verb: "The rabbi *bar mitzvahed* my son." Neither is it a past participle: "My daughter was *bat mitzvahed* last year."

Bar and bat mitzvah is what a young person *becomes,* simply by turning thirteen (or in Orthodox synagogues, twelve for girls). Bar and bat mitzvah literally translates as "son or daughter of the commandment." What it really means is "old enough to be responsible for *mitzvot.*" *Mitzvot* are the commandments that a Jew does not only to live a Jewish life, but also to sanctify life.

How Did Bar Mitzvah Begin?

Abraham, Moses, David—none were a bar mitzvah. The Bible seems to totally ignore adolescent rites of passage, with the exception that Abraham's oldest son, Ishmael, was circumcised at the age of thirteen (Genesis 17:25).

But does the Bible really ignore the passage into adolescence?

Genesis tells that Abraham's wife, Sarah, was barren, and she gave her handmaiden Hagar to Abraham so he could have children with her. The child that resulted from this union was named Ishmael. Sarah became increasingly disturbed by the continued presence in her household of Hagar and her son and persuaded Abraham to expel them into the wilderness, where a spring of water miraculously welled up in the desert and revived the almost-dying Ishmael.

Some Biblical scholars say that Ishmael's nearly fatal ordeal in the wilderness might have been an ancient Middle Eastern rite of initiation: A boy is tested in the wilderness, dies as a youth, and is reborn as an adult. Other scholars see an adolescent rite of passage implied in the story of the binding of Isaac in Genesis. God tells Abraham to offer Isaac as a sacrifice on Mount Moriah, but an angel intervenes to save the boy's life, and a ram is sacrificed instead. This story might possibly allude to an ancient ritual in which a boy is deliberately placed in danger, almost dies, and then is miraculously saved so he can advance toward maturity.

These stories may contain remnants of adolescent initiation rites. Although the Bible contains stories about adolescent boys (such as the story of Joseph), it pays no attention to the passage into adolescence. In fact, the Bible has far more references to weaning celebrations than to adolescent passages. Apparently, the passage from infancy was more important than the passage from childhood!

Modern Jews would reject this idea of such a brutal trial by ordeal as a way for our children to enter maturity. And yet, a secular Israeli once spoke about his son's supposedly nonreligious coming-of-age ceremony:

> On my son's thirteenth birthday, I awakened him at dawn. I had already packed a backpack with sandwiches, money, a flashlight, a knife, and a hatchet. My friends and I tied my son up, blindfolded him, put him in the back of our van, and drove him to the Negev. We then released him and told him: Now find your way home. Three days later, he knocked on our door in Tel Aviv, threw his arms around me, and sobbed, "Thank you, Abba. I love you."

We are never quite as secular as we think. This so-called secular Israeli had, perhaps unconsciously, internalized and combined the stories of Ishmael and Isaac—and he had acted them out on his son in the same geographical place where the ancient story had first occurred!

The bar and bat mitzvah experience certainly qualifies as a trial, although one far less dangerous than those faced by Ishmael or Isaac or, for that matter, our young Israeli teenager: A young person, preparing for a solo ceremony with the help of a tutor, struggles with learning Torah and presenting it to a community. Young people crave that experience of being tested. A Jew-by-Choice told me that when he was a teenager in his rural Wisconsin community, the local secular rite of passage was being allowed to hunt with the men for the first time: "I remember what it was like to hold the rifle for the first time, and to be surrounded by older boys and grown men. It was a real test."

Biblical tradition placed the age of majority at twenty years of age. This was the age of mandatory army service and of priestly service. Bar mitzvah, as a concept, actually emerged during the first centuries of the Common Era. It is an invention of the early rabbis, the sages whose interpretations of Torah created contemporary Judaism. We cannot be absolutely sure why these sages lowered the age of majority from twenty to thirteen, though certainly the connection to the age of puberty has some significance. When the term *bar mitzvah* appears in rabbinic literature, it simply refers to a young man who has reached the age of thirteen plus one day.

If anyone could be called the inventor of bar mitzvah, it would be the second century C.E. sage, Judah ben Tema. Judah envisioned the way that one's life of Jewish study and responsibility should unfold: "At five, one should study Scripture; at ten, one should study Mishnah; at thirteen, one is ready to do *mitzvot*; at fifteen, one is ready to study Talmud; at eighteen, one is ready for the wedding canopy; at twenty, one is responsible for providing for a family" (Mishnah, *Avot* 5:24).

Most references to the significance of the age of thirteen come from stories the rabbis told about characters in the Bible. Those stories constitute the body of Jewish interpretive literature known as *midrash*. It was the way that the rabbis continually breathed new life into the text of Torah and found new meanings within its stories.

What does the Midrash say about the significance of the age of thirteen? Consider the story that most Jews learned when they were little children. Abraham's father, Terach, is in the idol business in Ur, a city in ancient Sumer, which is the modern-day Iraq. He goes away on business, and leaves his young son, Abram, in charge of the idol shop. Abram, who is later called Abraham, shatters all the idols in the store with a stick, then places the stick in the hand of the largest idol. When Terach gets back, he sees the ruined merchandise.

"What happened?" he demands.

"Oh, father, it was terrible," says Abram. "The small idols got hungry and started fighting for food. Then, the large idol got angry and broke the smaller ones into little pieces. It was frightening. I don't want to talk about it."

"Wait a second," says Terach. "Idols don't get hungry. They don't get angry. They don't speak. They're just … they're just clay idols."

"So," Abram asks with a smile, "why do you worship them?"

Abram does this to create the ultimate break with idolatry. In so doing, he invents monotheism. The legend says that Abram was thirteen when the idol-smashing incident occurred. Today's Jewish parents might ask themselves: *What idols would you want your adolescent to smash in his or her life?*

Another midrash says that, at the age of thirteen, the twins, Jacob and Esau, went their separate ways: Jacob to the worship of God, Esau to idolatry. Each followed their true nature and inclinations. Parents might ask: *What choices should Jewish children make when they become bar or bat mitzvah?*

Finally, the Talmud says that Bezalel, the namesake of the famous art school now in Jerusalem, was thirteen when he designed the ancient tabernacle for worship in the wilderness. Parents might ask: *What should emerging Jewish adults build in their lives?*

These are more than nice little stories. They teach that the onset of adolescence can be a pivotal moment of becoming for a young person; that for Jews, this age of passage is pregnant with immense spiritual and moral depth. Bar and bat mitzvah says to our young people: Imagine yourself as Abraham, an idol breaker, rebelling against easy answers. Imagine yourself as Jacob and Esau, facing choices and ready (we hope!) to make the right ones. Imagine yourself as Simeon and Levi, ready to defend Jewish honor.

There is, of course, one problem: The above role models are all males. Where, in Jewish lore, are there role models for adolescent girls?

According to the Midrash, Moses's parents, Amram and Yocheved, decided to live apart in Egypt because they did not want to bring any more children into a world of slavery and oppression. Their daughter,

Miriam, convinced them to get back together. "This is wrong!" she said. "By refusing to live together and to have any more children, you are depriving our people of a future!"

One source says that Miriam was five years old when she did this courageous act. She may have been an exceptionally precocious child, but considering the healthy rebelliousness of adolescent girls, it has always seemed to me that she was closer to thirteen years old at the time. So, in our search for female role models, a thirteen-year-old Jewish girl could become Miriam and stand up for Jewish survival.

Thirteen: The Age of Choices

A certain prayer, *Baruch she-petarani me-onsho shel zeh* ("Blessed is the One Who has now freed me from responsibility for this one") is traditionally recited by fathers when their sons became bar mitzvah. Most scholars interpret it as meaning that the father is no longer responsible for his son's sins.

But it is also a kind of cosmic sigh—an admission that even sincere, competent, highly committed parents are limited in what they can do with their children. The rest is up to the child himself or herself. When parents say *Baruch she-peterani*, they say, in effect, "Whatever this young person does now, he is legally and morally culpable. Thank God, it's not my responsibility." At that moment, the parent becomes like Isaac, who, on looking at his sons, Jacob and Esau, realized that he had done all that he could for them. One son would worship God, the other would worship idols. There are limits to every parent's hopes and dreams, limits to every parent's ability to control and influence. The rest is up to faith, hope, and trust.

To the ancients, thirteen was the age of spiritual and moral choices. Some rabbinic sources say that only upon turning thirteen is a youth first able to make mature choices, because then the child becomes endowed with both the *yetser hatov* (the good inclination) and the *yetser hara* (the evil inclination), the dueling forces that Jewish theology perceives are within the human psyche.

Thirteen was also the age of religious achievement. The thirteen-year-old child could help constitute a *minyan* (the quorum of ten adult men needed for communal prayer). In addition, the thirteen-year-old could also fast on Yom Kippur. A minor tractate of the Talmud, *Sofrim*, mentions that in the era of the Second Temple (approximately the first century of the Common Era) there was a ceremony for twelve- or thirteen-year-olds who had completed their first Yom Kippur fast. In that ceremony, the elders of the community blessed the children on the occasion of completing this important *mitzvah*. Perhaps this was the first bona fide Jewish coming-of-age ceremony.

In one of the most religious conversations I ever had with a teenager, a thirteen-year-old told me she did not want to become bat mitzvah. I was initially not pleased with her decision. But, as we spoke, it was apparent that this was something about which she had thought long and deeply and that she had used her emerging maturity to reach a very mature and difficult decision.

She and her mother had come to see me eight months before she was scheduled to become bat mitzvah because she had changed her mind about proceeding with the ceremony and its accompanying celebration.

A little stunned, I asked her, "What's the problem?"

"There's no problem. I like learning Hebrew, so I'm not nervous about that. I like religious school, and I will go on to confirmation. I just don't want to become bat mitzvah."

The reasons that followed were intriguing. She didn't like what bat mitzvah had become for so many of her peers. The parties, the social pressures, the ostentation and superficiality turned her off. I reminded her that how she became bat mitzvah did not have to mimic what her friends and peers did.

She still refused. In doing so, it was clear that she wanted to make a statement.

I reminded her that bat mitzvah was what she would become, simply by becoming thirteen. Moreover, I assured her that her decision was not irrevocable. While thirteen is the traditional age of bar and bat mitzvah, many Jews celebrate that rite of passage when they are older—sometimes later in their teens, or in college, or as adult b'nai or b'not mitzvah.

I also said that I was proud of her. Reminding her of the legend about Abraham shattering his father's idols, I told her that, according to tradition, Abraham did this when he was thirteen years old. "Maybe you are shattering the idol that bat mitzvah has become for so many of your peers. Maybe today you really were bat mitzvah after all—in the true, ancient meaning of the term."

She smiled. Sure enough, she did not have a bat mitzvah ceremony. But she stayed in religious school, and she was confirmed with the other members of her tenth grade class. At her confirmation, I reminded her that she was a true daughter of Abraham, an idol smasher. That moment of idol smashing was the only bat mitzvah ceremony that she ever needed.

Thirteen also became the age of a kind of legal maturity. The Mishnah, the code of Jewish law compiled around 200 C.E., considers the vows of a boy aged thirteen plus one day as legally binding. At thirteen, a youth could be a member of a *bet din* (a Jewish court), and could buy and sell certain items of value, though apparently not real estate. The age of thirteen was therefore the crossroads of spiritual, moral, and religious maturity.

There is yet another opinion about the origin of bar mitzvah. Bar mitzvah may have its roots in the *brit milah* (ritual circumcision) ceremony that occurs when a boy is eight days old. At that ceremony, the father says, "As we have brought this child into the covenant of Abraham, so, too, will he be brought into the study of Torah, the *chupah* [the wedding canopy] and the performance of good deeds." Bar mitzvah was, therefore, the occasion when the community confirmed that the father had fulfilled the first part of the promise. Ideally, the same people who had attended the *brit* would also be present when the child became bar mitzvah.

Bar mitzvah, therefore, was a passage not only for the child, but also for the father (and in modern times, for both parents). It meant that they had fulfilled their Jewish responsibility to the child and to the Jewish community.

How Did Bar Mitzvah Customs Evolve?

A child who was younger than thirteen years old performed *mitzvot* as *options*. Once he turned thirteen, he performed them as *obligations*. As the Talmud taught, "It is better to do something when you're commanded to do so than to do something when you're not commanded to do so." The idea of *mitzvah* also implies responsibility and obligation. It connects us to the covenant of Abraham, Isaac, and Jacob, of Sarah, Rebecca, Rachel, and Leah, and of all Jews who preceded every thirteen-year-old. It is sacred and it deserves celebration.

Jews sensed this, and during the early Middle Ages, their practices began to change. In the twelfth century, the religious rights of minors began to disappear. We are not sure why this occurred. Perhaps it was because the carnage of the Crusades had created a shortage of men, and Jewish communities wanted to give them top priority in ritual matters.

By approximately the late Middle Ages, minors could no longer wear *tefilin* (phylacteries) or be called for *aliyot* to the reading of the Torah. Since those rituals became the defining elements of Jewish maturity, they later became the essential features of the bar mitzvah observance. In the sixteenth century, it became customary to call a boy to read the Torah on the Shabbat that coincided with or followed his thirteenth birthday. He read the last section of the Torah (*maftir*) that was read on that particular Shabbat and also the weekly section from the Prophets section of the Hebrew Bible (*haftarah*). Previously, the right of the minor to read the *haftarah* had not been restricted except on a few special Shabbatot.

Historically, bar mitzvah was a somewhat peripheral ceremony. But there were several exceptions even before modern times. The most poignant was the Marranos, the Spanish Jews who converted to Christianity under duress during the fifteenth century but secretly maintained certain Jewish practices and beliefs. Bar mitzvah became a crucial time for Marrano families: It was the moment when they informed the child that he was Jewish. If he had been informed of this earlier, his immaturity might have prevented him from keeping it as well-guarded a secret as it had to be. Yet, if he had learned later than this, the Christian element of his identity would have "taken," making any kind of link to Judaism much more difficult.

A Custom, Not a Commandment

If any ritual celebrates the diversity of Jewish expression, it is bar and bat mitzvah. The reason for this is clear—they are customs with no force of law. Standard in a bar or bat mitzvah ceremony, however, is the practice of the young person reciting the blessings for the Torah, reading or chanting that week's Torah portion, and reading the *haftarah* from a printed sheet. In the late Middle Ages, it became customary for the bar mitzvah to offer a *drashah* (sermonette or discourse) in the home. That *drashah* has been transformed into the bar mitzvah speech, which usually serves as a *devar Torah* (a sermonette on the Scriptural lesson) or as a personal prayer for the occasion. In many synagogues, the young person also leads the congregation in the Hebrew prayers in the service. In most synagogues, parents, grandparents, and other close relatives are given *aliyot* and other honors. While most bar mitzvah ceremonies occur during regular worship on Shabbat morning, Friday evening bar mitzvah ceremonies are not uncommon.

Bar and Bat Mitzvah as American Judaism's Spiritual Mirror

Traditionally, bar mitzvah meant a change in status, the attainment of religious maturity, and the assumption of additional religious responsibilities. In Europe and Russia, most Jews lived in communities that cherished learning, worship, responsibility, and obligation. When a young man was bar mitzvah, he was responsible for *mitzvot*. The community supported that value system. Today's Jews still want that kind of passage in our children's lives. One father of a recent bar mitzvah suggested that post-bar or -bat mitzvah teens should regularly help lead synagogue services, thus making their passage toward greater responsibility real and important. There are many religious schools that give post-bar or -bat mitzvah teens the opportunity to teach younger students, thus letting them use what they know and to transmit that learning to a younger generation.

Even though the observance of many Jewish traditions has waned in modern times, bar mitzvah is one of the few Jewish observances that has actually grown in importance. The closest parallel that we can find is in the holiday cycle. Until fairly recently, Chanukah had been a minor holiday. Contributing to its growing importance in post war America were its theme of religious freedom; its proximity to Christmas; and the rise of gift giving as a Chanukah custom.

The same is true of bar mitzvah. As Isaac Levitats, an observer of American Judaism, already wrote in 1949, "The bar mitzvah has become the most important milestone in a Jew's life in America. Never in our millennial history was so much importance attached to this ceremony."

Bar and bat mitzvah has not only grown in importance; it has also come to mirror trends in American Judaism. Take, for instance, "privatization"—the focus on the individual and the resulting diminishing of religious community. We see this in Reform Judaism's Shabbat morning service often being almost totally dedicated to the bar and bat mitzvah ceremony. This is certainly less so in Conservative, Reconstructionist, and Orthodox Judaism, in which the bar mitzvah ceremony is part of a service that would have been held whether or not there was a bar or bat mitzvah ceremony. It is also seen in the growth of Saturday evening bar and bat mitzvah ceremonies in Reform synagogues—the so-called *havdalah* bar and bat mitzvah that are held in conjunction with the service that ends Shabbat.

But the overwhelming consensus of religious opinion discourages such *havdalah* ceremonies. The reasoning is clear: The Torah is not traditionally read at that time; the timing of such ceremonies puts undue emphasis on the Saturday evening festivities; and a bar and bat mitzvah ceremony at *havdalah* convinces people that the service is "theirs," diminishing the centrality of the community in Jewish life.

Sometimes Jewish families choose to hold the bar and bat mitzvah ceremony in Israel. Such ceremonies certainly create a firm bond between the child and Israel. For many years, the favored site for these ceremonies was the Western Wall, the remaining wall of the ancient Temple Mount in Jerusalem. This has become less popular because of the enforced separation of women at the Wall, though it has become possible to have ceremonies at the southern wall of the Temple Mount, an area where such restrictions are not enforced. Some families will choose to celebrate a bar or bat mitzvah ceremony in an Israeli synagogue, to establish a connection with a worshiping community in the Jewish state.

An increasingly popular site for the ceremony is now the excavated synagogue at Masada, the Herodian palace overlooking the Dead Sea where the last Zealots held out against the Romans in 73 C.E. I am ambivalent about Masada as a place for a bar or bat mitzvah ceremony. One aspect of its symbolism is jarring and morbid: It is the site of the mass suicide of 960 Jewish men, women, and children. This is not the most hopeful image to convey at a bar or bat mitzvah ceremony.

Nevertheless, a ceremony at Masada can have lasting impact on a family. Several years ago, I officiated at a bar mitzvah ceremony at Masada for a young man in my congregation. This was particularly poignant, because his grandparents are Holocaust survivors. His Torah portion happened to include the *Sh'ma*, the classic Jewish watchword of faith that Jewish martyrs have said for centuries before their deaths. The boy's first words as a mature Jew were the *last* words of the martyrs of Masada. It all came together—his grandparents' story, the words he read, the location—and we wept. We understood, in a very palpable way that we hadn't before, that Masada symbolizes Jewish continuity in the face of hatred.

Some families have chosen for their children to celebrate bar or bat mitzvah in European synagogues located in the cities or countries in which their ancestors had lived, such as Poland or Germany. One boy from a Jewish Cuban-American family celebrated his bar mitzvah in the Havana synagogue where his grandfather had become bar mitzvah in the 1930s.

In many quarters of American Jewish life, bar and bat mitzvah still primarily means a youth can participate in rituals and that he or she is responsible for *mitzvot*. As an Orthodox rabbi noted:

> If their bar mitzvah speeches are any indication, my students really do believe that they are supposed to perform *mitzvot* now. I hear them saying, "Once I would try to fast as long as I could on Yom Kippur as an option. Now I do it as a responsibility." He now has to wear *tefilin*. He can now help make a *minyan*. Becoming bar mitzvah has a sense of immediacy with my people. There's a tangible change in status.

But in less traditional American Jewish circles, bar and bat mitzvah has other meanings. These may not be explicitly theological. But bar and bat mitzvah means, in all forms of contemporary Judaism, that Judaism survives in this youth, in this family and by implication, in the world at large. Making that survival coherent and meaningful is our task.

How Did Bat Mitzvah Begin?

Just as there are no real coming-of-age ceremonies for boys in the Bible, neither are there any such ceremonies for girls. But there is one biblical story that may contain a long-discarded "memory" of a coming-of-age ceremony.

It is the troubling story of Jephtah's daughter, found in Judges, chapter 11. Jephtah was a tribal leader in ancient Israel. Before he entered into battle with the Ammonites, he vowed that if he was victorious he would sacrifice the first living thing that came out of his house upon his return. Tragically, this turned out to be his daughter, and she implored him to fulfill his vow. The Bible tells us that she asked him to wait for two months so that she might mourn with her companions in the mountains. At the end of this period she met her tragic fate. The Bible states that it became customary for Israelite women to commemorate this event by an annual four-day mourning period; some scholars have wondered whether this is a lost memory of an ancient coming-of-age ritual for adolescent girls.

Starting in the second or third century of the Common Era, Jewish girls at the age of twelve had a legal responsibility to observe *mitzvot*. It was not until centuries later, however, that families would begin celebrating the girls' new status with some festivity.

By the 1800s, some families held a *seudat mitzvah* (a festive meal for a ritual occasion) on a girl's twelfth birthday. Sometimes the girl would deliver a talk and her father would recite the traditional *Baruch shepetarani* prayer. A great nineteenth century rabbinic authority, Rabbi Joseph Hayyim ben Elijah of Iraq, mentioned coming-of-age celebrations for girls in his legal writings. There were also such celebrations for twelve-year-old girls in Italy (where it was called "entering *minyan*") as well as such celebrations in Poland, Germany, and Egypt in the early twentieth century.

Despite these historical precedents, bat mitzvah has always been controversial among Orthodox Jews. Some believe that its status should be less than bar mitzvah because girls must be more demure than boys. Others realized that sound educational arguments support the custom of bat mitzvah.

In mainstream Orthodoxy, the bat mitzvah ceremony is basically a sermonette on the Torah portion, followed by a festive meal. Sometimes the girl does the *devar Torah* in the sanctuary, sometimes in the social hall. Girls are seldom allowed to read directly from the Torah scroll. In some Orthodox synagogues, girls lead the service and read from either the Prophets or Writings sections of the Bible. In Orthodoxy, bat mitzvah services may be held on Friday evening, Saturday evening, or Sunday morning, or even after the regular week-day morning service. Some modern Orthodox women have become bat mitzvah by chanting from the Torah as part of a women's service—no men allowed! In England, young Orthodox women sometimes become bat mitzvah as a group ceremony, in which the girls present essays and speeches, but do not read from the Torah. So, there is great diversity in the way Jewish communities have adopted this custom.

It is well known among Reform Jews that nineteenth-century classical Reform rejected bar mitzvah. Among the other reasons for its rejection, early American Reformers deemed it sexist (a word they could not have used), because only boys were allowed to become bar mitzvah. And yet, bat mitzvah did not begin with the Reform movement.

The first bat mitzvah ceremony in North America was that of the late Judith Kaplan Eisenstein, the daughter of Rabbi Mordecai Kaplan, the founder of Reconstructionism. It happened in May 1922, when, as she later recalled, she was "midway between my twelfth and thirteenth birthdays." Judith's grandmothers wrung their hands over the planned ceremony, each one prevailing on the other to persuade Rabbi Kaplan to abandon the idea.

Years later, she would remember that the night before the event, her father had still not decided on the exact form of the ceremony. The next day, as usual at a Shabbat service, Rabbi Kaplan read the *maftir* (the concluding portion of the Torah reading) and the *haftarah*. Then his daughter, "at a very respectable distance" from the Torah scroll (because girls traditionally did not read from the scroll), recited the first blessing and read the Torah selection from her own *chumash* (a book containing the Five Books of Moses).

Later she wrote, "The scroll was returned to the ark with song and procession, and the service was resumed. No thunder sounded, no lightning struck. The institution of bat mitzvah had been born without incident, and the rest of the day was all rejoicing."

Despite the family tensions over this auspicious occasion, and despite the fact that it would become a "first" in Jewish history, Kaplan was rather nonchalant about it when he noted in his diary:

March 28, 1922—Last Sabbath a week ago (March 16) I inaugurated the ceremony of the Bat Mitzvah at the S.A.J. [Society for the Advancement of Judaism] Meeting House (4 West 86 Street) about which more details later. My daughter Judith was the first one to have her Bat Mitzvah celebrated there.

Bat Mitzvah caught on slowly. According to Rabbi Daniel Zemel of Washington, D.C., in 1933 his aunt became the second known bat mitzvah in America, and his mother followed in 1935. Both became bat mitzvah at Anshe Emet Synagogue in Chicago, a Conservative synagogue, where their father, Rabbi Solomon Goldman, was the spiritual leader. Anshe Emet Synagogue became the first congregation in the United States to offer a bat mitzvah class for twelve-and thirteen-year-old girls. Other Conservative synagogues would follow suit in offering bat mitzvah: Ahavath Achim in Atlanta, Georgia (1941), Congregation Rodfei Zedek in Chicago, Illinois (1944), among others. By 1960, almost all Conservative synagogues celebrated both bar and bat mitzvah, and 96 percent of Reform synagogues did so as well.

Neither Reform Judaism nor Reconstructionist Judaism liturgically distinguish between bar mitzvah and bat mitzvah. In Conservative Judaism, practices range from the girl leading the service and reading from the Torah scroll to simply reading the *haftarah*. The time of the service might also vary. Some Conservative synagogues let a girl publicly celebrate becoming bat mitzvah on Shabbat morning. Others limit it to Friday evenings, or Monday, Thursday, and *rosh chodesh* (the first day of the Hebrew month) mornings when the Torah is also read.

Adult Bar and Bat Mitzvah

Recent decades have seen the growth of adult bar and bat mitzvah. (The term is somewhat of a misnomer, as one becomes bar or bat mitzvah at thirteen, regardless of whether or not a formal ceremonial marker of the passage takes place). Usually, adults who become bar or bat mitzvah lead a service or sections of it, read Torah and/or *haftarah*, and give a *devar Torah*.

Adult bar or bat mitzvah is a sign of a Jewish spiritual renewal since many of today's Jews grew up in assimilated or uninvolved Jewish households, or rebelled against going to religious school, or never learned Hebrew, or were not interested in religion as children. Others became bar or bat mitzvah when they were twelve or thirteen, but felt that the ceremony had no inner meaning for them. For such adults, an adult bar or bat mitzvah can help them become truly mature in a religious sense.

Also, there are many American Jews who began life as non-Jews, and who converted to Judaism as adults. For them, adult bar and bat mitzvah can deepen and celebrate their connection to the Jewish people.

This adult rite of passage is particularly powerful for women. Although bat mitzvah was "invented" in 1922, it took decades for it to become popular. Therefore, many Jewish women did not have the opportunity to become bat mitzvah at thirteen. The ceremony did not exist for them. Even after the advent of bat mitzvah, many women grew up in homes where Jewish education was required for boys, not for girls. As one fortyish woman in my congregation recently told me: "When it came to Judaism, girls just didn't count in my home."

Adult bat mitzvah has become an important way to redeem the Jewish past, and to atone for young women being previously barred from full access to Torah and *mitzvot*. It has become such an important part of many synagogues' continuing education programs that more than half of the non-Orthodox synagogues in America regularly conduct them. For women, bat mitzvah is an opportunity to affirm their role in the ritual life of Judaism in a way that they could not do when they were thirteen. For men, adult bar mitzvah is a symbol of Jewish growth and renewal. As a reporter recently wrote in the *New York Times*, "Adult bar and bat mitzvah is part high school equivalency diploma, part statement of spiritual intent, part celebration of ethnic roots in a polyglot society with increasingly tribal tendencies."

What, Finally, Does It All Mean?

I believe that most Jewish parents need to turn inward at bar and bat mitzvah time and ask themselves these thorny questions: "Why are we doing this? What does it all mean?" I have discovered that many parents and children have never discussed the meaning of bar and bat mitzvah with each other. What results too often is a ceremony that is essentially a performance, a demonstration of rudimentary linguistic competence in an ancient language. Scant attention is paid to its underlying meaning and beauty.

Yet, one thread links all the bar and bat mitzvah ceremonies throughout history, all the comings of age of every Jewish boy from Abraham on and of every Jewish girl from Sarah on. Bar mitzvah and bat mitzvah are a passage, but not one of puberty. "It's when I become a man," say so many bar mitzvah candidates. Curiously, bat mitzvah girls rarely say, "It's when I become a woman." Instead, they say, "Bat mitzvah is when I get new responsibilities." And they are right.

Bar and bat mitzvah is about ritual maturity. It is about growing up as a Jew. It is about becoming a fuller member of the Jewish community. But it is also about moral responsibility, about connecting to Torah, to community, to God.

Have each person in your family write down what he or she thinks bar or bat mitzvah should mean. Then, come up with a family definition for bar or bat mitzvah and write it in the space above. This will become a wonderful memento for your child.

2

"Speak to the Children of Israel"
How Bar and Bat Mitzvah
Speak to the Inner Life of Children

*A generation can only receive
the teachings in the sense that it renews them.
We do not take unless we also give.*

—Martin Buber

"Speak to the Children of Israel"

Some young people become *bar* or *bat* mitzvah. For me, the greatest moment of my adolescence was (forgive me) *car* mitzvah.

When I was sixteen and learning how to drive, my father took me out on the Seaford–Oyster Bay Expressway on Long Island. In those days, the speed limit was 65 mph—and I couldn't wait to get there. As I accelerated, the needle slowly moved up the speedometer. Suddenly, out of the silence, my father spoke.

"Jeff, let up on the gas a little bit. Let the car shift into high."

There was almost a sadness in his voice. I had never heard that tone before, and I have rarely heard it since.

Ever since that morning, I have thought a great deal about the meaning of that moment and analyzed the meaning of my father's words almost as if it they were a sacred text.

Whether he knew it or not, my father was saying, "Jeff, slow down just a bit. Look out the right window: There's your old elementary school. How I remember your first day there. How I remember the day you finally taught yourself how to ride a two-wheel bicycle, the day you realized that you could simply pick up your feet and pedal on your own. Just two weeks ago, you were slowly driving around the side streets of our neighborhood. Now you're racing along the expressway. Soon you'll be going to college—and you'll be gone. Ease up on the gas. Don't grow up so fast. Don't let me age so fast."

At the moment that the car hit 65, my father realized that I was no longer a little child—and he was no longer a young father. It was a true *secular* moment of passage.

That moment will always be with me. But my father and I never spoke about it. He and I were not alone in our silence: Many silences exist between parents and adolescents. In fact, the Torah is filled with such silences. There was silence between Abraham and Isaac. In Genesis 22, in the story known as the *Akedah*, Abraham and Isaac walked to the top of Mount Moriah where the patriarch had been instructed by God to sacrifice his son. What did they say during their climb? According to the Torah, Isaac asked Abraham, "Where is the lamb for the sacrifice?" Abraham responded, "God will see to the sacrifice, my son." They never spoke to each other again. The silence between Abraham and Isaac was echoed in the silence that emerged between Abraham and God. After the *Akedah*, the attempted sacrifice, God never again spoke to Abraham, who was previously God's greatest audience and dialogue partner.

There was also a silence between Jacob and his beloved son, Joseph. In Genesis 37, Jacob sent Joseph to spy on his brothers. Or perhaps the intention was for Joseph to reconcile with the brothers? When he found them, they stripped him of his multi-colored coat and sold him into slavery in Egypt. Despite Joseph's powerful love for his father, he never once communicated with him during his long exile in Egypt, which was a dress rehearsal for the Jewish people's later exile in Egyptian bondage. The silence between Jacob and Joseph begins that exile. In the words of the French author Andre Neher, it was an exile of *language* as well.

How powerful is that exile of language, of silence, between so many parents and adolescents. How powerfully we seek to overcome it.

Consider the young boy in my synagogue who would celebrate his bar mitzvah in three weeks. During his rehearsal in the sanctuary, I noted that his Hebrew—Torah, *haftarah*, and prayers—was flawless, yet he was still working on his *devar Torah*. He and his parents had neither discussed the meaning of the Torah portion nor read the translation of the Torah portion together. There was a general sense of *blankness* in him and even in his parents about the upcoming event.

"Have you and your parents discussed why you're becoming bar mitzvah?" I asked. There was silence. "So," I prodded, trying to elicit a reaction. "Why are they doing this? Why are you becoming bar mitzvah?" "It's what you do," he replied. "It's a tradition."

It was clear to me that they spent more time deliberating which video to rent than they had spent discussing the deeper meaning behind bar mitzvah. They are not alone in their reticence. Many

American Jews lack—yet secretly desire—a vocabulary to help them address the central questions behind God, prayer, Torah, and *mitzvot*. They are not exclusively to blame for this silence. They inherited a suburbanized, secularized, often trivialized American Judaism that had not adequately raised those questions. To the twentieth century Israeli poet Avraham Shlonsky, their Judaism was like a *mezuzah* from which the sacred parchment had been removed. It was spiritually empty. A generation ago, many Jews thought that being ethical or eating pastrami on rye would be enough to sustain Jewish identity. This hasn't been enough—not when anyone, Jew or gentile, can be ethical; and not when anyone, Jew or gentile, can enter a delicatessen.

How can parents break through the silence? How can we emerge from our exile of language? How can we start speaking to our children about what bar and bat mitzvah means?

Religious life is built on metaphors, symbols, and stories. We need to create new metaphors for our time. Truth be told, my own life never enjoyed the metaphor of having passed into maturity through the ceremony of bar mitzvah. Certainly, I had become bar mitzvah. Every Jewish boy does, whether or not he has a ceremony to mark the occasion. I just never had the ceremony.

The story is rather simple. My parents joined a Reform synagogue when I was in fifth grade. This is relatively late to start Jewish education, and not to be recommended. My parents asked me how I felt about becoming bar mitzvah. At that time, I was timid about learning Hebrew, so I told them I would rather concentrate on Jewish history and Bible, which I loved. My parents knew that Reform Judaism emphasized confirmation, and that became my Jewish goal.

As my thirteenth year approached, my male cousins started becoming bar mitzvah. (In the mid-1960s, it was relatively rare for girls to become bat mitzvah, and so none of my girl cousins went through this passage.) The pressure from great-aunts and great-uncles started: "Don't you want to become bar mitzvah like your cousins?" The implication in their question was: "Don't you want a party and presents like your cousins?"

The pressure worked. Six months before my thirteenth birthday, I consulted our rabbi. He told me that "quick" tutoring in Hebrew could "get me through" the ceremony. He also helped me understand that I coveted the *party*, not the *passage*, and that such a "rush job" would not be very conducive to my Jewish identity. It would have involved me in a meaningless ritual charade whose sole purpose was to compete with my cousins. It would not have deepened my connection to Judaism. I remember him fondly for helping me, as an impressionable thirteen-year-old, understand the truth about what I wanted.

The story does not end there. One day, as I was tutoring a group of adult *b'not mitzvah* students in Jewish theology, I revealed my secret to them—I had not celebrated bar mitzvah at the age of thirteen. They insisted that I join them in celebrating our passages together. We studied and learned together in seminar fashion in which I was not their teacher, but a fellow student. We all became adult *b'nei mitzvah* on the same cold winter morning. It was wonderful, even if it was thirty-five years late for me!

"Don't Let Down the Coach"

In the Midrash (*Kohelet Rabbah* 12:10), compiled in the eighth century C.E., we read: "The words of the wise are like a young girl's ball. As a ball is flung by hand without falling, so Moses received the Torah at Sinai and delivered it to Joshua, Joshua to the elders, the elders to the prophets, and the prophets delivered it to the Great Synagogue." That is how the ancient rabbis imagined the *shalshelet ha-kabbalah*, the great chain of tradition, that went from generation to generation: As a ball that is tossed, playfully, from teacher to student.

I once told a group of preteens that being Jewish means knowing about the Coach.

Once, I said, at a place called Mount Sinai, the Coach gathered us together, saying, "OK, you, Cohen, Schwartz, Goldberg, even you, O'Malley (whose descendants will someday join the Jewish people through conversion). Here's the plan. Go out for the long pass. I throw the ball to you, you catch it, then throw it to your kids, who will throw it to their kids. That is how the ball gets passed from generation to generation.

"The ball has gone from Israel to Spain to Germany to Poland to Russia to Northern Africa. We know the names of some of the ball throwers: Moses, Aaron, Deborah, David, Miriam, Ruth, Rabbi Akiba, Beruriah, Maimonides, and Henrietta Szold. All of our ancestors had his or her own way of catching the ball, of running with it, and then throwing it. Certain generations fumbled the ball, and almost let it slip through their hands. But they never completely lost the ball.

"Our generation won't drop the ball or fail to throw it to another generation. If we drop it, there are no guarantees that it will bounce again into our hands so we can throw it to future generations.

"There are rules to this 'game' of Judaism. *Number One:* Never forget that you are playing on a team that is larger than the people you see before you. It is a very, very big team. *Number Two:* Never let down your team members. You may not know them. If you do, you may not like some of them. But they need you, and you need them, for the ball to continue being passed through the generations. *Number Three:* Never let down the Coach."

Bar and bat mitzvah is a time when our young people get possession of the "ball." It is our job to make sure that they catch it, run with it well, and have enough knowledge and commitment to be able to throw it to their children, the next generation of ball throwers and ball catchers. It's the least we can do for God, for ourselves, for our children and their children and the Jewish future.

"Keep Up Your Part in the Choir"

A town in California traditionally began its monthly concerts with the singing of "The Star-Spangled Banner." One year, a guest conductor came to lead the orchestra. He was unfamiliar with the custom regarding the national anthem. As the opening bars of the first piece wafted through the auditorium, the audience realized that part of their tradition was missing.

Suddenly, a teenager rose and began singing "The Star-Spangled Banner." Slowly, others rose and also began singing. Soon, everyone was standing and everyone was singing. The singing was so powerful it drowned out the orchestra. Soon, the orchestra simply stopped playing. The musicians were dumbfounded. When the anthem was over, the orchestra applauded for the townspeople, for their performance was, in many ways, more exquisite than anything the professionals could have given.

All of us, even your child, are part of our Jewish community's "choir." The choir is comprised of every Jew now alive, and every Jew who has *ever* lived, and who will ever live. Every Jew has a piece of music with his or her part written upon it.

Some Jews will be tempted to walk away from the choir. This is not good. We need them. Some Jews will have the music in their hands, but they will merely stand silent while the rest of the choir is singing. This is also not good, for we need their voices. Every voice is unique. Every voice has something powerful to add to this millennial melody of the Jewish people. Think of what would happen if every person in the choir decided not to sing. There would be silence. And we have labored too long at our chorale of faith to let its message fall silent.

Some people will sing their part, and then improvise a little bit. This is fine. Judaism, like many kinds of music, is built less on rigidity than on informed improvisation. If we all sing our part, the result is a glorious harmony that can transform the world. Each of us has a voice. Each of us hears questions that are uniquely addressed to us: Where is *your* voice? What will *you* bring to our ancient melody?

Our voices can together meld into one large chorus. When they do, humanity, like that dumbfounded orchestra in a small town in California, will stand in awe.

"Don't Break the Chain!"

I once sat in my study with a girl who was debating whether to continue her Jewish education beyond the age of thirteen. She just wasn't sure. I asked her finally, "Have you ever received a chain letter?"

"Sure," she replied.

"How do you feel when you get a chain letter?"

"Actually, at first I feel pretty mad. After all, I didn't ask to get it."

"Right. What else is true about chain letters?"

"Well, there is usually some stuff in there about either good luck that comes to you if you continue the chain, or bad luck that happens to you if you break the chain."

"So, what do you do when you get a chain letter?"

"I usually sit down and send it on to five friends. Something bad could happen if I break the chain. Or, something good could happen if I *don't* break the chain."

"Exactly. But do you know the person who sent you the chain letter?"

"No ..."

"Then why continue with the letter?"

She fidgeted a bit. "Well, I guess I feel a sense of responsibility ..."

"You feel a sense of responsibility to people you don't even know and never met and may never meet. The Torah is like a chain letter. As with a chain letter, the process of passing it on has a lot of responsibility and a lot of power, and even a small amount of fear. Bad things could happen if we all crumpled up that chain letter and simply dropped it into the waste basket. The Jewish people could cease to exist. But great things could happen as well to the Jewish people and the Jewish faith."

There is a saying that everyone should have two truths in their pocket. One truth says, "I am only dust and ashes." The other truth says, "The world was created for my sake." This is *precisely* the time for our young people to hear the second truth. The Jewish world *was* created for the sake of each of our young people. Don't let them say it is not their responsibility to maintain the chain. It is.

Keep Your Corner Illuminated

Finally, a Hasidic tale.

In a mountain village in Europe many centuries ago, there was a nobleman who wondered what legacy he might be able to leave for his townspeople. At last he decided to build a synagogue. No one saw the plans for the building until it was finished. When the people came for the first time they marveled at its beauty and completeness.

Then someone asked, "Where are the lamps? How will it be lighted?" The nobleman pointed to brackets that were all through the synagogue on the walls. Then he gave each family a lamp which they were to bring with them each time they came to the synagogue.

"Each time you are not here," he said, "that part of the synagogue will be unlit. This is to remind you that whenever you fail to come here, especially when the community needs you, some part of God's house will be dark."

Bar and bat mitzvah can be the time when we teach our children that they have a responsibility to keep their part of God's house, and God's world, illuminated. For if they do not do so, their light will be missing, and the world will be just a little bit darker.

Write down your own ways of explaining bar and bat mitzvah to your children. What stories, images, and ideas would you use? What do you want to tell them about the meaning of this passage in their lives?

The River of Tears

How Bar and Bat Mitzvah Speak
to the Inner Lives of
Parents and Grandparents

May you live to see your world fulfilled
May your destiny be for worlds still to come,
And may you trust in generations past and yet to be.
May your heart be filled with intuition
and your words be filled with insight.
May songs of praise ever be upon your tongue
and your vision be a straight path before you.
May your eyes shine with the light of holy words
and your face reflect the brightness of the heavens.

—Talmud, Berachot 17a

The River of Tears

There is no such thing as a bar or bat mitzvah ceremony without tears.

The tears belong to several people. They belong to parents who are swelling with pride and relief. They belong to grandparents who may come up for their *aliyah*. They listen to their grandchild read or chant from the Torah, and by the time they utter the closing blessing, their lips are quivering and their tears are falling. I have seen tears fall right onto the Torah scroll. Of all the places where tears might fall, that is the holiest place of all.

Sometimes I tell the bar and bat mitzvah children about the River of Tears. It is an ancient legend that I invented.

There is a River of Tears at every bar or bat mitzvah ceremony. By definition, tears are salty. This River of Tears is sweet. This river flows with the tears of parents who have heard their children read from Torah. It is a very powerful river, for it is a very ancient river. It is a river that began in ancient Israel, and then flowed to Babylonia, and then to Spain and France and Germany and Poland and the United States and South Africa and Israel and Argentina. It is a river that flows from generation to generation. It is a river that flows wherever Jews have lived and worshipped. It gets mightier and sweeter with every passing Shabbat.

What is the source of these holy tears? What is it about bar and bat mitzvah that moves even "unreligious" Jewish parents and grandparents so deeply? How does bar and bat mitzvah speak to our own inner lives?

Tribal Tears

Jews are a tribe, in the highest and best sense of the word. Bar and bat mitzvah is the moment in the Jewish life cycle that most deeply defines who Jews are as a tribe. The Torah is their tribal wisdom.

Throughout history, the Jewish people have felt a sense of exile, and the Torah is our portable ancestral homeland. The Psalmist of almost two thousand years ago knew the feeling well: "By the waters of Babylon, we lay down and wept when we remembered Zion … How can I sing the song of the Eternal in a strange land?" (Psalm 137:1, 4).

Many American Jews, in particular, sense they are separated from a past once loved and now lost. Our exile is not only geographic, a function of living outside the land of Israel. It is spiritual. We live in a strange land of modernity, a land of dwindling communities and a land without social boundaries. Yet we want to retrieve that sense of rootedness that we, as a people, had when we sang the Lord's song. Its notes may have changed, but it is still, we sense deeply, very much the song of the Lord. And it can still, we sense deeply, console and reassure.

Some years ago, the Dalai Lama, the spiritual leader of Tibet, met for the first time with Jewish leaders and teachers. He had one main question for the Jews who visited him: "How have you managed to live for so long in exile from your homeland?" He hoped the answer would guide and inspire him as he led the scattered, demoralized, exiled Tibetan people. He was told that we Jews had brought into exile our values (such as righteousness, mercy, compassion, justice), our holy books (such as the Torah and the Talmud), and our ideas and ideals of the family.

The peak moments of life, when we experience the drama of passage, have an uncanny way of bringing us home. They can take us out of exile and show us the Jerusalem of the soul. They remind us that our lives have a rhythm and a purpose. The Protestant theologian Archie Smith once defined worship as the act of forgetting that you've forgotten. That is one reason for worship. To forget that we have forgotten. To forget that we are in exile from our roots. To reclaim our links to Jewish memory.

Judaism structures time and events for the Jew, the Jewish family, and the Jewish people. We could celebrate our thirteen-year-old child's birthday by taking ten of his friends to a football game. Instead, we observe the teachings of our tribal wisdom because, by giving us rhythm and structure, they are like a grid superimposed over the chaos of existence.

Not only at bar or bat mitzvah do we feel this structure. It is also how *Kaddish*, the prayer for the dead, functions. As Rabbi Neil Gillman, the eminent Conservative theologian, wrote, "Precisely at a time of our lives when we are most easily vulnerable to the threat of meaninglessness and chaos, our religious tradition gives us a ritual that puts order back into our lives in a very concrete way."

Immortal Tears

Personal immortality is the unspoken, unarticulated prayer at every life-cycle event. The prolific Talmudic scholar Rabbi Jacob Neusner spoke for many of us when he wrote, "At a bar or a bat mitzvah, a parent thinks not so much of the future as of the past, especially if a grandparent or a parent is deceased; the entire family one has known has assembled, and that is as much the past as the future."

At some level, often one that is deep and inarticulable, we know this. I remember a particular bat mitzvah in my last congregation. The father of the bat mitzvah had never struck me as a particularly emotional man, but at that service, standing over the Torah, he wept profusely. Standing next to him at the reading table, I was bewildered. Weeks later, he told me why he had cried:

"My father and my brother are both deceased. My kids are named for both of them. And now my daughters are both mature Jewish adults. I felt that the cycle was complete. Certain things touch you that persuade you of a Higher Power. For me, it was the memory of people who had died. I tell you, I could hear them taking pleasure in my daughter reading the Torah."

We know that our loved ones are immortal. We know that something intangible called "the soul" spans time and space. As the soul is to the individual body, so the Torah is to the Jewish people. It is the soul of the Jewish people. When we share moments of Torah, we guarantee the immortality of the Jewish people.

That dream of immortality for the Jewish people is as ancient as Ezekiel's vision of a valley of dry bones—the Jewish people after the destruction of Jerusalem in 586 B.C.E., miraculously coming back to life. Modern Jews, too, have seen dry bones come back to life. To the parents and grandparents of the generation after the Holocaust, the bar and bat mitzvah ceremony symbolizes that they are not the last Jews on earth. More than our mere ethnicity, the Torah and the reading from it at bar and bat mitzvah guarantee our immortality as a people.

It is precisely at such moments that parents and children see themselves as characters in Jewish history. I recall a conversation with the family of Bonnie, a bat mitzvah candidate, about her upcoming ceremony. She was to be the first bat mitzvah in her family's history. The girl's grandparents were Holocaust survivors. Her mother was born in a displaced persons' camp in Germany.

Bonnie and I were discussing the more mundane aspects of the ceremony when her mother noted, "There won't be many people there. Actually, there will be more from my husband's side than from mine." A silence fell upon us. Most of her side had disappeared in the camps.

I said to Bonnie, "Along with all the other important reasons for becoming bat mitzvah, there is another reason. When you stand on the *bimah* in the synagogue that morning, you will be spitting in Hitler's face."

I was restating the words of the theologian Emil Fackenheim, who wrote that after the Holocaust, the Jewish people had an additional commandment: Do not give Hitler any posthumous victories. Judaism lives—through Bonnie, her family, and their faith—and the faith of every Jew alive today.

When the Romans executed the Jewish sage Chananya ben Teradyon in the second century, they tied him to the stake with a Torah scroll and lit the pyre. As the smoke curled around him, his disciples asked him, "Our teacher, what do you see?"

Lifting his eyes and his voice, he uttered his last words: "The scroll is burning, but the letters are returning to heaven."

Scrolls have burnt. The letters of the Torah always return to heaven. Unfailingly, they always return to us as well, replenishing us, restoring us, and keeping us alive as a people.

Midlife Tears

The contemporary Jewish theologian Richard Rubenstein wrote that bar and bat mitzvah ceremonies are the occasion of parents' entry into middle age. Parents need rites of passage as much as their children do.

At the same time that children are going through their passage, their parents, who are usually just entering middle age, are pondering whether they are still useful and creative—or stagnating. In his classic *The Seasons of a Man's Life*, psychologist Daniel J. Levinson wrote that the task of midlife is to discern the polarity between being young and being old and to wrestle with a sense of mortality and a wish for immortality. Mid-life is close to the median age of parents of children who are bar and bat mitzvah. In our maturing children, we see both our own aging and our own immortality. We feel a greater sense of urgency to preserve through our children the values and traditions that we have cherished.

This transition occurs even on a purely mundane, social level. It may be the first time that many parents are hosting a large affair or are responsible for paying for such an event.

As I once asked a group of parents whose children had recently become bar and bat mitzvah, "For how many of you was this the first time that you had to do anything grown-up in your family? When your children were born and there was a *brit milah* or a baby-naming, I imagine that sometimes your parents ordered the platters for the meal. But this is different, isn't it?" And one father responded that his son's bar mitzvah "made me realize how old I am and that my kids are not that young anymore. It made me grateful for the consoling bond of religion."

"It made me grateful for the consoling bond of religion." Such is the often unspoken power of religion—to guide us through our passages and to give us meaning.

Tears of Passing Years

When grandparents bless the Torah at their grandchild's bar or bat mitzvah, they are often acutely aware of many things. They remember their own parents, which often means that they remember their own Jewish coming-of-age. They remember what it was like fifty, sixty, maybe seventy years before, when they were thirteen and their parents and grandparents stood over them. Many, if not most, of the grandmothers will not have those memories of becoming bat mitzvah. It matters little. They still feel the presence of their own parents and grandparents.

The grandparents sense the irretrievable passing of the years. They are not young anymore. Neither, they realize, are their own children. As grandparents look into the twilight of their lives, they struggle against despair. Their generation is no longer dominant, and they are less vital or vibrant than before.

The Talmud teaches that to hear your child's child reading Torah is like hearing the words from Sinai itself. Grandparents, even those that call themselves "unreligious," cry when their grandchildren read Torah. They sense that their grandchildren are speaking words that evoke Sinai. The modern Austrian Jewish author Stefan Zweig once wrote: "One who looks at his father is like one who sees God, because he can look beyond his father to creation. And one who looks at his children sees God, because he can look beyond his children through the generations to the Messiah."

Jewish Spirituality—Even for the "Unspiritual"

When all is said and done, what is it about bar and bat mitzvah that draws us—even when we tend to ignore the other sacred moments of Jewish time?

In reality, Judaism has two calendars—the public and the personal. The public calendar of Jewish sacred time is the festival cycle. The private calendar of Jewish sacred time is the life cycle—birth, maturity, marriage, and death. With the exception of Rosh Ha Shanah and Yom Kippur, Jewish spirituality has usually shifted from the festivals to the life cycle. When Jews experience *kedushah* (holiness), they invariably experience it in the life cycle—circumcision, baby-namings, bar and bat mitzvah, weddings, funerals.

Why has this shift happened? Because society has shifted its focus from the group to the self. Individualism has triumphed. The only community that we usually know well is our family. The synagogue may be a public space, but the meanings that we bring to it are often very private. As liturgist Lawrence Hoffman has said, "People attend synagogue now mostly for life-cycle liturgies to celebrate their selves ... the bar/bat mitzvah *minyan* kidnaps the sanctuary. The *mi sheberakh* [the traditional prayer for healing] becomes the center of the service." Even in the midst of massive unbelief and doubt, the Jewish life cycle is the context in which the Jew experiences "moment faiths," sacred moments in life when we realize that there is a God in the world.

The beauty of the Jewish life cycle is that it keeps the Jew connected to the Jewish people, to God, to Torah. During those moments when we might feel personally adrift and in need of Judaism, our potent tribal wisdom is there for us, with all its potential healing power.

The Jew is not alone at the *brit* ceremony. There, the *mohel* recites the words that God spoke to Abraham: *"Hithaleich lifanai veheyei tamim"* ("Walk before Me and be perfect"). Pointing to an empty chair, the *mohel* says, *"Zeh kisei shel Eliyahu hanavi"* ("This is the chair of Elijah, the prophet"). Elijah is "there" to ensure that the covenant lives. The *mohel* has already evoked Abraham, the first Jew. Elijah, the harbinger of the Messiah, is the last Jew. The newborn infant may yet be the Messiah, or may help usher in the Messianic Age. History and the Jewish people live through this child. Torah, also, potentially lives as well.

The Jew is not alone at the wedding. The Jewish wedding ceremony is more than two people celebrating and confirming their love. It is the reprise of the covenant between God and Israel. The bride and groom are no longer themselves. The seven wedding blessings urge the couple to imagine themselves as Adam and Eve, cradled yet again in the Garden of Eden. The blessings end by proclaiming that the marriage may help bring the Messianic Age. The groom's shattering of the glass is frequently interpreted as a memory of the destruction of the Temple in Jerusalem, a further link to Jewish history and experience.

And the Jew is not alone even at death. At a funeral service, usually a passage is read from Psalms, the oldest written Jewish liturgy. Then comes *Kaddish*, part of the inherited spiritual repertoire of every Jew, no matter how estranged. And finally, the service ends with the community saying to the mourners: *Hamakom yenachem etchem betoch shear avelei Tzion viYerushalayim* ("May God comfort you among those who are mourners for Zion and Jerusalem"). The liturgy links across space and across time the individual mourner's anguish to that of the larger Jewish people.

Bar and bat mitzvah ceremonies are far more crowded than anyone can imagine. At the bar and bat mitzvah ceremony, the visible and, even, the invisible generations are present, just as they were present for the sealing of the covenant. The silent, implicit message of bar or bat mitzvah is the revelation that each parent understands: *I am not the last Jew in the world.*

Bar and bat mitzvah is so popular because it is the tangible sign that the youth before us embodies all that passed before him or her, that this thirteen-year-old incarnates Jewish triumphs, tragedies, wisdom, virtues, and the soaring hopes of a people who have seen themselves decimated only to rise again from the blackest of ashes. This child is now a constant reminder of Jewish yesterdays that were fulfilled or frustrated, and of Jewish tomorrows still to come.

What are your feelings as your child prepares to become bar or bat mitzvah? What changes are you going through at this time? How do you think Judaism can help you get through the different cycles of life? Write your answers here and above.

CHAPTER

4

Hearing God's Voice
The Meaning of Torah

The divine word spoke to each and every person
according to his or her particular capacity:
the young according to their capacity,
the old in keeping with their capacity.

—MIDRASH, *Pesikta de Rav Kahana*

Hearing God's Voice

Something uplifting, something inarticulately holy occurs when a child reads from the Torah scroll on the day when he or she becomes bar or bat mitzvah.

Like many words from religious traditions, Torah has multiple meanings. It literally means "teaching." When we speak of reading from *the* Torah, we generally mean reading from the *sefer Torah*, the Torah scroll itself. The scroll contains the Five Books of Moses. Each book has a name in Greek or English, and also a Hebrew name, which corresponds to the first or second words of the book. Therefore, Genesis, the Greek name, is *Bereshit* ("When God began to create") in Hebrew. Exodus becomes *Shemot* ("These are the names"); Leviticus is *Vayikra* ("And God called"); Numbers is *Bemidbar* ("In the wilderness"); and, Deuteronomy is *Devarim* ("The words").

What Torah Portion Will Your Child Read?

It takes a full Jewish year, starting in the fall with the festival of *Simchat Torah*, to read the Torah. Bar and bat mitzvah candidates read (or chant, according to the custom of their synagogue) the *parashah*, the Torah portion for that particular week. If your child celebrates bar or bat mitzvah during a festival (Sukkot or Pesach, or on the second day of Shavuot, or on Rosh Chodesh, the first day of the Jewish month), there will be special Torah and *haftarah* readings that will not conform to the usual weekly cycle.

If your child's thirteenth birthday falls roughly between October and the end of December, he or she will probably read from Genesis, which spans the years from the Creation to Joseph's death in Egypt. Much of the Hebrew Bible's richest narrative material is in Genesis— Creation; Cain and Abel; Noah and the Flood; and the tales of the patriarchs and matriarchs, Abraham, Isaac, Jacob, Sarah, Rebecca, and Leah. It also includes the oldest complete novel in history, the story of Joseph, which takes up more than one-quarter of the book of Genesis.

If your child becomes thirteen between January and the end of February, he or she will read a section from Exodus. This tells of the Jews' enslavement in Egypt; the rise of Moses and the liberation from slavery; the crossing of the Red Sea; the giving of the Ten Commandments; the idolatry of the Golden Calf; and the design and construction of the Tabernacle, the desert sanctuary for the original tablets of the Law. Exodus also includes various ethical and civil laws, such as the instruction "not [to] wrong a stranger or oppress him, for you were strangers in the land of Egypt."

If your child turns thirteen between early March and the end of May, he or she will read a section of the book of Leviticus. The book contains the laws of sacrifice, ethics, and purity. Leviticus is the "user manual" of ancient Biblical Judaism.

If your synagogue has summer bar and bat mitzvah ceremonies, a child born during June or July will read from the book of Numbers, which recounts the wanderings in the wilderness and various rebellions against the authority of Moses.

With the end of summer comes the end of the yearly reading of the Torah. Deuteronomy, the last book in the Torah, is essentially Moses's farewell address to the Israelites as they prepare to enter the land of Israel. Various laws that were previously discussed are repeated, sometimes with different wordings. Deuteronomy ends with the death of Moses on the summit of Mount Nebo as he looks across the valley into the land that he would not enter. On *Simchat Torah*, the scroll goes from the death of Moses to the creation of the world without missing as much as a breath.

What Else Is Torah?

The first part of the Hebrew Bible is the Torah. But there is much more to it than these five books. The accurate term for the Hebrew Bible is the *Tanach*, an acronym for *Torah*, *Neviim* (the Prophets), and *Ketuvim* (the later Writings). In Hebrew, the Torah is also referred to as the *Chumash*; in Greek, it is known as the *Pentateuch*. Both terms are derived from the word for "five" in their respective languages.

In the broadest sense, Torah means Judaism's entire literary and legal tradition. Studying Torah means not only studying the Torah (the *Chumash*, the *Pentateuch*, the *Scroll*), but the entire Hebrew Bible, as well. We can extend this to post-Biblical Jewish law and lore, such as the *Mishnah*, the *Talmud*, and the *Midrash*, and can speak even more broadly when we speak of studying Torah. We can mean studying medieval commentary, philosophy, poetry, mysticism, and Hasidism. We can mean studying modern scholars, teachers, and philosophers. We can mean *everything* that Jews have thought about, struggled with, and created during their history.

In effect, when we say *Torah*, we mean Judaism. We also mean anything that emerges out of our open encounter with those sources. When we study secular literature, we reflect on it by noting "Shakespeare *said*"— in the past tense. But when we study Judaism? "The ancient rabbis, or Rashi, or Maimonides, *says*"—in the present tense. Judaism is an ongoing conversation in which the insights of our ancestors are as real to us as if they had been said today. As *Pirke Avot* (the ethical maxims of the early rabbis, who lived in the first two centuries of the Common Era, as recorded in the *Mishnah*) says, "Every day a voice goes forth from Sinai." Every day, at least, if we can train our ears to hear the truth and the power and the beauty of the Torah.

Judaism is not just the words of the written Torah. It includes oral traditions. Jews are not fundamentalists. We do not lock ourselves into a prison of the text and exclude all external experience. The insights of modern science have prompted us to reexamine the creation story of Genesis. Archeology has raised new questions about the historical accuracy of the Biblical texts. Feminist thinkers have inspired us to reconsider some of the Torah's views on women. Psychologists and sociologists have encouraged us to ask whether some of the Torah's teachings on human sexuality are still accurate.

Judaism has shaped and reshaped itself since its ancient days. Many of its practices have changed radically since Biblical days. For instance, Jews no longer celebrate Passover by sacrificing a lamb. The Torah tells us to refrain from working on the Sabbath and on the sacred days of the major festivals. Yet it never defines work. Rituals that now seem essential to Shabbat—candle lighting and *kiddush*—are nowhere in the

Torah. *Kippah* or *yarmulke*, traditional Jewish ritual head coverings, are not in the Torah. The Torah does not mention several holidays that we now think are essential to Judaism, such as Chanukah and Purim. And it did not anticipate the Holocaust and the rebirth of the Jewish state, which have become pivotal to modern Jewish self-understanding.

Judaism begins with *the* Torah, the scroll that young Jews read as they become bar and bat mitzvah. Ideally, Torah becomes their Sacred Story, the lens through which they view themselves as Jews. These stories have survived because they are timeless.

Parents and children shudder when they hear the story of the binding of Isaac. The shuddering goes back to our very beginnings as a people. Every infertile couple inwardly weeps when hearing of Rachel's difficulty in bearing children. Her cry to her husband Jacob—"Give me children, or else I die!"—echoes across the centuries. Single parents who struggle to raise children "know" the story of Hagar and Ishmael, Abraham's maidservant and her son, who were cast out into the desert. Every one who has had but an instant of spiritual understanding and intuition has been with Moses at the burning bush that was not consumed. Every Jew who has become successful while living in a non-Jewish culture knows what Joseph experienced in Egypt. And many aged persons who hear the tale of the death of Moses knows what it is like to die before reaching one's greatest goal.

In the Shabbat morning service, we read these words—*tein chelkeinu b'Toratecha*, "Give us our portion in Your Torah." Each of us has a verse in the Torah that "has our name on it." Each of us has a verse that is about us. If we are fortunate, we will find that verse and make it a part of our lives. In every Torah portion, there is a verse that can speak uniquely and directly to our young people as they become bar and bat mitzvah.

The Haftarah: The Rest of God's Call to Us

The Scriptures are more than the Torah. After the Torah is read in the synagogue, the congregation hears the *haftarah*, which literally means "the conclusion." The *haftarah* comes from the *Neviim*, the

Prophetic books, the second part of the Hebrew Bible, the *Tanach*. It is read from a Hebrew Bible, or in the case of a bar or bat mitzvah, sometimes from a photocopied sheet.

The Torah is read sequentially, from Creation to the death of Moses. But the *haftarah* is read selectively, from any number of prophetic and historical books. Those *haftarah* passages were chosen because of their thematic connection to the Torah text.

Not all Books in the Prophetic section of the Hebrew Bible are prophecy. Several are historical. The Book of Joshua recounts the story of the conquest and settlement of Israel. One *haftarah* passage speaks about Joshua's succession to leadership after the death of Moses. Another tells the exciting story of the spies who entered the city of Jericho before the Israelite conquest of the land of Israel.

Judges speaks of the time of anarchy when "no king ruled in Israel." Some judges are well known through literature and history—Deborah, the great prophetess and military leader; Samson, the great Biblical strong man; Jephtah, who vowed to sacrifice the first animal (or person) that he saw after winning a decisive battle and ended up sacrificing his only daughter.

The Books of Samuel tell of the transition from the period of Samuel, the last judge and prophet, to the monarchy under Saul and David. The Books of Kings tell of the death of King David, the ascension of King Solomon, and the Israelite kingdom's rupture into the northern kingdom of Israel and the southern kingdom of Judah.

Above all else, these historical books are noteworthy for their striking sense of *normality*. Jews emerge as a holy people, but only in their potential. Their kings and generals are people of flesh and blood, with real-life urges, failures, weaknesses, and triumphs.

Then in the *haftarah* come the words of the prophets, those spokesmen for God whose words fired Jews' consciousness and conscience. Their names are immortal—Isaiah, Jeremiah, Ezekiel, Amos, Hosea.

A religious writer, Frederick Buechner, once quipped that "there is no evidence of any prophet being invited back a second time for dinner." Some of them would not last long as rabbis in modern congregations.

No prophet ever won a popularity contest. The prophets were powerful and passionate truth tellers—both to ordinary people and especially to the rulers. They were the spiritual ancestors of such contemporary religious leaders as Reverend Martin Luther King, Jr. and Rabbi Abraham Joshua Heschel—great voices of religious and social conscience.

The prophets reminded the Jewish people that God cares more about ethical behavior than about ritual accuracy; that God chose the Jewish people not for privilege but for duty; that we have a religious obligation to build a society that will guarantee justice and peace; and that, with our help, history can move toward an ultimate, redemptive conclusion, which we call the days of the Messiah or the Messianic age.

Why Your Child Reads Torah

Torah is more than the Scroll. It represents everything that Jews hold sacred. So, let us consider: What is the significance of reading Torah during a worship service?

I once asked a group of parents of pre-bar and bat-mitzvah candidates, "What does it mean for your child to read Torah when he or she becomes bar or bat mitzvah?" Among their responses:

- "That my son has completed his studies and achieved his goal that was taught in Hebrew and Sunday school."
- "He learns values from the Torah that can be applied to real life."
- "It signifies that she has come of age in the Jewish religion."
- "A link with his ancestors in a common bond that dates back for thousands of years."
- "A special moment in her life to read from such a special and sacred scroll."

There were more than a few answers of one word: "Tradition."

I found the responses troubling. As I read "skills" and "accomplishment" and "educated," I wondered: How was this particular skill and accomplishment and educational achievement different from others that the child would experience?

One quality separates this act of learning, reading and interpreting Torah to a congregation from all other experiences and learning and accomplishments. That quality is God.

Modern Jews are notoriously hesitant about speaking of God. They fear that accepting God as the source of Torah might lead to a dangerous flirtation with fundamentalism. "If God is in it, doesn't that mean God wrote it? If God wrote it, how can I even think of disagreeing with it?"

Jews have always perceived Torah through the eyes of great commentators and interpreters, such as Rashi, the great medieval sage who lived in the Rhineland in the eleventh century. Judaism treasured the idea that it must constantly reinterpret the tradition it had inherited. This is the opposite of fundamentalism, which believes in the unchanging, literal nature of a sacred scripture.

Some people believe that Torah is simply the great literature of a great people. That position is common and respectable. That is what college students learn when they take courses on "The Bible as Literature." As literature, Torah is, indeed, wonderful. But *simply* as literature, it becomes as spiritual as, say, Mark Twain. It loses its fire and its passion.

Traditional Judaism holds that God dictated the entire text of Torah to Moses. This view sees revelation as a singular event, not a constantly evolving process.

There are, of course, other views. Modern scholarship sees the development of literary traditions within the Torah itself. Yet, this knowledge hardly detracts from the sanctity of what we read. Similarly, we do not need to know exactly how Picasso chose to paint *Guernica* to feel the full impact of the painting.

Where do we get this sense that God is *in* the text, even if we believe that God did not write the text?

God's Presence in the Scroll

The Torah is great literature. Shakespeare and Tolstoy are also great literature. So is Dickens, yet no contemporary English person would open *Oliver Twist* to find spiritual uplift in its pages. The *Odyssey* is great literature, yet we cannot imagine a modern Greek running into a burning building to rescue a manuscript of it, as generations have done for the Torah scroll. If we were to look at the Torah as simply the great literature of our people, then it would not command or move us as it does.

The fact that we American Jews use the Torah scroll indicates that we have not become entirely secularized. We Jews understand, often purely intuitively, the power of the Scroll. It evokes history, continuity, tradition—and it does so in a way that no other Jewish ritual object can.

Consider, first, the *halachah* (traditional Jewish law) regarding how a Torah scroll must be treated. There is one law that almost every Jew knows: a person who accidentally drops a Torah scroll must atone through fasting or giving charity. Some say the person who witnesses the dropping of the Torah must also fast as an act of mourning. As the late scholar Rabbi Daniel J. Silver wrote, the Torah "had become revelation, resplendent in divine mystery, symbol and substance of God's wisdom, the source too holy to be handled with any but the most reverent humility." The Nazis delighted in desecrating Torah scrolls and transforming them into such profane objects as shoes and, even, a banjo. Photographs from *Kristallnacht* of November 1938 show thugs unraveling Torah scrolls out of synagogue windows. On that Night of Broken Glass, countless Jews ran back into burning synagogues to rescue Torah scrolls. Some were learned; some were religiously ignorant. They all felt the pull of the Scroll, the same pull that each generation of Jews had felt dating back to Sinai.

How Do We Experience God in the Service?

The liturgical high moment of Shabbat morning worship is the Torah service. And the emotional "center" of that service occurs when the Torah is removed from the *aron hakodesh* (the Holy Ark). What *is* the Ark? And what does it mean to Jews?

To Daniel Silver, a divine choreography is performed before the Ark. The curtain in front of the Ark, he explained, recalls

... in purpose and name, the *parochet*, the curtain that had fronted the Holy of Holies in the Temple, where the ark containing the Tablets of the Ten Commandments was said to have been kept ... and where in the Second Temple there had been an empty space filled with God's presence. ... The *sefer Torah* was understood as God's immanent presence. Men bowed when they crossed in front of the Ark and rose when it was opened, because of its sacred contents.

But the Ark itself has even greater significance. The late mythologist Joseph Campbell wrote that sacred stories connect us to sacred places. Each culture believes that its sacred place is the center of the earth. Jews are no exception. The Holy of Holies in the ancient Temple on the Temple Mount in Jerusalem was the very navel of the earth. It was where the tablets of the covenant were kept. Some traditions say that place is the birthplace of Adam, or where Noah made his first sacrifice after the flood, or where Abraham bound Isaac as a sacrifice, or where Jacob dreamed of a ladder of angels. Moslems say it is where Mohammed ascended to heaven.

Since the ninth day of the Hebrew month of Av in the year 70 c.e.—the day the Romans destroyed the Temple—Jews have lacked this sacred geographic and spiritual center. But on each day the Torah is read—Monday, Thursday, Shabbat morning and afternoon, and festival mornings—Jews go before the Ark, the holiest spot in the holiest area in the holiest room in the holiest building that they know. And there, something happens.

Just what occurs when the rabbi removes the Torah from the Ark and prepares it for reading? More than meets the eye. The Ark in the synagogue "becomes" the Ark in the ancient Temple in Jerusalem. Every time the Torah is taken out to be read, Jews reenact the moment when God gave the Torah to Moses. In a sense, when a rabbi hands the scroll to a child, he or she re-creates the giving of the Torah to Moses to be read to the Jewish people.

The Scroll is held aloft after it is read or chanted and the congregation sings: "This is the Torah that Moses placed before the children of Israel to fulfill the word of God." Literary theorists suggest that the observers of such symbolic acts participate in an imaginative process called "the willing suspension of disbelief." It doesn't matter that the congregants saying these words may be sitting in a suburban synagogue wearing a suit or a dress. During services, we are one with all Jews everywhere in the world in all times. The synagogue may be only half full. But present is every Jew who has ever lived and who ever will live. For a few moments, when we stand at the open Ark, we are no longer in our synagogue. We stand before Sinai with our ancestors, witnessing the majestic and the awesome and the ineffable.

Note, finally, the magic of the Scroll itself. No parents would let their child read or chant his or her Torah portion from a printed page or even from a bound book. The Torah scroll is our link to the God who loves us and who made and keeps a Covenant with us.

As Blu Greenberg, the Orthodox Jewish feminist, wrote: "God revealed the Torah to the Jewish people at Sinai. ... Some part of my DNA was also there at Sinai, in the crowd. Reading the weekly portion of the Torah, week after week, year after year, I never cease to be amazed at this treasure."

Did God Write the Torah?

Because I believe in a pluralistic approach to Jewish sources, I believe that there are several ways of hearing God in the text. The first possibility is the supernaturalist interpretation regarding divine revelation. Most often called Orthodox, this position states that God revealed the Divine Will at Sinai in both a written form (the written Torah, *Torah she-bichtav*) and oral form (*Torah she-be-al peh*, which was ultimately written down as the *Mishnah* and the *Talmud*). The oral tradition is the authoritative interpretation of the written Torah.

Rabbi Norman Lamm, the great Orthodox scholar and chancellor of Yeshiva University in New York, explained the Orthodox position:

The Torah is divine revelation in two ways: It is God-given and it is godly. By "God-given," I mean that He willed that man abide by His commandments and that that will was communicated in discrete words and letters. ... I accept unapologetically the idea of the verbal revelation of the Torah. ... *How* God spoke is a mystery;

how *Moses* received this message is an irrelevancy. *That* God spoke is of the utmost significance.

Conservative Judaism, which occupies the centrist position in American Judaism, offers a spectrum of positions regarding God's role in revelation. Some Conservative theologians, such as the late Abraham Joshua Heschel, hold that God revealed the Divine Will at Sinai. Those revelations, however, were transcribed by human beings, which accounts for the wide variety of biblical traditions, and which also accounts for the occasional contradiction of these traditions.

Other Conservative theologians, such as the late Ben Zion Bokser, hold that *divinely inspired* human beings wrote down the Torah. Still others, such as the late Seymour Siegel, say Torah is the *human* record of the encounter between God and the Jewish people at Sinai. Since it was written by human beings, it contains some laws and ideas that we might reject as anachronistic.

In general, Conservative Judaism sees Torah as rooted in a transcendent reality, yet constantly evolving. Francine Klagsbrun, a prominent Conservative lay leader and author, has written: "The texts are the lifeblood of our tradition. What happened at Sinai is a mystery I cannot fathom, but something did happen to assure the people of Israel that divine purpose informed every aspect of their existence. The Torah may have had several authors over time, but at its core it remains inspired by a people's conviction of their encounter with God."

Conservative Judaism, true to its name, *conserves* much of the traditional view of Torah, though accepting that our view of it is affected by the time in which we live. It looks at what Jews have done, at the practices they have abandoned, and approaches tradition while it is cognizant of contemporary realities. When changes are to be officially made, they must evolve through the Committee on Jewish Law and Standards of the Rabbinical Assembly, which is Conservative Judaism's rabbinic body.

Reconstructionist Judaism was the intellectual child of one of the most extraordinary Jews of the twentieth century, Rabbi Mordecai Kaplan (1881–1983). His writings also greatly affected the Conservative movement. Kaplan believed that Judaism was the *creation* of the

Jewish community, influenced by the God Who, existing within nature, cannot violate its laws. Kaplan also taught that Torah emerges from the life of the Jewish people.

Reconstructionists believe that revelation is the process by which the Jewish people discover God's purpose. The earliest record of this search is contained in the Torah. As Ira Eisenstein, Kaplan's son-in-law and successor as the leader of the Reconstructionist movement, has written:

> Despite what the Torah claims for itself, I believe that it is a human document, reflecting the attempt of its authors to account for the history of the Jewish people, and for the moral and ethical insights which its geniuses acquired during the course of that history. It is "sacred literature" in the sense that Jews have always seen in it the source and the authority for that way of life and that view of history which gave meaning and direction to their lives.

Finally, there is the approach of Reform Judaism. Professor Michael Meyer of Hebrew Union College–Jewish Institute of Religion, summarizes that approach this way: "The Torah is not for me divine revelation in any literal sense. Rather the Pentateuch, the Prophets, the Writings, and the rabbinic literature represent our people's ongoing historical endeavor to verbalize their experience of a God Who represents the objective reality of justice, mercy, and love."

Hearing God in the Torah: Sometimes It Is Very Easy

There are certainly moments when I hear the authentic voice of God—metaphorically—in the Torah. And I believe that those are moments when our young people can hear God's voice as well. There is little that compares with the opening words of the scroll: *Bereshit bara Elohim* ("When God began to create heaven and earth"). One does not have to be a fundamentalist to feel the power in this one sentence. It transcends geology and astronomy and suggests an order and a meaningfulness in the world. Since God made the world, *Bereshit* suggests that we who are made in God's image are stewards of God's creation. And since God included rest in the order of creation, *Bereshit* tells us that Shabbat is holy.

Many other stories with God's presence permeate the Torah. From them, our young people can find that God's voice truly sings forth— Abraham setting forth at God's command to a land that he did not yet know. The revelation of the Ten Commandments. Moses dying in solitude on Mount Nebo.

Why is God in those stories? Because their meaning has survived the centuries. Because they have an overwhelming literary beauty. Because of the emotions they elicit. And most often, because their implicit values have survived intact, though not unchallenged, into our time. When our young people interpret those stories and find their own place within those values, that is God's voice speaking once again.

We seek out—and cherish—those moments when our youth hear God in Torah. That happens when the stories of Torah become *their* stories. A few years ago, I taught Marcie, a twelve-year-old girl, the story of how Miriam, the sister of Moses, prevailed upon her parents to maintain their relationship, even in the face of the stress brought upon by the oppression of Jews in Egypt. As a result, she cajoled her own parents, who were having marital difficulties, into reconciling their differences.

When Robert Coles, professor of psychiatry at Harvard University, was researching his book *The Spiritual Life of Children*, he asked the Jewish, Christian, and Muslim children whom he interviewed, "What story in the Bible (or the Koran) is *your* story?" He writes: "Biblical stories have a way of being used by children to look inward as well as upward…. The stories of Adam and Eve, Abraham and Isaac, Noah and the Ark, Cain and Abel, Samson and Delilah, David and Goliath, get linked in the minds of millions of children to their own personal stories." Those stories help them explore such issues as family relationships, sexuality, awe, envy, and anger.

We—and our children—need to feel connected to a story that goes beyond us, a story that predated us and that will last long after we are gone.

As the philosopher Alasdair MacIntyre writes: "I can only answer the question 'What am I to do?' if I can answer the prior question 'Of what story or stories do I find myself a part?'"

Twelve-year-old Marcie had found her own story, her own life, and her own struggle in the scroll, and that story had told her what to do.

Sometimes It Is Very Hard

Sometimes it is very hard to hear God in a text. But when young people try, in their trying they hear God telling them to strive for inspiration, to find the deeply imbedded jewel in a place that seems devoid of such jewels. When we seek to find meaning in a morally or aesthetically difficult text, we make a conscious effort to hear what the text might be saying to us. We are saying that there might be more wisdom before us than meets the eye. This is the essence of the Jewish search for wisdom—knowing that we do not have all the answers and believing that they may yet come through sincere inquiry and struggle.

I have two favorite examples of wisdom in unlikely places in the Torah. One is in Leviticus, which is a problematic book. Most of us Jews feel more connected to the Torah's stories than to its laws, and truth be told, there is really only one story, one event in the book. Fire consumes Aaron's sons, Nadav and Avihu, as they make the wrong kind of incense offering. It is an interesting story with some tantalizing commentaries. At its best, it makes a wonderful detective story, as we wonder aloud, "Who or what killed Nadav and Avihu? Why did they have to die?" But, on the whole, the story is not very uplifting.

That is the problem. Most of Leviticus is concerned with laws. It's one thing for our children to read the Torah's laws about compassion for strangers and widows and orphans, or to read the details of the construction of the Tabernacle. But the laws of Leviticus are something else again. Sacrifice. Blood. Altars. Purity. Impurity. Sexuality.

And then, there's the portion known as *Tazria*, sometimes combined with the subsequent portion *Metzora*. Here we encounter the Torah in all its real-life nakedness. Some bar or bat mitzvah candidate always gets this portion since it is almost impossible to schedule around it. This Torah portion comes around in the spring, the most popular season for a bar or bat mitzvah ceremony.

Consider the topics of *Tazria-Metzora*. Ritual impurity after child-birth. Menstrual flows. Various bodily emissions. A detailed description of a disease that may be leprosy or psoriasis. Not the most attractive subjects in the world—and virtually guaranteed to elicit a "yuk!" from any thirteen-year-old.

Yet, sometimes I hear some excellent bar and bat mitzvah speeches about this portion. Our teenagers are fascinated by the Torah's description of psoriasis and the accompanying social fear and ostracism. They integrate their growing sense of social justice and compassion into the words of the Torah portion. They know that the revulsion that the Torah describes is too often identical to our contemporary revulsion to such diseases as cancer, epilepsy, AIDS. They understand the antiquity of their own discomfort with people who are handicapped, deformed, or, for whatever reason, different. When our young people make the connection, Torah comes alive before their eyes. God has "spoken" again.

Genesis 34: The Rape of Dinah

It had once been the practice in my former congregation to let b'nai mitzvah choose the passages they want to read from the assigned Torah portion for their Shabbat. Jessica, a thirteen-year-old, made a rather unusual choice. Her thirteenth birthday happened to fall in early December. *Parshat Vayishlach* from the book of Genesis was her Torah portion. *Vayishlach* contains several narrative gems, especially Jacob's wrestling with the unnamed stranger at the banks of the Jabbok River and his subsequent reunion with his brother, Esau. Yet, when presented with those literary options, she stunned me.

"No," she said, "I read the Torah portion and I want to read the part about Dinah. Didn't you once give a sermon about how she was raped? People should know about Dinah. I want to read her story."

Dinah? Hardly the story that a thirteen-year-old girl would want to share with friends and family. Mind you—this was years before Anita Diamant wrote her novel *The Red Tent* about Dinah. Who knew about Dinah back in those pre-Diamant days?

Why don't most Reform Jews know about Dinah, even those who attend synagogue frequently? The reason is clear: Most Reform synagogues do not read the entire weekly Torah portion. The Torah readers choose to read a passage that seems to be spiritually uplifting and will not be too jarring to modern sensibilities. Even in traditional synagogues, my guess is that the Torah reader tends to rush through the story of Dinah, betraying a certain embarrassment with the tale.

For that reason, years may pass in a Reform synagogue before the Torah scroll is opened to Genesis 34: "And Dinah, the daughter of Leah, went out to see the daughters of the land. Shechem, the son of Hamor the Hivite, prince of the land, saw her and he took her and he lay with her and he humbled her."

Apparently, Shechem loved Dinah and wanted to marry her. But first, Shechem's father, Hamor, had to agree that Shechem and all the males of his clan would be circumcised. On the third day after their circumcision, while they were still in pain, Simeon and Levi, Jacob's sons, slaughtered the men of Shechem and rescued their sister from Shechem's household. It is a tale of sexuality and the dark impulses of vengeance.

And yet, on the day she became bat mitzvah, Jessica read the story of Dinah proudly and well. Jessica helped me understand that we can again redeem Dinah's story. We hear Dinah's voice frequently these days.

Some say that Dinah's story is not about rape, but about seduction. It is clearly about the place of one woman's sexuality in our sacred literature and in our imagination. Dinah says nothing in the story, and so the text is about the muteness of women and how this must be fought. The story is about violence and ethical profanation, themes that, regrettably, are alive and more than relevant today.

Jessica struggled with the tale of Dinah. In her *devar Torah*, she reminded the congregation that Dinah is silent and passive both in the Biblical tale and in more than a thousand years of rabbinic interpretation and retelling of her tale. She taught that Dinah's muteness symbolized the role of Jewish women in traditional society, a muteness that she thought must no longer exist. It was a sparkling morning of reclaiming Torah.

Through the act of interpretation, we discover why the Torah is written without vowels. It needs us to add our own voice to it. The Torah we are given is revelation only in potential. It needs our voice, our presence, our interpretation. Then, and only then, does it become complete. When Jessica struggled with the story of Dinah, and then so wonderfully interpreted it for the congregation, she added her voice to the Torah. By doing so, she helped complete it.

Young People Feel God

Through study or interpretation or teaching the congregation what he or she has learned, young Jews deeply and profoundly feel God in the Torah. I once asked a group of post-bar and -bat mitzvah teens, "How did you feel the presence of God in your bar or bat mitzvah ceremony?" If you think that our children are entirely secularized and cynical, read how some young people answered me:

- "I felt that God was around when I held the Torah and when I was reading it. The Torah scroll symbolizes a special closeness to God."

- "Reading from the Torah was like God giving Moses the Torah. It's come down to us, and we're taking its laws into our hands. Because the Torah symbolizes God."

At such moments we understand the Torah blessing, *Baruch attah Adonai, notein hatorah*, "Blessed are You, Adonai, Giver of the Torah." God did not just give Torah at Sinai. God gives Torah today. This is Torah's magical potency that has spoken through the ages.

And that is what I say to the young person who is about to become bar or bat mitzvah, to a thirteen-year-old who is trembling, just as the Jews trembled when God revealed the Ten Commandments at Sinai. I hand the scroll to him or her and say, "Centuries ago, our people stood at Sinai. There in the wilderness, we met God. Centuries later, when we reflected on that presence and on that encounter, our people wrote these words that are found in this scroll. This scroll is the closest thing to what we know God wants of us. In this scroll are many of our stories, our laws, our teachings, even our very names. This scroll is the secret of our survival."

One more secret is that the scroll lets us hear God speak, either with hushed, comforting quiet or with a great cosmic peal that humbles. It is the way we hear God. It is the way we stand at Sinai once again. All that the Jewish people have been and all that we will be is on the *bimah* as a youth reads from the scroll. It is a scroll that has been battered and burned and torn through the ages. But it has survived because the Jewish people have cherished it.

The Talmud puts it this way: "We were sitting and discussing the Torah, going from the Torah to the Prophets, and from the Prophets to the Writings, until the words became as radiant as when they were first imparted at Sinai" (Palestinian Talmud, Hagigah 2:1). That is how studying Torah can be for us as well—a moment of feeling the radiance that our ancestors felt when they first stood at Sinai and received the words for the first time.

Ask each member of your family to answer this question: What does Torah mean in my life? What do I believe the source of Torah to be? Agree on an answer that speaks for your entire family and write it here.

Putting the Mitzvah Back in Bar and Bat Mitzvah

God is hiding in the world.
Our task is to let the divine emerge
from our deeds.

—ABRAHAM JOSHUA HESCHEL, *God in Search of Man*

Putting the Mitzvah Back in Bar and Bat Mitzvah

Jewish children become bar or bat mitzvah because of God's covenant with the people of Israel. The *mitzvot* are our end of the covenant. *Mitzvah*, in fact, is one of the most important ideas Judaism gave to the world: A relationship with God entails mutual responsibility. Traditionally, there are 613 *mitzvot* derived from the Torah. Ritual *mitzvot*, such as observing Shabbat and keeping the dietary laws of *kashrut*, connect us to God. Ethical *mitzvot*, such as not murdering or gossiping, govern our relationship with people. Some *mitzvot* are in positive language: "Thou *shalt* ..." Others are in negative language: "Thou shalt *not* ..." The idea of *mitzvah* is central to Jewish identity. It is the essence of the Covenant, our end of the agreement made at Sinai, the summit of Jewish existence.

The Difference between Mitzvah and Mitzveh

There is one problem with *mitzvah*. Many people don't know how to pronounce the word. There seem to be two pronunciations. Is it *mitzvah*? Or *mitzveh*?

One small vowel makes all the difference. *Mitzveh* is a Yiddish term that comes from the original Hebrew. Hebrew contributed almost 5,000 words to Yiddish, which often made slight changes in the original meaning of the Hebrew words. *Mitzveh* is a classic example. As author Moshe Waldoks once wrote, "*Mitzveh* encompasses moral deeds not explicitly enjoined by the religious teachings of Jewish tradition. *Mitzveh* means doing something for someone else; feeling communal solidarity by imitating God's concern for the world."

Mitzvah means something deeper. Traditionally, *mitzvot* are of divine origin. But somehow during the past century, we Jews lost the sense of *mitzvah* as a holy obligation. Meanwhile, *mitzveh* was alive and well, usually in casual Jewish conversation: "Why don't you do a *mitzveh* and call your great-uncle?" People rarely used the term *mitzveh* to mean something more binding than what you should do simply because it was a nice thing to do.

But as Rabbi Arnold Jacob Wolf of Chicago once said, "Judaism is more than the Boy Scout Handbook." It is more than niceness. *Mitzvah*, "obligation," is essential to Jewish living. It is a religious commandment, a link between God and humanity, a sacred obligation.

Sometimes we learn that what we thought was a *mitzveh* was really a *mitzvah*. My wife's grandmother would always take strangers from the streets into her home for Shabbat dinner. My mother-in-law thought that she was doing it because she was being nice; she was performing a *mitzveh*. Looking back, her daughter (who is now my wife) knows that a *mitzvah* was being enacted; that a holy obligation linked her grandmother to Jewish traditions.

Why Perform Mitzvot?

Traditional Judaism sees only one real reason to perform *mitzvot*— God commanded them through the Torah and through generations of Jewish legal literature (*halachah*) that describes *how* the *mitzvot* should be done.

Conservative, Reconstructionist, and Reform Judaism have produced many other reasons for doing *mitzvot*. Among these:

- *Mitzvot* are done to genuinely feel the Presence of God. As Rabbi Abraham Joshua Heschel wrote, "A *mitzvah* is a prayer in the form of a deed." Lighting Shabbat candles imparts a feeling of inspiration. *Havdalah*, the ceremony that ends Shabbat, uplifts us. Performing a *mitzvah* invites God into the human soul. Knowing that the *mitzvah* will continue to bring God's Presence is an impetus to do it again and again.

- *Mitzvot* are done because of what happened at Sinai. Sinai established a patterned way of Jewish life, a sense of discipline. Every *mitzvah* echoes that original Covenant. Jews perform righteous deeds not only because of the dictates of the conscience, but because an external force *compels*, a force that returns them to Sinai.

- *Mitzvot* are done to feel connected to Jews, past and present. History has a voice, and, to a Jew, *mitzvah* gives that voice its timbre, its weight. One Jew recently explained his refusal to eat pork precisely that way to me: "Sure, I like pork. I used to eat it. Then, I thought about the enemies of our people who forced us to eat pork as a kind of torture. In solidarity with those Jews, I stopped eating it."

- Finally, *mitzvot* are done because they connect Jews to Jewish tradition. That several-thousand-year-old tradition has produced some of Western civilization's greatest values. For that reason, they are not to be cavalierly disregarded or discarded. Shabbat, for example, can help restore the Jewish soul and also provide an oasis in time for the Jewish family. *Kashrut* can help Jews retain their identity. By establishing limits to what we eat, it teaches that there are boundaries in life, and kosher slaughtering teaches avoiding unnecessary cruelty to animals. Torah study can be intellectually invigorating and soul-elevating. Space does not permit discussing all of the ethical *mitzvot*, such as business ethics, that are increasingly relevant with every passing year. Those *mitzvot*, at the very least, deserve the benefit of the doubt.

  As the Reconstructionist leader Rabbi David Teutsch has written: "The *mitzvah* system leads to an awareness of the transcendent value in human life and guides us to living in a moral and spiritual fashion that has redemptive power not only for us as individuals, but for us as a collective. Those actions recommended by Jewish tradition—both old and new—which achieve that end are truly *mitzvot*."

Just one of these reasons for doing *mitzvot* might be powerful enough to command more than simply "doing a good deed." But all four are compelling and persuasive. As the social commentator Leonard Fein wrote in *Where Are We? The Inner Life of American Jews*: "I am open to the language, to the question, and to the life of a Jew. I will not permit my problems with the tradition to separate me from it. I will enter the tradition, and its ritual elements, without a chip on my shoulder. The methods of the tradition have sustained very many people in very many places over centuries of time. So I must study. And wrestle. And listen. And err. And rejoice. And listen."

Mitzvah: The Torah's Active Voice

Mitzvot teach us to sanctify life. They foster altruism and self-esteem, so crucial to the life of a young Jew. They can bring Jewish families closer to the Jewish people, to all people, and to God.

Not each *mitzvah* will speak to every Jew. Ultimately, the vast majority of non-Orthodox Jews pick and choose among *mitzvot*. As the Reform leader, Rabbi Eric Yoffie, has said, "As a *mitzvah*-inspired liberal Jew, the only option that I have is to decide for myself what binds me. I will seek guidance from rabbis and teachers, but ultimately I must examine each *mitzvah* and ask the question: do I feel commanded in this instance as Moses was commanded?"

Each *mitzvah* that we do is sacred. So, too, is the idea that *what we do shapes who we are,* that the deed shapes the heart more than the heart shapes the deed. It's like sports or playing an instrument. The only way to get good at what you do is to practice.

Most Jewish parents want their children to feel Jewish and to somehow be connected to the Jewish past and the Jewish future. Judaism teaches that only through the *doing* can there be a genuine, rooted, profound feeling of Jewishness.

A Jew's actions, then, create a Jewish world. Such actions have consequences. Perhaps the most powerful Jewish idea is *kiddush hashem,* which I translate as "adding to the holiness of God's reputation." In some contexts, *kiddush hashem* means martyrdom for the sake of one's Jewish identity and Jewish ideals. But its deeper meaning is that when Jews act admirably, when Jews act like *menschen,* their lives serve as living testaments for God. We might almost say that when we perform *mitzvot,* we become part of God's "P.R. campaign" in the world.

More than anything else, *that* is the goal of bar and bat mitzvah, and that is the goal of all Jewish life.

Doing Mitzvot Makes Jewish Values Real and Brings Greater Meaning to Bar and Bat Mitzvah

Take a look at the best-seller lists, and you will notice that one of the most popular topics for current books is *values* and *virtues*. In any bookstore, you can buy collections of stories about such virtues as self-discipline, compassion, responsibility, friendship, work, courage, perseverance, honesty, loyalty, and faith. Not only are these books available, they sell well: Several have been on the best-seller lists for months.

To the current American conversation about virtues and values, Judaism has much to add about inner life, dignity, relationships, sanctity, public and private fidelity, gratitude, commitment, and the family. Many Jewish *stories* embody those virtues. But, in reality, we learn less from *maiseh* (story) than from *mitzvah*. The *mitzvot* are the most effective teaching tools about the search for goodness because they are simple, immediate, and concrete. They do not require *interpretation*. They require doing. Some Jewish stories, like the parting of the Red Sea, elicit the response: "Did that *really* happen?" *Mitzvot* elicit the response: "Can I *really* do that?"

Since Judaism lacks a catechism of values, any attempt to list them is almost, by its very nature, highly arbitrary and selective. Decades ago, the Jewish essayist Hayim Greenberg said, "A Jew who can name all the plants in Israel in Hebrew possesses one qualification for useful service in the State of Israel, but if he does not know to their deepest sounding such Hebrew expressions as *mitzvah, tzedakah, chesed, kiddush hashem,* he cannot carry a part in that choir that gives voice to the Jewish melody. These are the powers that build a Jewish personality."

The following list represents both ritual *mitzvot* and ethical *mitzvot*. It represents the Jewish tradition's best ways of building a Jewish personality and deepening human character.

Under each *mitzvah* are projects that give those *mitzvot* shape and meaning. Appendix 2 at the end of this book lists groups and *tzedakot* (charities) that can help families fulfill many of these *mitzvot*. Young people can do some of those *mitzvot* by themselves; others will be more appropriate for the entire family to do together. Through them, one can apply Jewish wisdom to daily life.

Be creative in your choices of *mitzvot*. Read through your child's Torah portion and *haftarah*. Is there something in those portions that suggests a particular kind of *mitzvah?* The Abraham stories talk about hospitality; the stories of liberation from Egypt suggest various kinds of social justice causes; the construction of the desert sanctuary in Exodus lends itself to support of your local synagogue; *Kedoshim* (Leviticus 19) is a laundry list of *mitzvot,* including *tzedakah,* caring for the elderly, economic justice, caring for immigrants, and the like. Let your deeds speak with the Torah's voice —it will be a wonderful way of adding meaning to your bar and bat mitzvah experience.

Gemilut Chasadim: Acts Of Loving-kindness

Gemilut chasadim is best understood as *nonfinancial giving.* So powerful is *gemilut chasadim* that the Torah begins with it: God makes garments for Adam and Eve. And the Torah ends with it: God buries Moses. So powerful is *gemilut chasadim* that performing acts of loving-kindness is the closest that humans can come to a genuine imitation of God.

- Encourage your child to visit someone who has lost a loved one. This fulfills the *mitzvah* of *nichum aveilim* (comforting mourners.)

- Encourage your child to visit or call on someone who is ill. This fulfills the *mitzvah* of *bikur cholim* (visiting the sick).

- Your daughter (or your son!) can grow her or his hair long and contribute their excess tresses to Locks of Love, an organization that creates wigs for people who have temporarily lost their hair through chemotherapy.

- Encourage your child to learn games, magic, clowning, or balloon-animal-making skills to use in the pediatric ward of a hospital.

- Arrange to have leftover food from your bar or bat mitzvah celebration taken to a soup kitchen that feeds the homeless and the hungry.

- Arrange for a barrel for cans and boxes of food to be placed in your synagogue.

- Bring *chametz* (leavened food products that are forbidden on Pesach) from your home to a local food pantry. Encourage congregants in your synagogue to also do this.

- Volunteer as a family at a soup kitchen for the homeless.

- Ask guests to bring canned food or such toiletries as soap, toothpaste or shampoo to your bar or bat mitzvah party for subsequent distribution to the homeless.

- Welcome an inner-city child to your home for the summer through the Fresh Air Fund, thus fulfilling the mitzvah of *hachnasat orchim* (welcoming guests).

- The debate on the acceptability to Jews of Halloween continues. The holiday, after all, has its roots in pagan and Christian practices. But many Jewish youngsters do go trick-or-treating. That is a reality of life in America. To help transform Halloween into a holiday with some ethical values, have children collect food for the hungry rather than candy for the well-fed.

- Give three percent of the cost of your bar and bat mitzvah celebration to MAZON, The Jewish Hunger Fund (for more details, see Appendix 2).

- Encourage your child to write to an elected official about an important social or political issue. This fulfills the *mitzvah* of *mishpat* (justice). Use a Jewish idea in the letter.

- Participate as a family in a clothing drive for the needy.

Tzedakah: Sacred Giving

Some Jews say *tzedakah* is the highest *mitzvah*. It is usually translated as "charity," "justice," or "giving." I prefer translating it as "sacred giving." *Tzedakah* is not what we give; it is what we owe as part of our covenant with God. Though many American Jews have dropped a variety of ritual practices, they cling to the practice of *tzedakah* as they would to a precious heirloom. Perhaps this is because, as Proverbs says, "*Tzedakah* redeems from death." It not only potentially saves individuals from a physical death. It also redeems the giver from a death of the soul.

- Choose a *tzedakah* from Appendix 2. Contribute it to honor your child becoming bar or bat mitzvah, or encourage him or her to set aside for *tzedakah* a portion of money received as gifts at the bar or bat mitzvah.

- Give away or sell old toys in a garage sale, using the proceeds for a charitable cause. (In Africa, newly emerging adolescent boys of the Maasai tribe give away childhood possessions as part of their rite of passage into adulthood.)

- Contribute some *tzedakah* every Friday night before Shabbat into a family *puschke*, or a *tzedakah* container. Decide as a family where the money should go. Decent, gracious, loving human beings are made, not born. This is the easiest, most economical, most hands-on way of teaching the value of *tzedakah* to a child.

- Participate in a gleaning at Sukkot, and give your harvest to the poor.

- Time, as well as money, can be given. Set aside time each week for a socially redeeming purpose. Encourage your child to do the same.

Talmud Torah: The Study of Torah

Jewish learning should extend beyond the words of the Hebrew texts. One can learn that Jewish wisdom can walk through all kinds of doors in our lives.

- Children can give some of their old and useable religious school textbooks to younger children. It could be done in a ritualized form, even at a public worship service. It's a way for those young people to say to themselves and to the community: "I have grown. The old me has vanished. I am passing on my sources of earlier wisdom to another generation."

- Attend concerts of Jewish music or lectures on Jewish subjects.

- Read Jewish books together as a family.

- Sing Hebrew songs together as a family.

- Visit a Jewish museum or the Holocaust museums in Washington, D.C. or Los Angeles as a family.

- Collect Jewish books, recordings, and computer programs.

Hidur Penei Zakein: Honoring the Elderly

The elderly deserve respect regardless of their accomplishments or status. They are often part of our own families. Their stories and their lives are closely interwoven with our own.

- Your child can call, write, or visit an elderly relative or friend.

- Your child can help nursing home residents hold services for Shabbat and Jewish holidays and Passover seders.

- Your child can deliver flowers to a nursing home before the start of Shabbat.

- Your child can make weekly visits to a resident of a nearby nursing home whom he or she has "adopted."

- Donate old books, records, audiotapes, CDs, books on tape, or videotapes to a nursing home.

- Older members of the community could help teach Hebrew, Torah, and other skills to bar and bat mitzvah candidates. Those older role models should be open and available for our youths to be able to ask them the questions of life and the questions of Jewish living and belief. The community could honor the elder tutor at the bar or bat mitzvah ceremony.

Zicharon: Memory

So precious is the *mitzvah* of memory that Torah commands us no less than 169 times to remember. Perhaps there is mystical significance in 13 being the square root of 169. At the age of thirteen, Jewish children have a fairly extensive memory, one that is both tribal and individual. They remember Shabbat and the major Jewish holidays. They especially remember that Jews were slaves in Egypt. Jewish parents must remember to teach their children to remember.

- Make sure your child knows his or her Hebrew name and the person for whom he or she was named. What special Jewish qualities did that person have that you hope your child would emulate?

- Find out your family's name in "the old country." Do not let it fade into oblivion.

- Find out the name of the town, city, or village that your family came from in its country of origin. Someone in your family may know this, and it is more than simply "someplace in Russia." Look up the town in the *Encyclopedia Judaica* and learn something about the town and what it gave to the Jewish world.

One young man in my congregation is the grandson of Holocaust survivors. In our congregation, bar and bat mitzvah candidates must complete a *mitzvah* project, comprised of the many categories of *mitzvot* found in this chapter. During his project—researching his family history—he found a photograph of the Holy Ark from his grandfather's synagogue in Poland, now destroyed. Imagine the power that moment had for him and his family.

- Many Jews are now immigrating to this country. Most are from the former Soviet Union and Argentina. Collect clothing, food, furniture, books, and such Jewish items as menorahs for needy immigrants. Tutor immigrants in English.

Shabbat: Honoring the Sabbath

The Zionist thinker Achad Ha-Am once wrote: "More than Israel has kept the Sabbath, so has the Sabbath kept Israel." Every Jewish life should have more than a small taste of Shabbat.

- Have Shabbat dinners as frequently as you can in your home, preferably every Friday night. Light the Shabbat candles, recite the *motzi*, *kiddush*, and bless your children (and have them bless you, as well). Sing *birkat hamazon*, the blessing after the meal. Invite friends to share in your Shabbat celebration.

- Encourage your child to cook a traditional Shabbat dish. If you are deficient in the arts of Jewish cooking, ask an older person in the synagogue to come to your home and teach your family how to do it.

- As a family, jointly discuss and create *mitzvot* for Shabbat. Decide what you should do or should not do. Some families may decide to avoid commercial transactions on Shabbat, such as business and shopping. Some may decide to turn off the television or their computer. Some may decide to make

Shabbat into a day for visiting friends and family, and not on which to engage in entertainment or other diversions.

- Attend synagogue services as a family.

- Reserve a half-hour on Saturday to study together as a family, either from *Pirke Avot* (which is found in most prayer books), or from the Torah portion of the week.

- End Shabbat with *havdalah* (the service early Saturday evening that marks the end of Shabbat). *Havdalah* is a beautiful, brief, sensuous home-based service that uses candles, wine, and spices. It is a wonderful way to say farewell to Shabbat.

Kedushat Ha-aretz: Sanctifying Our Relationship with the Land of Israel

Few things bind the Jewish people together more than our historic love of the land of Israel. Bar and bat mitzvah can be the age when we teach our children the meaning of Zionism, to strengthen our connections to the land of Israel, to support and nurture it.

- March or demonstrate for Israel.

- Purchase and use Israeli products.

- Plant trees in Israel. (See Appendix 2 for the address of the Jewish National Fund, which has long helped reforest Israel.)

- Give *tzedakah* to Israel. (See Appendix 2 for the names and addresses of various *tzedakot*, including the United Jewish Appeal and the New Israel Fund.)

- Travel to Israel as a family.

Kedushat Halashon: The Sanctity of Speech

Most people assume that sanctity of speech means prayer. But sanctity of speech is much more profound. Joseph Telushkin, the author of *Words That Hurt, Words That Heal: How to Choose Words Wisely and Well*, suggests that if you can't go twenty-four hours without saying something unkind about someone else, then you have a real problem. Many people have such a problem: The Torah's most violated commandment is Leviticus 19:16: "Do not go about as a talebearer among your people."

Kedushat halashon means teaching our children to watch their mouths just as we teach them to watch their hands, teaching them to avoid gossip, tale-bearing, rumor-mongering, and other acts of verbal violence just as we teach them to avoid physical violence. In Hebrew, Jews call such prohibited speech *lashon hara* ("the evil tongue"). It is a negative, yet truthful statement about others.

- Urge your child to be careful about what he or she says about other people.

- Discuss with your family a time when you or your children did not observe this Jewish value. What could you or they have done differently?

- Discuss with your family the acceptability of certain kinds of speech. Discuss the quality, the content (and the volume!) of speech in your home. Consider how speech can be used for healing, not hurting.

Kedushat Hazeman: The Holiness of Festivals and Sacred Seasons

To be a Jew is to feel a part of Judaism's entire festival calendar. To be a Jew is to go through the cycle of the seasons as a Jew.

- Participate in a Passover Seder with your family. Ask your child to write a special reading to be used at the seder.

- Ask your child to write a prayer to use when your family lights its Chanukah menorah.

- Build a *sukkah* in your backyard. Decorate it. Have dinner in it, or, at least, make *motzi* and *kiddush* in it. If the weather is warm, encourage your children to sleep in it overnight.

- Have the entire family attend Purim services dressed as characters from the Megillah.

- Plant a tree in Israel each year on Tu B'Shevat, the New Year of trees.

Tzar Baalei Chayim: Avoiding Cruelty to Animals

Judaism teaches us to treat animals with dignity. They cannot be wantonly destroyed; animals of unequal strength cannot be yoked together; an animal collapsed under the burden of a load must be helped even if it belongs to an enemy. Judaism even addresses the psychological pain of animals and advises that a mother bird must be sent away to spare her the pain of seeing the eggs being removed from her nest. Kosher slaughtering ensures swift, painless deaths for animals.

- Become involved with an organization that deals with animal rights.
- Become conscious of the type of clothing that you wear. Debate the "kashrut" of fur and leather clothing.
- Give money to the local animal shelter.
- Adopt a dog or cat.

Tikkun Hanefesh: Repairing the Self

An important part of becoming bar and bat mitzvah is growing as an individual. Ancient rabbis believed that the ultimate goal of the *mitzvot* was nothing less than *letzaref haberiot*, refining the individual into better human material. Encourage children to:

- Eliminate a bad habit.
- Patch up a bad relationship by establishing *shalom* with another person.
- Transform a negative attitude into a positive attitude.

Darchei Shalom: The Paths of Peace

Seeking peace is considered the greatest of *mitzvot*. So powerful is peace that our tradition tells us that *shalom* is one of God's names.

- Think about the effect of violent television shows, films, music, toys and games, especially video games, on our psyches, attitudes, and behavior. Do a *"shalom* inventory" of your own home, and try to revise your amusement habits.

- Try to bring a greater sense of *shalom* into your daily life and the daily life of your children.

- Be aware of the words that you and your children use. Try to temper and moderate those words. Be aware of the sources of foul or offending words, especially from electronic and print media, and try to minimize or eliminate those sources from your lives.

Mitzvah: The Path to Self-Esteem

One reason for doing *mitzvot* is not often articulated or understood. *Mitzvot* create a sense of human and spiritual competence in the person who does them.

Frequently, certain learning disabilities impede a young person's ability to learn Hebrew and therefore to prepare for bar and bat mitzvah. But many children who are learning-disabled do learn Hebrew. When I work with such children, I give them as much as they can do, even if it means less Torah to read or fewer prayers to lead at the ceremony. This practice emerges from my conviction that bar and bat mitzvah is a status and a process. It does not depend on how much Hebrew you can learn.

But there is a larger question. What if a child is *incapable* of learning Hebrew? Surely this problem is not unique to our day. In the past, a child in a traditional Jewish society who could not learn Hebrew was given a task to do: Going from house to house to collect wax for candles that would burn in the synagogue. Without candles, the synagogue would plunge into darkness; physically as well as spiritually. When the synagogue candles were lit, the worshippers would remember the adage, *Torah or*, "Torah is Light." The child might not be able to *read* Torah, but he could help the community.

The lesson was that children owed something to the Jewish community. How do we translate that lesson to our time? Children who cannot learn Hebrew often *can* learn Jewish history and culture. Using the practices of our ancestors as a model, I suggest involving such a child in *mitzvot* in the community. At the bar and bat mitzvah ceremony, the child could speak about the *mitzvot* performed while preparing for truly becoming bar or bat mitzvah, for being old enough to understand the meaning of *mitzvah*.

The Path to Maturity and Community

The word *mitzvah* comes from the root *tzavah*, which means not only "to command," but "to connect." *Mitzvot*, then, are the connective tissue that bind us with God, with the better parts of ourselves, and with other people.

I learned much about the meaning of *mitzvot* when a close relative of my great-uncle Harry died. One evening during the *shiva* period, among those sitting *shiva* was a young boy in his early teens. He went over to my great-uncle Harry and said to him: "May God console you on your loss." He then distributed prayer books to the mourners in the living room and began to lead the evening service.

After the service was over, he went into the dining room, helped himself to some cookies, returned to my great-uncle's side, shook the old man's hand, and left. I turned to my great-uncle and asked, "Who was that boy?" Uncle Harry shrugged his shoulders and answered, "A kid from the *shul*."

That simple response from my great-uncle was almost as beautiful as a Psalm. I thought of all the other possible responses: "Oh, him? He lives next door." "That boy? He lives across the street from us. He rakes our leaves in the autumn and shovels our snow in the winter." "Him? He lives down the block. We've known him all his life."

Instead, the response was far more eloquent: "A kid from the *shul*." That was the context in which he knew the boy. Suddenly, it all made sense. The boy was about thirteen or fourteen. He was, therefore, bar mitzvah—old enough to do *mitzvot*. Someone in the synagogue—the rabbi, the cantor, the director of education, or a knowledgeable lay person—must have taken him aside and said, "Now that you are bar mitzvah, and old enough to do *mitzvot*, we're going to teach you the most delicate *mitzvah* imaginable. We're going to teach you how to go into a house of mourning and use your prayer-leading skills to walk people through the valley of the shadow of death. A lot of Jewish kids can lead a service. But this skill will help heal the world."

I have often thought about what that youth learned about Jewish community and how this experience may have helped him confront death more honestly and more maturely. That is yet another purpose of *mitzvot*: Bonding us with the community.

Parents are powerful teachers. We have the power to teach our children what the synagogue and the community can really mean. It can mean something that exists above and beyond us, something that we are born into, and live within and *through*.

The Jewish educator Joel Grishaver once told me about a young boy who became bar mitzvah. In the moments before the service started, his parents could not figure out how to make his oversized *tallit* drape properly over his shoulders. Nevertheless, the boy proceeded with his ceremony, the *tallit* dangling unceremoniously over his shoulders.

The boy began his speech: "As I prepared to become bar mitzvah, my parents gave me a choice between two gifts. I could either get a piece of jewelry, like a Star of David, or I could have a leaf with my name on it on the synagogue's Tree of Life in the lobby, which means that my family made a donation to the synagogue in honor of my becoming bar mitzvah. I have decided to choose the Tree of Life for three reasons. First, it is *tzedakah*. Second, it will always be here. And third, I have often stood in the lobby and looked at the names on the Tree of Life. I know those people. I want to be in their company."

As he concluded his speech, suddenly the oversized *tallit* magically fell into place and fit perfectly. The boy was now clothed, beautifully, in a *tallit* that symbolizes the commitment to the *mitzvot*.

That is what it means to become bar or bat mitzvah.

Which mitzvot *will you choose to do as a family? What are the* mitzvah *resources in your community? Use this space as a* mitzvah *journal to help you plan what you will do and record your experiences.*

6

Rites and Wrongs of Passage
Putting the Party in Perspective

Bernie's Bar Mitzvah:
It's a show, it's food, fantasy.
It's an audience participation extravaganza.

Rites and Wrongs
of Passage

During a conversation on other matters, the talk suddenly turned to plans for a bar mitzvah ceremony to be held in two years. My friend heaved a massive sigh. "It's really terrible," she said, "being under this much pressure to put on a big show, to keep up with what everyone else is doing. The caterer's first question for me was, 'What theme do you want?'"

Every Jew in America has a "Can you top this?" tale about the Worst Bar Mitzvah Party of the Year. We need not list the contenders here. Someday, when the definitive volume of American Jewish Folklore is written, such fables of unmitigated ostentation will constitute a large and (almost) funny chapter.

The bar and bat mitzvah party has been much criticized over the years. And for good reason. Yet, most Jews do not know that the party is an integral part of the bar and bat mitzvah ritual. The first mention of the bar mitzvah party in any Jewish text is in the *Shulchan Aruch* (the classic sixteenth-century code of Jewish law): "It is the religious obligation of the father to tender a festive meal in honor of his son's becoming bar mitzvah, just as he might do when the boy marries."

From a *halachic* (Jewish legal) point of view, then, the party has a proud lineage. But references to bar mitzvah parties go back even further than the Middle Ages, and scholars have had a field day trying to locate the genuine seed of the custom.

Some say the celebration goes back to Isaac's weaning. Genesis 21:8 says Abraham threw a feast to celebrate that event. One ancient source suggested that Isaac was weaned at the age of thirteen (Midrash, *Bereshit Rabbah* 53:10)! Therefore, the party. And, therefore, the connection to the age of thirteen.

Elsewhere, the Midrash suggests that Abraham regretted that he had rejoiced and had made others rejoice at the feast for Isaac, yet did not make an offering to God. God said to him: "I know that even if I

commanded you to offer your only son to Me, you would not refuse."
(*Bereshit Rabbah* 55:4). This midrash teaches that the binding of Isaac
was God's way of showing Abraham that he had not lost the capacity
to make an offering to God.

Some say the tradition of the bar mitzvah party goes back to Rabbi
Yosef in the Talmud (*Kiddushin* 31a). Rabbi Yosef was blind. In Jewish
law, the blind were exempt from doing *mitzvot*. But Rabbi Yosef realized that he was already doing the *mitzvot*. Why not get credit for doing
so? He wanted to change his status from someone who didn't have to
do the *mitzvot* to someone who had to do the *mitzvot*.

So Rabbi Yosef made an offer. If some skilled sage could prove that
a blind person had an obligation to do *mitzvot*, he would host a great
celebration to mark his change in status. A little more than one thousand years later, the sixteenth-century legal authority, Rabbi Solomon
Luria, drew on his knowledge of this Talmudic discussion. He reasoned
that if Rabbi Yosef could celebrate that he was now obligated to do the
mitzvot, shouldn't we celebrate and give thanks to God that a bar mitzvah was now obligated to fulfill the *mitzvot*? Rabbi Luria ruled that the
bar mitzvah meal is a *seudat mitzvah* (a religiously commanded festive
meal) on the same spiritual level as the wedding feast. The boy would
have to give a religious discourse during the banquet. In Poland, the
bar mitzvah discourse (*derashah*) became part of the festive meal. This
was probably the origin of the bar and bat mitzvah speech, which, in
the public imagination, eventually became transformed into the
famous "Today, I am a fountain pen" speech of classic Jewish comedy.

The bar mitzvah feast occurred in the afternoon as the third meal of
the Sabbath. An hour before the afternoon service (*minchah*), the lad
would go to the homes of his guests to invite them to the third meal.
At the meal, the lad would discourse on the customs of bar mitzvah
and would lead the grace after the meal.

A Choice:
Celebration or Conspicuous Consumption

Modern American Jews are not the first Jews to confront the ethical
overtones of conspicuous consumption. Even in medieval times, there

were excesses in celebration. But in the sixteenth century, Solomon Luria didn't like what he saw. In his commentary on the Talmud, he condemned bar mitzvah parties as "occasions for wild levity, just for the purpose of stuffing the gullet" (*Yam Shel Shelomo, Baba Kama*, 7:37).

The rabbis of the Middle Ages eventually enacted laws to limit spending on festivities. They did this to protect the dignity of the less wealthy. This was identical to the original reason for a plain wooden casket at a funeral: So no one would be humiliated by having a less-than-opulent coffin. It also parallels the original reason for communal *kiddushin* (wedding) rings. Communities would own such rings, and they would be briefly placed upon the finger of each new bride in the community, so that poor families would not be humiliated.

Beyond this, I suspect that the rabbis worried about the jealousy of gentile neighbors, who might use displays of Jewish opulence as an excuse for a pogrom. Saul ha-Levi Morteira, a leading rabbi in seventeenth-century Amsterdam (and the teacher of philosopher Baruch Spinoza), made this point in a sermon he gave around the year 1622:

> The first generation of our ancestors who left the land of Canaan knew that they were resident aliens, who had departed from their own land and come to a land not theirs. They continued to think of themselves as aliens, and they did not overreach. The Egyptians loved them and bore them no envy. But after their death, the following generation thought of Egypt as the land of their birth. They grew arrogant and became so provocative in their behavior that they aroused the envy of the Egyptians, who decreed harsh laws against them and enslaved them.

Finally, some historians suggest that these laws kept the emerging *nouveau riche* in their places so they did not threaten the status of the Jewish old guard.

In the early decades of the twentieth century, when Jews were first becoming comfortable in America, bar mitzvah parties became especially opulent. Soon, the bar mitzvah's social component would eclipse its ritual function. The 1920s and 1930s saw the growth of the catering industry, which encouraged the transformation of bar mitzvah from a ceremony to an affair. This era also saw the growth of gift giving in connection with bar mitzvah.

The Ethics of Jewish Celebration

Soon, the materialism that had become attached to bar mitzvah was decried. In 1938, the noted Orthodox rabbi H. Pereira Mendes insisted that the bar mitzvah "not be allowed to deteriorate into merely a day for perfunctory observance or for merry-making or gifts." Twenty-six years later, the Central Conference of American Rabbis condemned the

> deterioration in the character of the bar mitzvah "affair." The extravagant consumption, the conspicuous waste, and the crudity of many of these affairs are rapidly becoming a public Jewish scandal. The lowering of standards as reflected in many bar mitzvah celebrations is in direct violation of the teaching of the Torah. The trend toward the abandonment of aesthetic standards can lead to the abandonment of ethical standards as well.

Concerns about the taste and aesthetics of bar and bat mitzvah are with us today. Bar and bat mitzvah has become a multi-million dollar industry: Catering halls, musicians, dancers, photographers and videographers, caricaturists, comedians, party planners, so-called party enhancers to encourage guests to have a good time, personalized color-coordinated *kippot*, party favors for the kids, florists, *ad nauseam*. The implicit message is that your party should be different. It should be unique. That is how you will measure your own difference and uniqueness. Instead, parents should be thinking critically: "Do we really need all this?" Just consider this: Jews have been celebrating the sacred moments of life for centuries without any of this stuff. And they all did just fine.

But there is a larger issue of the Jewish ethics of celebration. Such ethics help us understand the way that Jews view the world.

The Czech-born German author Max Brod taught that there were essentially three religious ways of viewing the world: paganism, Christianity, and Judaism. Christianity—particularly early Christianity—believed that man should behave as an *angel*: Reject good food, fine wine, and possessions. Enter a monastery to be ascetically sealed away from the temptations of the world. Paganism believed that man was an *animal*: Seek pleasure, good food, fine wine, and possessions.

Early Christianity still has a voice in our world. It is the voice of abstinence. We heard it in the Prohibition movement, and we still hear it in certain quarters of the antiabortion and antigay rights movement. (To be fair, such voices exist within the Jewish world as well.) Paganism also still shapes our world. We find it in beer commercials, in *Food and Wine* magazine, in the *Playboy* ethic, on tabloid television, in the consumerism of American society that proclaims "whoever dies with the most toys, wins."

Judaism's great contribution to the moral vocabulary of the world was that it produced a middle way between those extremes, the way of *mitzvah* and *kedushah*. God made us a little lower than the angels, but much higher than the animals. Judaism advises that we neither *reject* nor *hoard* pleasure. We *sanctify* pleasure. We sanctify what we eat through *kashrut* (dietary laws), what we own through *tzedakah* (holy giving), what we drink by *kiddush* (blessing the wine), and by drinking moderately on Shabbat and on Pesach and other holidays and somewhat immoderately on Purim. We touch a drop of wine to the lips of the newborn baby. We remember the exhortation that goes with the lifted cup: "*Lechayim*—To life!" Wine may sweeten our life, but should not be used to the point that it becomes addictive.

Modern Judaism (and by extension, all modern liberal religions) faces the dilemma of the split self, by which I mean: "*This* is my religious self. *That* is my nonreligious self. I will let religion enter certain areas of my life. But there are many areas of my life that religion will not enter. I will not let religion enter those places because I have arbitrarily ruled that those areas are off-limits to religion."

The split self says of the bar and bat mitzvah: "The religious part of this moment is what happens in the sanctuary that morning. But then comes the closing song of the service. We say *shabbat shalom* to each other. We leave the sanctuary. We are in profane territory, and *profane* comes from *pro fanum*, meaning 'away from the sanctuary.' Then we can do anything we want. Briefly, we were in the world of text, Torah, and holiness. But now, we are back in the real world, when the lessons and Torah of the real world will be heard in all their glory."

This is not far, really, from those who say, "I don't care what the Torah says about treating employees. When I want to hear Torah, I'll go to synagogue. In my business, I don't want to hear Torah."

A genuine pity. More than a pity—a Jewish scandal. Of her cousin's bloated bar mitzvah rock and roll theme party, author Joanne Greenberg wrote, "Any serious religious or questing Jewish person contemplating my cousin's bar mitzvah as a 'Jewish' event might be forgiven for bolting the faith and ceasing to consider it as a fit repository for his questing spirit."

When I attend such affairs, I say to myself, "I *don't* want to be puritanical, but is this *really* about a sacred Jewish passage?" Should thirteen-year-old girls (or any women, for that matter) be wearing strapless dresses, with plunging necklines, on the *bimah*? I am not saying that they have to look like something out of an Isaac Bashevis Singer novel, with covered heads and long sleeves. But there is a Jewish value known as *tzniyut,* modesty in dress and comportment. We should avoid inappropriate clothing before the Torah. That value does not belong just to the Orthodox. It belongs to all Jews.

Do thirteen-year-old children really need to stay at bar and bat mitzvah parties until two o'clock in the morning? Why are these children being pushed into a pseudo-adulthood?

Do we think carefully, if at all, about how bar and bat mitzvah glitz affects young adolescents? Do we ask what happens when kids get bored at these weekly events? Are we somehow contributing to youngsters vandalizing synagogues, catering halls, and restaurants at bar and bat mitzvah celebrations? Are they to blame? Or are we?

We must remember that everything we do with our children teaches *something*. For example, how do we sanctify the act of eating? Many families say blessings over the food that they serve at their celebrations—by making *kiddush* and *motzi* and singing *birchat hamazon,* the blessing after the meal. Blessing our food is how we remember that we are linked to a divine presence that sustains us.

How do we handle the issue of *kashrut* in our celebrations? *Kashrut* is the system of Jewish dietary laws which includes abstaining from biblically prohibited foods, like pork or shellfish; not mixing milk and meat; and eating only meat that has been slaughtered according to Jewish law. For Conservative and Orthodox Judaism, *kashrut* is a mandatory part of a Jewish life style. Both movements officially expect that bar and bat mitzvah parties—indeed, *any* celebration—will be kosher. Reconstructionism maintains *kashrut* as an important value. While Reform Judaism does not demand *kashrut* of its adherents, it is increasingly open to the spiritual benefits of the Jewish dietary laws and encourages Reform Jews to choose to observe *kashrut*. By having a kosher bar or bat mitzvah celebration, we teach our children that God cares about what we eat; that we can sanctify *what* and *how* we eat; that Judaism enters every sector of our lives, not only what we do in the sanctuary; and that all Jews should be able to eat at our celebrations, thus emphasizing the unity of the Jewish people.

Do we think about the messages we send even through the *music* that accompanies bar and bat mitzvah celebrations? Or about the lyrics of the rap music that is often played at these parties? Or about the volume of the music? Should guests have to shout while trying to converse with whomever is sitting next to them?

We may say, "Listen, there's Judaism—and then there's the real world." Or, as one father said to his daughter right after the ceremony, "OK, let's boogie!"

Let us not forget that "boogying" (or, as we Jews call it, *simcha*, or celebratory joy) has a proper and sanctified place in Judaism. There probably isn't enough of it. But when we make distinctions between Judaism and "the real world," we are also saying that we don't take Judaism very seriously, that Judaism is for dress-up occasions, that Jewish values are for public liturgy but not for private performance, that we are willfully participating in an idolatry of the self.

Toward the Middle Way: How to Sanctify Our Celebrations and Put God on the Guest List

What do we do? Putting God on the guest list means that God calls to us to conquer, in some small way, the polarities between the sacred and the profane. Early in the planning stages for a bar or bat mitzvah, it is important for parents to ask themselves, "What Jewish values do we hope this bar or bat mitzvah celebration will embody?" Make a list of them. Your list might include compassion, dignity, justice, learning, social action, generosity, humility, moderation, a love for the Jewish people and the Jewish homeland. These are the essence of Judaism's middle way between early Christianity and ancient paganism. Plan your celebration *around* these values, and stick to them.

I know a family that put the emblems of the twelve tribes on the luncheon tables at their son's bar mitzvah party. It was their way of teaching about our ancient roots in the land of Israel. Another family put information about various social service agencies and *tzedakot* on each table, along with prestamped envelopes and asked their guests to make contributions to those worthy causes in honor of their child. Another family bought trees in Israel in honor of each of its bar mitzvah guests.

I know one family that asked relatives and friends to help light the candles on the bar mitzvah cake. (The candle lighting ritual is a modern invention that emerged from the catering industry. The Jewish scholar Vanessa Ochs surmises that it may have started as an addendum to the *aliyot* during the Torah service, or as a birthday party ritual.) This family chose to do it in a different way. As each guest came up to light a candle, he or she offered the bar mitzvah boy a blessing, or a word of encouragement, or a Jewish value that the young man might embody.

In some communities, parents of bar and bat mitzvah children make a pact with each other about how they will celebrate this rite of passage. Since their children are all in the same class, and will therefore be exposed to each other's celebrations, they want to ensure that there is a set of standards. So they agree: "No themes. No parties until the wee hours. No outrageous music or spending."

In some communities, parents create a party co-op, in which they help create bar and bat mitzvah celebrations for each other—planning menus, cooking, transporting children, providing hospitality for out-of-town guests, even ushering at each others' bar and bat mitzvah ceremonies.

In some communities, bar and bat mitzvah parents who have just completed the experience become coaches for the next set of parents whose children will become bar and bat mitzvah. Their rabbis and educators train them to guide these new families through the ethics and aesthetics of bar and bat mitzvah. The parents share successes and disappointments, and the entire experience becomes one of shared striving.

All of these are wonderful ways to build community. Community is more than "warm fuzzies." It is more than friendship. It is about shared values and visions. Some even sidestep the entire culture of catering by having the party at their homes or at a summer camp.

Best yet, I know families that travel to Israel in lieu of a party. They correctly surmise that their child would soon forget a party, but never a trip to Israel.

Sometimes, God enters our celebrations when we ask the right questions about how to celebrate. I know a family whose son was to become bar mitzvah on the Shabbat after the September 11 catastrophe. In the shadow of such a monstrous event—an event that had deeply touched our community—the boy's mother asked me if it was even appropriate for the family to celebrate their son's ritual coming-of-age.

We discussed the ethics and aesthetics of celebration in such a situation. Clearly, her son's bar mitzvah ceremony merited some sort of merriment, even muted merriment. Ultimately, the family decided to tone down the level of the music, making the party festive but somehow subdued. I consider it a blessing that this woman cared enough to ask the hard questions about how Judaism intersected with the world and with her life.

Ultimately, the educational and religious spirit of bar and bat mitzvah can extend beyond the final hymn or prayer at the service. It can permeate the lives of our young, and it can enrich what they take with them into the world. Jewish celebrations that truly celebrate Jewish values implicitly erode the distinctions that so many erect between the "Jewish world" and the "real world," between our daily lives and the relatively scant amount of time so often devoted to overtly religious issues and rituals. It can help remind us that the religious and the spiritual are everywhere, and cannot be relegated to certain places and certain times.

A friend told me that when a caterer inevitably asked, "What's the theme of your daughter's bat mitzvah going to be?" he responded, "How about Judaism?"

It's a good answer, simple yet elegant.

What are some things that you might do to "put God on the guest list" at your celebration? Write some of your ideas here.

7

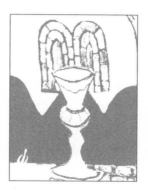

To a Skeptical Jewish Parent

He drew a circle that shut me out
Heretic, rebel, a thing to flout.
But love and I had the wit to win
We drew a circle that drew him in.

—EDWIN MARKHAM, "OUTWITTED"

To a Skeptical Jewish Parent

People once lived lives of faith occasionally disrupted by moments of unbelief. Today, it is somewhat the opposite. We have moments of unbelief that are sometimes interrupted—*blessedly* interrupted—by moments of faith. Traditional roads to faith seem to be incessantly blocked or hopelessly detoured.

Nowhere in Jewish life do we sense this doubt more than with the ambivalent Jewish parent. Something about the years preceding bar and bat mitzvah brings those doubts and questions to the surface.

Some parents acutely feel the social pressures for their child to have a bar or bat mitzvah: "Our neighbors are renting the state of Delaware for the reception, and Michael Jackson is singing, and the President of the State of Israel is flying in to do *motzi*."

Some parents start wondering about the meaning of Judaism and Jewish wisdom in their lives and in the lives of their children. I would even go so far as to call it *Torah-phobia*. As one father of three said to me recently about the Joseph story, a tale of sibling rivalry, "How do you make this stuff relevant, anyway?"

Some parents remember their own bar and bat mitzvah experiences with anger or boredom, or a combination of both. There is no end to the conversations that start with, "I went through this when I was a kid, and I swore that I would spare my child this dreariness."

Some parents simply become cynical about the whole enterprise, using something resembling atheism as an instrument of escape. As a parent recently said to me, "I have some real doubts about the Jewish idea of God. I've spent a long time looking at all the terrible things that have been done in the name of religion and the walls that it erects between people. It makes me wonder whether my daughter should learn this stuff and become bat mitzvah. Maybe I'm wrong to lay my stuff on her, but I can't be a hypocrite."

The Jew who sincerely struggles with the life of faith and the life of Torah is in good company. For Judaism is the only religion that has, in the words of writer Dennis Prager, "canonized its critics." Jewish literature is filled with stories about those who struggled with God: Abraham confronted God about Sodom and Gomorrah. Moses, during the incident of the golden calf, demanded that God spare the Jewish people, "or else blot my name out of Your book." Job, after losing all that was precious to him, could only listen for the voice of God that emerges "out of the whirlwind."

Elisha ben Avuya, the heretic of the second century C.E., lost his faith in God when he saw a child die. The child had fallen out of a tree as he was shooing the mother bird away from the nest before taking the bird's eggs. Sending away the mother bird from the nest is one of only two *mitzvot* in the Torah that promises long life to those who fulfill it. His rabbinic colleagues called him *Acher* (the "apostate"), yet he was never read out of our history. His anguished wrestling with God is emblematic of the larger Jewish story. More recently, Elie Wiesel emerged from the Holocaust to recreate his life with the mission of forcing humanity to rethink both God and itself.

Many claim that religion divides people and is responsible for most of the world's evil. Moreover, they assert, the Jewish idea of God is intellectually and spiritually bogus. So these Jews say they are "areligious," "nonreligious," "New Age," *anything* but "religious." And, sometimes, anything but Jews. Some, certainly, greatly care about the Jewish people. Some, surely, care deeply about something called Jewish culture, though we are increasingly uncertain what that means. But believers in God, believers in the Covenant and in Jewish destiny, they are not.

One day, the great writer Franz Kafka was strolling in a park in Berlin, when he saw a little girl crying because she had lost her doll. Kafka tried to comfort her, telling her that the doll had merely gone on a trip, and that he had just seen the doll and had spoken to it. The doll had promised Kafka that it would stay in touch with the girl and would send a letter to her from time to time. Whenever she would come to the park, Kafka said he would bring her a letter from the doll.

As you can imagine, Kafka himself wrote letters to the little girl, letting her think that the doll had written them. Eventually, he sent her a new doll. He told her that the new doll was the old doll but its appearance had changed since the last time she saw it because of the great adventures she had had.

The doll is a metaphor for religious faith. The old doll has indeed changed, just as we may not be able to reclaim the old, seemingly naive faith of our ancestors. But by struggling with our faith, we can reclaim a new belief for ourselves and for our children.

Do Religions Divide People?

Those who claim that religions divide people ask, "Why can't there be a universal religion?" But what would a universal religion exclude? What pearls that are peculiar to a certain tradition would be overlooked or rejected? Think of the potential theological fender-benders such a religion would have. If you think that the world is made right by believing in Jesus, then it can't be made right by doing Torah. The two mutually exclude each other.

A generic religion is impossible because there is no such thing as a generic human being, and there won't be until the Messiah merges us into a great rainbow of humanity. In the interim, we all view life through the lenses of our tribes, be they ethnic, racial, or theological.

As F. Forrester Church, a Unitarian minister, put it: We all stand in the cathedral of the world. In the cathedral are a multitude of stained glass windows. We are born in one part of the cathedral, and our parents and our grandparents teach us how to see the light that shines through our window, the window that carries the story of our people. The same light shines through all the windows of the cathedral, but we interpret its story in many different ways. The light is the presence of God. And the ways we see its colors are the ways of our tribe.

There are different responses to life in the cathedral of the world. Relativists say, "All the windows are basically the same, so it doesn't matter where you stand." They may even wander from window to window. Fundamentalists say, "The light shines only through my window."

And fanatics break all the windows except theirs. But the fact remains, our view of truth and reality is tempered by the way that our people view the world. The light that comes through our Jewish window is the light of Torah and of *mitzvot*. It is not the whole light. But it is our refraction of the light, and that is why it is holy.

The Messiah will show each person that the light that they have been viewing is for everyone, and that ultimately there will be one window in the cathedral of the world. Then we will have the same view of reality, one that is holy and complete. But until that day, individual peoples bask in the light that is refracted through their own particular window. Bar and bat mitzvah is the time when we bring our children to our window, point to the light, and teach them that Torah is our stained glass window.

As Rabbi Jonathan Sacks, chief rabbi of Great Britain, has said: "Covenant tells me that my faith is a form of relationship with God—and that one relationship does not exclude any other, any more than parenthood excludes a love for one's children."

Do Religions Create Evil?

I once heard a bar mitzvah boy trip over one of the readings in the Reform prayer book, *Gates of Prayer*: "In a world torn by violence and *prayer*." He meant to say: "In a world torn by violence and *pain*." History, especially recent history, has often taught us how effectively prayer can tear the world apart. People have killed for their gods. And people have died for their gods.

Yes, many people have died, and continue to die, in the name of religion. You would have to be blind and deaf, without access to media or newspapers, to deny that terrible and sobering truth.

But, imagine two grisly piles of bodies. One pile would be of those who have died in religious wars over the millennia, and one pile would be of those who have died in the name of the secular ideologies of the past century—Nazism and Communism. If we would count the victims, we probably would discover that more people have died at the hands of those demonic antireligious regimes than at the hands of all the religious leaders of history combined.

There are times when we are tempted to hum John Lennon's song "Imagine": "Imagine no religion ..." If a religious zealot shoots a doctor who performs abortions, it makes the news. But on that same day, countless millions of Americans prayed and sang and studied and chanted and meditated and taught and acted—without even a mention from anyone. When a terror bomb explodes in Israel, there are pious ultra-Orthodox men who collect the precious shards of flesh, because people are made in God's image. Are not those men heroes of the spirit?

The columnist and political commentator E. J. Dionne, Jr., writes:

> I think religious faith cannot be supported just because it brings comfort in times of anguish. But neither can it be discredited by horrid acts committed in its name. Faith is suspect, I think, when God is harnessed to immediate human ends and identified entirely with a personal or political or national cause. Faith is brought down by a pridefulness that expresses an unwavering conviction that our own desires and interests coincide perfectly with the divine. Faith, I'd argue, is more credible when it stands as a challenge, when it insists on aspirations beyond those of our own political movements or communities or nations. The prayers of this faith do not express certainty that God is on our side. Only the hope that because we try to seek justice and mercy ourselves, that might prove to be true.

We should train our eyes to look at the strength that faith can instill, and not the pain or death it can impart? Simon Wiesenthal, the determined Nazi hunter and a secular Jew, has said that his lack of faith goes back to Dachau. There, in that Kingdom of Darkness, he once saw a man charge people bread to use the *siddur* (prayer book) that he had smuggled into the camp. "If that's religion," Wiesenthal said to himself at the time, "I don't want to be religious."

Upon later hearing that story, someone asked Wiesenthal, "You may be right. It is horrible, unthinkable, for someone to charge another person bread to use a prayer book. But what about the people who freely gave their bread away? What does it say about them?"

Bar and bat mitzvah is the time when we say to our children: "Listen, there is more than enough to be cynical about in the world. So why not learn about the sources of hope from the people who first brought the idea of hope into the world?"

The Jewish Idea of God?

Finally, some Jews scoff that they "can't believe in the Jewish idea of God." Fine, but which God don't they believe in?

There are many gods that a Jew might not believe in: the highly personal God of the Bible and rabbinic literature. The God of Jewish mysticism. The God of Baruch Spinoza, the God Who is inseparable from the laws of nature. The God of Martin Buber, Who is found in an intimate relationship. Or the God of Mordecai Kaplan, Who is the Power that assures individual salvation and personal enhancement.

This cursory journey through Jewish thought reveals something indispensable about Jewish self-understanding—whichever vision of God a Jew rejects, he or she is in good company, since Judaism has never had a strict catechism of belief. The essence of Judaism is not the idea of God. A *midrash* (*Pesikta de Rav Kahana* 15) imagines God saying, "Would that they deserted Me and kept My Torah." This is not explicit permission for atheism, because the rest of the verse concludes, "For when they keep My Torah, they would have come back to Me." Let us not be reckless. Jewish theology must not be discarded as alien or irrelevant to the Jewish quest for meaning. But Jewish living is more powerful than being able to articulate a finely nuanced theology. We and God find each other in those moments when we, even in the midst of overwhelming doubt, self-consciousness, and cynicism, can begin to live a Jewish life.

Bar and bat mitzvah is a time when we can truly find God—despite it all. Someone once said that there are no atheists in fox holes. I think that there are also no atheists on the *bimah* at a bar or bat mitzvah.

You May Be More Religious Than You Think

The Protestant theologian Karl Barth once said that we should never take unbelief at face value. The surprising truth is that most Jews *think* that they don't believe. Their actions belie their suspicions.

Beyond Israel Bonds and fund-raising and the latest headlines about the Middle East, something about Jews' return to Israel calls out to us in a deep, profound way. The resurrection of a people from the pits of despair reminds us of God's redeeming presence in the world. It says to us, deeply and profoundly, that God does not lie. There is a purpose to history. There is hope. The Jew who gives his or her children a Jewish education, even the parent who does so despite serious reservations and ambivalence, is saying: "I want my child to stand in the light refracted through the Jewish window. I know that my child might wander. I know that my child might become curious about other windows. But I want my child to know where home is, as well."

Consider the words of feminist Letty Cottin Pogrebin. Her children lacked even a minimal Jewish education, and therefore, were not bar or bat mitzvah. Pogrebin regrets that decision mightily:

> I did offer the children the opportunity to go to Hebrew school, but my invitation was desultory and lackluster.... All three [children] refused my offer, contenting themselves with the vicarious pleasures of their friends' bar or bat mitzvah celebrations.... My children felt Jewish, but had little sense of being part of a historical constituency.... Like many of my anti-religion decisions, I have come to view this as a grievous error of judgment. Because I had a feminist axe to grind, I cheated my children out of a Jewish education and allowed them to reject a rite of tribal inclusion whose significance they were not equipped to evaluate.... All three ... are paying for my commitment to their pain-free non-religious childhoods with the shallowness of their ethnic foundations.

The Jewish educator Dr. Ron Wolfson once quipped that we can learn much about the tasks of Jewish education by observing the flight attendants on airplanes. Why do they always announce that you should put your own oxygen mask on first, and then your child's? Because if a child is gasping for air, it does no good for the parent to also be gasping for air. The parent should tend to himself or herself first, and then help the child.

That's how it is with Jewish education as well. There is a shortage of air out there, a shortage of oxygen of Jewish learning and commitment. Parents should emulate airplane passengers by first tending to their own Jewish and spiritual growth. That will prepare them for helping their children grow as Jews as well.

Which of the issues described in this chapter have been real to you? How have you confronted them? How have you dealt with them? What are some other spiritual doubts that you have encountered? Use this space to write them down.

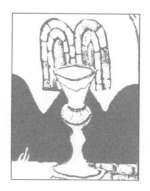

The Shabbat Morning Worship Service

Finding Your Place in the Words

I do not understand
the book in my hand.

Who will teach me to return?
Loss of custom, ruin of will,
A memory of a memory
thinner than a vein.

Who will teach us to return? …

We do not want to come back.

We do not know where we are.

Not knowing where we are,
how can we know where we should go?

—Cynthia Ozick, "In the Synagogue"

The Shabbat Morning Worship Service

It is the same in every Jewish congregation in North America. Many Jews are uncomfortable with Jewish worship. Only one piece of evidence is needed to prove this assertion—the Shabbat morning bar and bat mitzvah service.

Guests arrive late, sometimes timing their arrival to their estimate of when the Torah reading will start. People don't pray. Sometimes they don't even open the prayer book. They often seem lost, and may even have no idea what the service is about or what it is supposed to accomplish. They don't know what to do, where to read, what to read, what page to turn to, when to stand, when to sit, when to sing. The acerbic words of author Annie Dillard ring true: "Why do people in churches [and synagogues] seem like cheerful, brainless tourists on a tour of the Absolute?"

America is the most religious nation in the Western world. According to a worldwide study based at the University of Michigan, 44 percent of Americans attend church once a week, not counting funerals, christenings, and baptisms, compared with 27 percent of people in Great Britain, 21 percent in France, 4 percent in Sweden, and 3 percent in Japan. Fifty-three percent of the Americans say that religion is very important in their lives, compared with 16 percent, 14 percent, and 13 percent, respectively, of the British, French, and Germans.

But Jews lag well behind the general population in congregational membership, in worship attendance, and in the importance they place on religion in their lives. Of all Americans, Jews have the lowest attendance at weekly religious services—about half the national average.

In too many synagogues on too many Shabbat mornings at too many bar and bat mitzvah ceremonies, there is too little participation. Jewish congregations have too often become audiences, while cantors and rabbis have become performers, masters of ceremonies, talk show hosts. People are there for *something*, but it's not the service, and it is certainly not prayer. Bar and bat mitzvah candidates were meant not only to lead the prayers, as a *skill*, but also to *pray*, as a *value*.

Worship—true worship—was intended to be different—to inspire, to ennoble, to induce awe. As the contemporary Jewish theologian Rabbi Eugene B. Borowitz suggests, "The Jewish service is primarily an expression and a renewal of the Jewish people's Covenant with God. The unique feature of communal worship is sharing an experience of transcendence with other Jews as a historic community."

How is this goal to be achieved? When people pray with *kavvanah* (with sacred intention). They care about the words that they are praying. That is the meaning of the words that are written over the *bimah*, the raised platform in the synagogues: *Da lifnei mi attah omed* ("Know before Whom you stand"). When Jews pray with *kavvanah*, they know that they stand before God.

Prayer is a universal human need. Yet for many Jews, prayer is difficult. There are many reasons for this difficulty. We live in a time that is increasingly uncomfortable with poetry. There is a valuable, beautiful treasure embedded in the words of the prayer book, but too few people are looking for that treasure. Jews are often estranged from the words in the very prayer books that they hold in their hands, thinking they are for other Jews, in other times, in other places. Not only are many of us liturgically illiterate, we are also not comfortable with Hebrew. Furthermore, Jews often settle into the comfortable cushion of ethnicity, saying that they are Jewish by sociology, gesture, and cuisine, but not by theology.

American Jews can find meaning in the poetry and the ancient words of prayer. We can add our words to the words of the ancients, our voices to their voices, our harmonies to their harmonies. And, if we approach prayer with the right attitude, the right knowledge, the right spirit, it may embrace us and inspire us. And, yes, it may even enlighten us.

Is the Service Theater?

When someone goes into a synagogue, it is often difficult to know how to even begin approaching the seemingly weighty task of Jewish worship. So, start by thinking of the Shabbat morning service as *participatory theater*.

What happens at the theater? You watch a performance on a stage, complete with props, choreography, and gestures. The actors know the lines that they have learned from their scripts. The audience is passive and applauds the actors at appropriate times.

But what happens in the "theater" experience that is the Shabbat morning service? There is also a script, a script that tells a story. As in the theater, the service has its own staging, props, choreography, and script.

Take the staging, for example. Where participants in a service stand is very important. The moment when a Jewish child stands before the Ark is a moment of extreme sanctity. The Ark is much more than where the Torah is stored. It symbolizes the Ark in the ancient Temple, the holiest place in the world.

Take props, for example. The prayer book, in one sense, is a prop, as are the Torah scroll, wine goblets, and on Friday evening, candles.

Take the choreography. We stand at the holiest moments of the service. We bow. We bend our knees. Some worshippers even ascend onto their toes at certain points in the service.

Finally, the script. Our script is the *siddur* (the Jewish prayer book). The word *siddur* comes from the Hebrew word "order." The *siddur* was first compiled during the eighth and ninth centuries C.E., though the forms of the service and of many prayer texts already existed by about 200 C.E., and even earlier for others.

The *siddur* is a living, breathing, and continually changing document. That is why there are so many translations and adaptations. The *siddur* we use might be the Reform movement's *Mishkan T'filah* or *Gates of Prayer* or *The Union Prayer Book* or any of the new Reform liturgies that are being developed, or the Conservative movement's Silverman *siddur*, or *Siddur Sim Shalom*, or the Reconstructionist *siddurim*, *Kol Haneshama* and *The Sabbath Prayerbook of the Jewish Reconstructionist Foundation*. It might be the *siddur* used in Orthodox synagogues, like the one edited by Birnbaum or published by Art Scroll. Many congregations have developed their own unique prayer books. Some have more Hebrew than others. Some translate the traditional texts poetically or literally. Some reinterpret theological ideas.

Many congregations have developed their own unique prayer books. Some offer greater opportunities for congregational participation than others. Some refuse to describe God as "He" or "King" or "Lord." Some are explicit about the choreography in the service—when to rise, when to be seated.

The differences between these *siddurim* are less important than what they have in common—they tell the story of what Jews hold most precious. The Jewish prayer book teaches and communicates. For centuries, it was our people's source of theology. As Rabbi Henry Slonimsky, former dean of the Jewish Institute of Religion (which later merged with Hebrew Union College) once wrote: "I regard our old Jewish *siddur* as the most important single Jewish book. It is a closer record of Jewish sufferings, Jewish needs, Jewish hopes and aspirations, than the Bible itself. If you want to know what Judaism is, you can find out by absorbing that book."

There are also actors in the Jewish service—ourselves. We perform a sacred drama that reflects our beliefs, our needs, our dreams, our values. As liturgist Rabbi Lawrence Hoffman has noted, when the actor playing Macbeth goes home, he takes off his costume and refrains from plotting another murder. But for Jews, the parts that we play in worship are not simply roles: They are identity. "Worshippers," wrote Hoffman, "are expected to believe their liturgy even after they leave the synagogue; or, if not to believe it literally, at least to know that the story is theirs. They are to own it; it is their sacred biography."

In this sacred drama, God is omnipresent. In this sacred drama, God is talked both *about* and *to*. For God is also an actor in the service—unseen and off stage, but always present. In fact, as Hoffman notes, God even has "lines" in this "drama." We must sometimes strain to hear these lines, but they are definitely there, waiting to be heard, sometimes *demanding* to be heard.

One more thing about this idea of worship as theater—it's not theater in the sense that you buy your ticket and wait to be entertained. It is more like the living theater movement of the 1960s and 1970s—that modern experiment where there is no difference between the actors and the audience, and where there is no real distance between the stage and the seats.

It is a theater where everyone is involved. It is a theater in which there is no real audience. There are only participants, and everyone has a role to play.

The Acts of the Script

Our script is broken into acts, which correspond to the traditional sections of the worship service. Our script tells a story, which is the world view of the Jewish people.

Act One is the *Shema* and its blessings. In this section, beginning with the *Barechu*, the service contains words that teach us *what Jews believe*. This section condenses the core of Jewish belief. It includes prayers to the God Who creates; to the God Who shows love to the Jewish people through the gift of Torah; and to the God Who redeems the Jewish people from Egyptian bondage. The God of Act One is Creator, Revealer of Torah, and Redeemer.

Act Two is *Tefilah* ("prayer" or even "self-judgment"). It is the essence of Jewish prayer. This section is also known as the *shemoneh esreh*, the prayers of the traditional daily liturgy. It is also called the *amidah* (the "standing" prayer) because it is traditionally recited standing. *Tefilah* evokes *what we need* as Jews: to be linked to our ancestors; to believe that there is a reality that transcends the grave; to feel part of God's Holiness; to give thanks; to find fulfillment and *shalom* (peace). Little is requested of God during the Shabbat service. There are many more requests in the daily *tefilah*—pleas for healing, sustenance, forgiveness, the restoration of Jerusalem. But on Shabbat, which is a dress rehearsal for the Messianic Age, we rehearse what it will be like not to need much of anything.

Act Three is the Torah reading. It is *what we learn*. This act takes place on Mondays, Thursdays, festivals, Rosh Hodesh (the first day of the Jewish month), and of course, Shabbat. During this section of the service on Shabbat mornings, the *haftarah* is read.

Act Four is *what we hope*. It contains *Aleinu* and *Kaddish*—prayers for the ultimate universal recognition of God's unity and the coming of God's kingdom.

These are the four basic acts of the worship service. In many synagogues, especially those that are Conservative and Orthodox, there is also a prologue to the service consisting of introductory prayers, *Birchot Hashachar* ("the morning blessings") and *Pesukei Dezimra* ("verses of song"). In Conservative and Orthodox synagogues, an additional service, *musaf*, corresponds with the additional sacrifice in the Temple and repeats some themes of the earlier liturgy. It is customarily recited after the Torah service.

Becoming Liturgically Literate

There is an old story about a convention of comedians who had been getting together for many years. Over the years, they had all heard the same jokes, so they no longer needed to tell them. They assigned every joke a specific number, and a comedian would stand up, call out the number, and people would laugh.

One comedian got up and said, "Forty-two." There was a howl of knowing laughter. "Thirty-seven." Again, guffaws. "Fifty-two." Knee-slapping all around. On a roll, he thought, he tried one more: "Ninety-seven." Nothing. No response. He sat down, dejected.

"What happened?" he asked an old crony. "That was a very funny joke. Why didn't anyone laugh?"

"You told it wrong," his friend answered.

The same goal applies to Jewish worship: To know prayers so well that so many associations are connected with them that they barely need explanation. They should be as familiar to the Jewish worshipper as those numbered jokes were to the comedians. Their elucidation should be as unnecessary to the worshipper as the meaning of "The Star-Spangled Banner" is to the average American on the Fourth of July.

Worship can again become the way that the Jewish people passes its knowledge about itself from generation to generation. Such a task requires a common liturgical language that the praying community can share.

Here, then, are the most important Jewish prayers. The list is selective. Different Jewish movements will highlight different prayers, adding some, deleting others. But, in essence, these prayers form the theological underpinning of the worship experience. Each prayer has a historical meaning to Jews. But more than this, each prayer is filled with potential meaning to the Jew who is prepared to embark on a search for that meaning.

I have chosen to revive a venerable custom. In mystical prayer books, the margins contained *kavvanot*, meditations that prompted the worshipper to focus more clearly on the inner (and often esoteric) meaning of the prayers. I have added meditations after the explanations of each prayer. For each of us, in our own ways, also need *kavvanot*. We need to focus. We need to ask questions. When you attend synagogue, either for ordinary services or for a bar or bat mitzvah service, remember this chapter. Ask yourself the questions that accompany each prayer. Those moments of focus and questioning will help you pray. They will help you reach the heights.

Don't let this mini-encyclopedia of Jewish liturgy deceive you— Jewish worship cannot be learned like a vocabulary list or the multiplication tables. Knowing the meaning of the prayers out of their intended context—the worship service itself—is like knowing musical notes but never hearing them strung together to become the symphony that they were intended to be.

There is, in the final analysis, only one way to truly learn the worship service, to feel comfortable with it, and to feel competent with it. You have to pray it and sing it with a congregation. Anything else is theological voyeurism, and you and your child will know it. Even if it is not explicitly required by your rabbi, I unequivocally recommend that you and your child attend services regularly during the year before (and it goes without saying, after) your child's bar or bat mitzvah ceremony.

Barechu
Praise!

בָּרְכוּ אֶת־יְיָ הַמְבֹרָךְ!

בָּרוּךְ יְיָ הַמְבֹרָךְ לְעוֹלָם וָעֶד!

Praise Adonai, the Blessed One!
Praised be Adonai, who is blessed for ever!

Barechu is the call to worship. This set of responses indicates that the formal part of the worship service is ready to begin. Formal Jewish worship requires a *minyan* of at least ten Jewish adults (in some communities, ten men).

Meditation

What distracts me and keeps me from being completely present for prayer and worship? How can I remove these distractions? What is this community with which I am ready to pray?

Yotzer*
Creator

בָּרוּךְ אַתָּה, יְיָ אֱלֹהֵינוּ, מֶלֶךְ הָעוֹלָם, יוֹצֵר אוֹר וּבוֹרֵא חֹשֶׁךְ, עֹשֶׂה שָׁלוֹם וּבוֹרֵא אֶת הַכֹּל. הַמֵּאִיר לָאָרֶץ וְלַדָּרִים עָלֶיהָ בְּרַחֲמִים, וּבְטוּבוֹ מְחַדֵּשׁ בְּכָל־יוֹם תָּמִיד מַעֲשֵׂה בְרֵאשִׁית.

מָה רַבּוּ מַעֲשֶׂיךָ, יְיָ! כֻּלָּם בְּחָכְמָה עָשִׂיתָ, מָלְאָה הָאָרֶץ קִנְיָנֶךָ. תִּתְבָּרַךְ, יְיָ אֱלֹהֵינוּ, עַל־שֶׁבַח מַעֲשֵׂה יָדֶיךָ, וְעַל־מְאוֹרֵי־אוֹר שֶׁעָשִׂיתָ: יְפָאֲרוּךָ. סֶלָה. בָּרוּךְ אַתָּה, יְיָ, יוֹצֵר הַמְּאוֹרוֹת.

Praised are You, Adonai our God, Ruler of the universe, who fashions light and creates darkness, who establishes peace and creates all things. You illumine the earth and all its inhabitants with compassion, and with goodness renew the work of creation daily.

*This is one of several versions of this prayer.

How manifold are Your works, Adonai; You have made all of them in wisdom; Your creations fill the earth. You are praised, Adonai our God, for the splendor of the work of Your hands; and for the glowing lights that You have made, You are glorified for ever. Praised are You, Adonai, the Creator of the lights.

Yotzer is the morning prayer of creation. Its theme is the creation of light and darkness. It affirms that God creates and re-creates the world every day.

The popular author Robert Fulghum tells the following story in his book *It Was on Fire When I Lay Down on It*. During World War II, Nazi paratroopers who had invaded Crete were attacked by peasants wielding kitchen knives and farm tools. In retaliation, the population was rounded up, executed, and buried in a mass grave. Years later, in response to the darkness of the past, Dr. Alexander Papaderos formed the Institute for Reconciliation, which is devoted to furthering human understanding. To remind himself of the meaning of life, Dr. Papaderos carries in his pocket a small, round piece of glass, no larger than a quarter. It is a piece of a mirror from a German motorcycle that as a small boy he had found shattered on the road. He used to delight in shining its reflective light into dark places where the sun would never shine, in deep holes and crevices and dark closets.

"It became a game for me to get light into the most inaccessible places I could find," he said. "I kept the little mirror and as I went about growing up, I would take it out in idle moments and continue the challenge of the game. As I grew to manhood, I came to understand that this was not just a child's game, but actually a metaphor for what I might do with my life. I came to understand that I am not the light or the source of light. But the light is there, and it will only shine in the dark places if I choose to reflect it."

Meditation

How am I making light shine into the dark places in my life? How am I separating light from darkness? How have I felt a sense of creative purpose operating in me and in the world?

Shema Yisrael
Hear, Israel!

שְׁמַע יִשְׂרָאֵל: יְיָ אֱלֹהֵינוּ, יְיָ אֶחָד!
בָּרוּךְ שֵׁם כְּבוֹד מַלְכוּתוֹ לְעוֹלָם וָעֶד!

Hear, O Israel: Adonai is our God, Adonai is one!
Blessed is the glorious realm of God for ever and ever!

It is hard to sum up the power of the *Shema*. The sages called it *kabbalat ol shamayim* ("the acceptance of the yoke of Heaven"). It is the central statement of Jewish faith, the realization that an eternal covenant bonds us with God. Every time we sing or recite it, we re-covenant with God and with each other. We say that we are a part of a community whose task is to bring the reality of God into the world by living ethically and by God's teachings.

The *Shema* forges us into a community that transcends time and space and circumstance. Elie Wiesel tells of a group of Jews who wanted to celebrate *Simchat Torah* in a barracks at Auschwitz. But they lacked a Torah. An old man asked a young boy, "Do you remember what you learned in *cheder*?"

"Yes, I do," replied the young boy.

"Really?" said the old man. "You really remember *Shema Yisrael*?"

"I remember much more," said the young boy.

"*Shema Yisrael* is enough," said the old man. And he lifted the boy from the ground and began dancing with him, as though he was the Torah.

"Never before," Wiesel later wrote, "had Jews celebrated *Simchat Torah* with such fervor."

That is the *Shema's* power, and it is on our lips twice daily, morning and evening. The *Shema* has been on the lips of our martyrs. It has been on the lips of those who have sought strength. It has been on the lips of those who are about to depart from this world.

> ## Meditation
>
> *What words do I live by in my life? What words are sufficient to sustain me? What does it truly mean for God to be One? How can I feel my life to be part of a larger, lasting Unity? When have I felt connected to something beyond me?*

Ve-ahavta
You shall love …

וְאָהַבְתָּ אֵת יְיָ אֱלֹהֶיךָ בְּכָל־לְבָבְךָ וּבְכָל־נַפְשְׁךָ וּבְכָל־מְאֹדֶךָ. וְהָיוּ הַדְּבָרִים הָאֵלֶּה, אֲשֶׁר אָנֹכִי מְצַוְּךָ הַיּוֹם, עַל־לְבָבֶךָ. וְשִׁנַּנְתָּם לְבָנֶיךָ, וְדִבַּרְתָּ בָּם בְּשִׁבְתְּךָ בְּבֵיתֶךָ וּבְלֶכְתְּךָ בַדֶּרֶךְ, וּבְשָׁכְבְּךָ וּבְקוּמֶךָ.

וּקְשַׁרְתָּם לְאוֹת עַל־יָדֶךָ, וְהָיוּ לְטֹטָפֹת בֵּין עֵינֶיךָ, וּכְתַבְתָּם עַל־מְזוּזוֹת בֵּיתֶךָ, וּבִשְׁעָרֶיךָ.

לְמַעַן תִּזְכְּרוּ וַעֲשִׂיתֶם אֶת־כָּל־מִצְוֹתָי, וִהְיִיתֶם קְדֹשִׁים לֵאלֹהֵיכֶם. אֲנִי יְיָ אֱלֹהֵיכֶם, אֲשֶׁר הוֹצֵאתִי אֶתְכֶם מֵאֶרֶץ מִצְרַיִם לִהְיוֹת לָכֶם לֵאלֹהִים. אֲנִי יְיָ אֱלֹהֵיכֶם.

You shall love Adonai your God with all your heart, with all your soul, and with all your might. These words, which I command you this day, shall be upon your heart. Teach them faithfully to your children; speak of them in your home and on your way, when you lie down and when you rise up. Bind them as a sign upon your hand; let them be symbols before your eyes; inscribe them on the doorposts of your house, and on your gates. Thus may you remember all of My mitzvot, and do them, and so consecrate yourselves to your God. I, Adonai, am your God who led you out of Egypt to be your God; I, Adonai, am your God.

Ve-ahavta, which is part of the *Shema* unit, immediately follows the *Shema* in the service (as well as in Deuteronomy 6) and it is also called *kabbalat ol hamitzvot* ("the acceptance of the yoke of the *mitzvot*"). The *Ve-ahavta* tells us that it's not enough to know that there is a God. That knowledge must be manifest in specific actions.

What actions do we list aloud in the *Ve-ahavta*?

"Teach them to your children." Don't contract the job out to someone else. Be a living role model of the search for Jewish wisdom and Jewish values.

"Speak of them in your home and on your way, when you lie down and when you rise up." If the presence of God is to mean anything in our lives, then it must mean everything in our lives. Torah cannot only be internal. It must be external also, it must live in our homes through ritual, through *tzedakah*, through the values that we teach. It must live through the way we treat our employees, our business colleagues, even our competitors. It must live in society as a prod and a guide.

"Bind them as a sign upon your hand; let them be symbols before your eyes." These words would become the scriptural rationale for *tefilin* (the phylacteries or the leather boxes that contain words of Torah and which are worn on the forearm and on the forehead). The *tefilin* are worn during the weekday morning service. They are worn between our eyes so Torah becomes our way of seeing the world, and so that our vision is in accord with God's higher vision for the world. They are worn on our arms so Torah informs our way of acting in the world. They face the heart to connote that Torah will ultimately be inside us.

"Inscribe them on the doorposts of your house and on your gates." This is the scriptural rationale for the *mezuzah* that marks the doorposts of the Jewish home. It marks the intersection between the public and the private, between the internal and the external, between us and the world.

Meditation

What would it mean to love God "with all my heart"? How am I serving as a conduit of God's love? How am I bringing God into my home? Into my business? Into the world?

Geulah
Redemption

אֱמֶת וְיַצִּיב, וְאָהוּב וְחָבִיב, וְנוֹרָא וְאַדִּיר, וְטוֹב וְיָפֶה הַדָּבָר
הַזֶּה עָלֵינוּ לְעוֹלָם וָעֶד. אֱמֶת, אֱלֹהֵי עוֹלָם מַלְכֵּנוּ, צוּר יַעֲקֹב
מָגֵן יִשְׁעֵנוּ.

לְדֹר וָדֹר הוּא קַיָּם, וּשְׁמוֹ קַיָּם, וְכִסְאוֹ נָכוֹן, וּמַלְכוּתוֹ
וֶאֱמוּנָתוֹ לָעַד קַיֶּמֶת. וּדְבָרָיו חָיִים וְקַיָּמִים, נֶאֱמָנִים
וְנֶחֱמָדִים, לָעַד וּלְעוֹלְמֵי עוֹלָמִים.

מִמִּצְרַיִם גְּאַלְתָּנוּ, יְיָ אֱלֹהֵינוּ, וּמִבֵּית עֲבָדִים פְּדִיתָנוּ.

עַל־זֹאת שִׁבְּחוּ אֲהוּבִים וְרוֹמְמוּ אֵל, וְנָתְנוּ יְדִידִים זְמִירוֹת,
שִׁירוֹת וְתִשְׁבָּחוֹת, בְּרָכוֹת וְהוֹדָאוֹת לַמֶּלֶךְ, אֵל חַי וְקַיָּם.

רָם וְנִשָּׂא, גָּדוֹל וְנוֹרָא, מַשְׁפִּיל גֵּאִים וּמַגְבִּיהַּ שְׁפָלִים, מוֹצִיא
אֲסִירִים וּפוֹדֶה עֲנָוִים, וְעוֹזֵר דַּלִּים, וְעוֹנֶה לְעַמּוֹ בְּעֵת שַׁוְּעָם
אֵלָיו.

מִי־כָמֹכָה בָּאֵלִם, יְיָ!

מִי כָּמֹכָה, נֶאְדָּר בַּקֹּדֶשׁ,

נוֹרָא תְהִלֹּת, עֹשֵׂה פֶלֶא!

שִׁירָה חֲדָשָׁה שִׁבְּחוּ גְאוּלִים לְשִׁמְךָ עַל־שְׂפַת הַיָּם. יַחַד כֻּלָּם
הוֹדוּ וְהִמְלִיכוּ וְאָמְרוּ: יְיָ יִמְלֹךְ לְעוֹלָם וָעֶד.

צוּר יִשְׂרָאֵל, קוּמָה בְּעֶזְרַת יִשְׂרָאֵל, וּפְדֵה כִנְאֻמֶךָ יְהוּדָה
וְיִשְׂרָאֵל. גֹּאֲלֵנוּ, יְיָ צְבָאוֹת שְׁמוֹ, קְדוֹשׁ יִשְׂרָאֵל. בָּרוּךְ אַתָּה,
יְיָ, גָּאַל יִשְׂרָאֵל.

*This will for ever be true and everlasting, beloved and precious,
awesome, powerful, good and beautiful for us: The Eternal God
truly is our Sovereign, the Rock of Jacob our protecting Shield.*

*You endure from generation to generation, as Your name endures;
Your throne remains, as Your sovereignty and faithfulness abide
forever.*

Your words live and endure, for ever a precious part of our faith, now and to all eternity.

You redeemed us from Egypt, Adonai our God, and set us free from the house of bondage.

For this Your beloved praised and exalted God; Your precious people rendered melodies, songs and praises, prayers and thanks to the Ruler, the living and eternal God.

You who are high and exalted, great and awesome, who can raise the valleys and lower the mountains, O free the captive and redeem the oppressed, and answer Your people when they cry out to You.

Who is like You among the gods, Adonai!

Who is like You, adorned with holiness, awesome in splendor, doing wonders!

Your children witnessed Your sovereignty as You parted the sea before Moses. "This is my God!" they exclaimed. "Adonai will reign for ever and ever!"

For as it has been said: "Adonai delivered Jacob, redeeming him from the hand of an overpowering aggressor." Praised are You, Adonai, the Redeemer of Israel.

The *Geulah* prayer speaks of the redemption from Egypt. It climaxes with the triumphant singing of *Mi Chamocha*: "Who is like you, among the gods, *Adonai*?" Moses and the Israelites sang this at the shores of the Sea of Reeds. This prayer is in the form of a responsive reading. It therefore echoes the experience at the Sea, during which the Israelites sang responsively with Moses and Miriam.

As we sing *Mi Chamocha*, we try to imagine walking through the parted waters of the sea. A Hasidic sect marks the last day of Pesach by pouring vats of water on the floors of its synagogue so worshippers can walk through it and relive the experience of the Sea of Reeds. Other peoples have also tried to wade through those parted waters. They symbolize freedom and liberation, both internal and external. This prayer reminds us that the tyrants of history, whether ancient or modern, do not have the last word.

> ## Meditation
>
> *What waters separate me from my goals in life? When have I felt redeemed by a force more powerful than me? How have I struggled for freedom? What are those things in my life that tyrannize me? How have I helped those seeking freedom?*

Avot
Fathers or Ancestors

בָּרוּךְ אַתָּה, יְיָ אֱלֹהֵינוּ וֵאלֹהֵי אֲבוֹתֵינוּ, אֱלֹהֵי אַבְרָהָם, אֱלֹהֵי יִצְחָק, וֵאלֹהֵי יַעֲקֹב הָאֵל הַגָּדוֹל, הַגִּבּוֹר וְהַנּוֹרָא, אֵל עֶלְיוֹן.

גּוֹמֵל חֲסָדִים טוֹבִים, וְקוֹנֵה הַכֹּל, וְזוֹכֵר חַסְדֵי אָבוֹת, וּמֵבִיא גְאֻלָּה לִבְנֵי בְנֵיהֶם, לְמַעַן שְׁמוֹ, בְּאַהֲבָה.

מֶלֶךְ עוֹזֵר וּמוֹשִׁיעַ וּמָגֵן. בָּרוּךְ אַתָּה, יְיָ, מָגֵן אַבְרָהָם.

Praised are You, Adonai our God and God of our ancestors: God of Abraham, God of Isaac, God of Jacob; great, mighty, and awesome God, God supreme. (Some versions: Praised are You, Adonai our God and God of our ancestors: God of Abraham, God of Isaac, God of Jacob; God of Sarah, God of Rebecca, God of Rachel and God of Leah.)

Grantor of love and kindness, You care for us all by remembering the devotion of our ancestors, and in love, bringing redemption (Some versions: "a Redeemer") to their descendants for the sake of Your name.

Our Ruler helps and saves and protects us. Praised are You, Adonai, the Protector of Abraham.

The *Avot* prayer connects us to our ancestors. They had a faith, a way of life, a way of standing resolute in the face of overwhelming odds, each with their own relationship with God.

Avot is not only about Abraham and Sarah, Isaac and Rebecca, Jacob and Rachel and Leah. It's about praying to the God of your parents and your grandparents and your great-grandparents. You are praying all the way back into history. Praying is not only speaking to God. Praying is remembering that all the generations of the Jewish people are connected to God in a covenant that does not die, but which becomes eternally reborn every time we worship as a community.

But this does not mean that we walk in lockstep with the generations. The prayer says: "*God* of Abraham, *God* of Isaac, and *God* of Jacob." It does not state: "God of Abraham, Isaac, and Jacob." As Martin Buber noted, every generation must come to its own conception of God. Our way of looking at God may be different from our parents'. It may be different from our grandparents'. Yet, we are all part of the same covenantal pattern.

Meditation

What did my parents teach me? What did my grandparents teach me? What stories have they left me? What moral legacies have they left me? When do I feel their presence? What was God to them? What is God to me?

Gevurot
Powers

אַתָּה גִבּוֹר לְעוֹלָם, אֲדֹנָי, מְחַיֵּה הַכֹּל אַתָּה, רַב לְהוֹשִׁיעַ.
מְכַלְכֵּל חַיִּים בְּחֶסֶד, מְחַיֵּה הַכֹּל בְּרַחֲמִים רַבִּים. סוֹמֵךְ
נוֹפְלִים, וְרוֹפֵא חוֹלִים, וּמַתִּיר אֲסוּרִים, וּמְקַיֵּם אֱמוּנָתוֹ
לִישֵׁנֵי עָפָר.

מִי כָמְוֹךָ בַּעַל גְּבוּרוֹת, וּמִי דוֹמֶה לָךְ, מֶלֶךְ מֵמִית וּמְחַיֵּה
וּמַצְמִיחַ יְשׁוּעָה.

וְנֶאֱמָן אַתָּה לְהַחֲיוֹת הַכֹּל. בָּרוּךְ אַתָּה, יְיָ, מְחַיֵּה הַכֹּל.

Eternal is Your power, Adonai, giving life to all [or, traditionally, "giving life to the dead"] through magnificent salvation. With faithful love, You sustain the living, and with great compassion give life to all. You support the fallen and heal the sick, free the captive and keep faith with those who sleep in the dust.

Who is like You, Master of Might, and who can compare to You, our Sovereign, who rules death and life, causing salvation to flourish!

You faithfully give life to all. Praised are You, Adonai, who gives life to all [or, traditionally, "who gives life to the dead"].

The main theme of *Gevurot* is the ultimate Messianic resurrection of the dead. Traditional versions of the prayer make that belief explicit and speak of God as *mechayeh hametim* ("the One who resurrects the dead") since traditional Jewish theology believes that God will return the dead to life in the Messianic era. The new Reconstructionist version is *mechayeh kol chai* ("Who gives life to all that lives"). Reform versions have traditionally spoken of God as *mechayeh hakol* ("Who gives life to all") since Reform Judaism has traditionally not accepted the notion of bodily resurrection.

But even here, an increasing number of Reform Jews are willing to think about resurrection as something that really happens. It might be through the rhythms of nature—through the constant flow of the seasons that revives those things that are dormant. It might be through relationships—for Judaism teaches that a friendship regained or revived is similar to resurrection of the dead. And yes, it might be the traditional Messianic era resurrection of the dead—in ways that the mind cannot imagine but that might nevertheless be real.

"God keeps faith with those who sleep in the dust." You don't have to literally believe in resurrection to sense that there is something nonmaterial, something beyond our bodies, that lives forever. It's called our souls. Because we have souls, we are endowed with eternal worth and eternal hope.

In 1962, an Israeli submarine sank off the coast of Israel. All the sailors were drowned. Soon after, the father of one of the sailors attended a basketball game that his son's old team won. "When my son comes back, I will tell him of your victory," he said to his son's old teammates. His son was dead, but his words were an assurance that there is a hope that transcends the grave.

Meditation

What unseen presences are with me when I pray? When have I felt the reality of my soul? When have I sensed that the human soul can transcend death?

Kedusha
Sanctification

נְקַדֵּשׁ אֶת־שִׁמְךָ בָּעוֹלָם, כְּשֵׁם שֶׁמַּקְדִּישִׁים אוֹתוֹ בִּשְׁמֵי מָרוֹם,
כַּכָּתוּב עַל־יַד נְבִיאֶךָ: וְקָרָא זֶה אֶל־זֶה וְאָמַר:

קָדוֹשׁ, קָדוֹשׁ, קָדוֹשׁ יְיָ צְבָאוֹת, מְלֹא כָל־הָאָרֶץ כְּבוֹדוֹ.

לְעֻמָּתָם בָּרוּךְ יֹאמֵרוּ:

בָּרוּךְ כְּבוֹד יְיָ מִמְּקוֹמוֹ.

וּבְדִבְרֵי קָדְשְׁךָ כָּתוּב לֵאמֹר:

יִמְלֹךְ יְיָ לְעוֹלָם, אֱלֹהַיִךְ צִיּוֹן, לְדֹר וָדֹר, הַלְלוּיָהּ.

לְדוֹר וָדוֹר נַגִּיד גָּדְלֶךָ, וּלְנֵצַח נְצָחִים קְדֻשָּׁתְךָ נַקְדִּישׁ.
וְשִׁבְחֲךָ, אֱלֹהֵינוּ, מִפִּינוּ לֹא יָמוּשׁ לְעוֹלָם וָעֶד. בָּרוּךְ אַתָּה,
יְיָ, הָאֵל הַקָּדוֹשׁ.

*Let us proclaim the sanctity of Your name here on earth, just as it is
proclaimed in the high heavens; as recorded by Your prophet, let us
cry out one to another:*

*Holy, Holy, Holy is Adonai of Hosts; the fullness of the whole earth
is God's glory!*

We respond with blessing:

Blessed be God's seat of glory!

Following Your sacred words we say:

*Adonai shall reign forever, your God, O Zion, from generation to
generation. Halleluyah!*

*From generation to generation we will tell of Your greatness, and to
the ends of time proclaim Your holiness. Your praise, O God, shall
never leave our lips. Praised are You, Adonai, the holy God.*

The *Kedusha* is best known by the refrain *Kadosh kadosh kadosh
Adonai Tzevaot, melo kol haaretz kevodo.* "Holy, holy, holy is the Lord
of Hosts. The whole earth is full of God's glory." It is Isaiah's vision of
the divine beings that surround the Divine Throne (Isaiah 6:3). Some
worshippers rise on their toes as they sing "Kadosh" in order to imitate
the ascent of the angels to the Divine Throne.

And then, *Baruch kavod Adonai mimkomo* ("Blessed is the Glory of God in heaven and earth"), which was Ezekiel's response to his vision of the Celestial Chariot that carries the Divine Throne (Ezekiel 3:12). This was the most profound of Jewish mystical visions.

Those two private prophetic visions of God continue into *Yimloch Adonai le-olam, elohayich Tziyon, ledor vador, Halleluyah* ("Adonai shall rule forever, Your God, O Zion, from generation to generation. Hallelujah!", Psalm 146:10). It triumphantly affirms that God is not just the God of the individual prophet's vision. God is the God of the entire Jewish people.

Meditation

What are those moments when I have felt exalted? What are those moments when I have felt the reality of God's Sovereignty? What are those moments when I have transcended myself and felt one with the Jewish people?

Kedushat Hayom
Sanctification of the Day

Yismechu:

יִשְׂמְחוּ בְמַלְכוּתְךָ שׁוֹמְרֵי שַׁבָּת וְקוֹרְאֵי עְנֶג. עַם מְקַדְּשֵׁי שְׁבִיעִי כֻּלָּם יִשְׂבְּעוּ וְיִתְעַנְּגוּ מִטּוּבֶךָ. וְהַשְּׁבִיעִי רָצִיתָ בּוֹ וְקִדַּשְׁתּוֹ. חֶמְדַּת יָמִים אוֹתוֹ קָרָאתָ זֵכֶר לְמַעֲשֵׂה בְרֵאשִׁית.

Those who keep Shabbat and call it a delight shall rejoice in Your reign. The nation that keeps the seventh day holy shall be delighted by Your goodness. For you favored the seventh day and sanctified it, calling it the most precious of days, a memory of the act of creation.

Veshamru:

וְשָׁמְרוּ בְנֵי־יִשְׂרָאֵל אֶת הַשַּׁבָּת, לַעֲשׂוֹת אֶת־הַשַּׁבָּת לְדֹרֹתָם בְּרִית עוֹלָם. בֵּינִי וּבֵין בְּנֵי יִשְׂרָאֵל אוֹת הִיא לְעֹלָם, כִּי שֵׁשֶׁת יָמִים עָשָׂה יְיָ אֶת־הַשָּׁמַיִם וְאֶת־הָאָרֶץ, וּבַיּוֹם הַשְּׁבִיעִי שָׁבַת וַיִּנָּפַשׁ.

The people of Israel shall keep Shabbat, observing Shabbat through-out all their generations as an eternal covenant. It is a sign between Me and the people of Israel for ever, because in six days Adonai cre-ated the heavens and earth, and on the seventh day ceased from work and rested.

Our God and God of our ancestors, favor our rest. Sanctify us with Your commandments and let us share in Your Torah. Satisfy us with Your goodness, gladden us with Your salvation, and purify our hearts to serve You in truth. Adonai our God, in Your gracious love let Your holy Sabbath be our heritage, that in it all of Israel, hallow-ing Your name, may find rest. Praised are You, Adonai, who sancti-fies the Sabbath.

Kedushat Hayom sanctifies the Shabbat day, either through the singing of *Yismechu* or *Veshamru*. We link God's holiness to the holi-ness of this moment in Jewish time.

Meditation

How do I sanctify time in my life? What are the holiest moments in my life? How have I made Shabbat a holy time?

Avodah
Worship

רְצֵה, יְיָ אֱלֹהֵינוּ, בְּעַמְּךָ יִשְׂרָאֵל, וּתְפִלָּתָם בְּאַהֲבָה תְקַבֵּל,
וּתְהִי לְרָצוֹן תָּמִיד עֲבוֹדַת יִשְׂרָאֵל עַמֶּךָ. אֵל קָרוֹב לְכָל־
קֹרְאָיו, פְּנֵה אֶל עֲבָדֶיךָ וְחָנֵּנוּ. שְׁפוֹךְ רוּחֲךָ עָלֵינוּ, וְתֶחֱזֶינָה
עֵינֵינוּ בְּשׁוּבְךָ לְצִיּוֹן בְּרַחֲמִים.

בָּרוּךְ אַתָּה, יְיָ, הַמַּחֲזִיר שְׁכִינָתוֹ לְצִיּוֹן.

Take pleasure, Adonai our God, in Your people Israel, and accept our prayer with love. May our worship always be acceptable to You. God is close to all who call; turn to Your servants and be gracious to us. Pour out Your spirit upon us, and may our eyes behold Your return to Zion in compassion. Praised are You, Adonai, Who returns the wandering in-dwelling Divine Presence to Zion.

Avodah focuses our attention on a distant part of our history—the sacrificial offerings in the ancient Temple in Jerusalem. We also remember that although we no longer have a Temple, every Jewish home is a *mikdash m'at* (a miniature sanctuary), in which the mundane can be transformed into the sacred.

My love for this prayer has little connection with any Messianic longing to rebuild the Temple and restore the sacrifices held there. I love it because of its *chatimah* (the "closing" or "sealing" of the prayer): "Praised are You, Adonai, Who returns the wandering in-dwelling Divine Presence to Zion." That is the prayer that I say, tears in my eyes, when I see the shore of Israel from the descending El Al jetliner. This is what I say whenever I remember that we live in an age in which Jews have come home to Israel, where, once again, we have met God. Some sages say that God's Presence was in exile with us. If that is true, then God has returned with us to Zion.

Meditation

What might it feel like to bring an offering to prayer? What would my offering be? How can I create holy places in my life? Have I had a holy experience in Israel?

Hodaah
Thanksgiving

מוֹדִים אֲנַחְנוּ לָךְ, שָׁאַתָּה הוּא יְיָ אֱלֹהֵינוּ וֵאלֹהֵי אֲבוֹתֵינוּ לְעוֹלָם וָעֶד. צוּר חַיֵּינוּ, מָגֵן יִשְׁעֵנוּ, אַתָּה הוּא לְדוֹר וָדוֹר. נוֹדֶה לְךָ וּנְסַפֵּר תְּהִלָּתֶךָ, עַל־חַיֵּינוּ הַמְּסוּרִים בְּיָדֶךָ, וְעַל־נִשְׁמוֹתֵינוּ הַפְּקוּדוֹת לָךְ, וְעַל־נִסֶּיךָ שֶׁבְּכָל־יוֹם עִמָּנוּ, וְעַל־נִפְלְאוֹתֶיךָ וְטוֹבוֹתֶיךָ שֶׁבְּכָל־עֵת, עֶרֶב וָבֹקֶר וְצָהֳרָיִם. הַטּוֹב כִּי לֹא־כָלוּ רַחֲמֶיךָ, וְהַמְרַחֵם: כִּי־לֹא תַמּוּ חֲסָדֶיךָ, מֵעוֹלָם קִוִּינוּ לָךְ.

וְעַל כֻּלָּם יִתְבָּרַךְ וְיִתְרוֹמַם שִׁמְךָ, מַלְכֵּנוּ, תָּמִיד לְעוֹלָם וָעֶד.

We acknowledge that You are Adonai our God and the God of our ancestors, forever. You are the Rock of our life, our Protector in salvation from generation to generation. And so we thank You and sing Your praises, for our lives which are in Your hand, and for our souls, which are entrusted to You; for Your miracles which are among us daily, and for Your wondrous and great acts of every hour, morning, noon, and night. You are beneficent, for Your mercy is unending; You are merciful, for Your love is unending. You have always been our hope.

For all these things, our Ruler, may Your name be blessed and exalted, for ever and ever.

Hodaah asks us to remember to be thankful for what we have. Because it is Shabbat, there is little that we ask of God. Shabbat is a dress rehearsal of Messianic times, affording us the opportunity to imagine what life would be like without asking for anything, to have all our needs satisfied. We give thanks for all that we have, for all that we might have, for the ability to give thanks.

Meditation
For what am I particularly grateful? When have I truly felt a sense of humility? How do I know Whom to thank?

Birchat Shalom
The Blessing of Peace

שִׂים שָׁלוֹם, טוֹבָה וּבְרָכָה, חֵן וָחֶסֶד וְרַחֲמִים, עָלֵינוּ וְעַל־כָּל־יִשְׂרָאֵל עַמֶּךָ.

בָּרְכֵנוּ אָבִינוּ, כֻּלָּנוּ כְּאֶחָד, בְּאוֹר פָּנֶיךָ, כִּי בְאוֹר פָּנֶיךָ נָתַתָּ לָּנוּ, יְיָ אֱלֹהֵינוּ, תּוֹרַת חַיִּים, וְאַהֲבַת חֶסֶד, וּצְדָקָה וּבְרָכָה וְרַחֲמִים, וְחַיִּים וְשָׁלוֹם.

וְטוֹב בְּעֵינֶיךָ לְבָרֵךְ אֶת־עַמְּךָ יִשְׂרָאֵל בְּכָל־עֵת וּבְכָל־שָׁעָה בִּשְׁלוֹמֶךָ.

בָּרוּךְ אַתָּה, יְיָ, הַמְבָרֵךְ אֶת־עַמּוֹ יִשְׂרָאֵל בַּשָּׁלוֹם.

Grant peace, goodness and blessing, grace, love, and mercy, for us, and for all of Israel, Your people. Bless us, Loving Parent, one and all, with the light of Your presence; for by that light You gave us the law of life, and a love of kindness; justice, blessing, compassion, life and peace. May it be pleasing in Your sight to bless Your people Israel at all times and seasons with Your peace. Praised are You, Adonai, who blesses the people Israel with peace.

Birchat Shalom reminds us that there is one thing that we do not have—peace. It calls for an end to violence, war, and bloodshed. Some versions of the prayer ask for peace not only for the Jewish people, but for all the nations of the world as well. We remember that the accurate translation of *shalom* is not simply "peace," but "completeness," "fulfillment," and "wholeness."

Meditation

What am I doing to bring shalom into the world? Into my family? Into my life? What would give me a true sense of fulfillment and completeness?

Aleinu
It is incumbent upon us ...

עָלֵינוּ לְשַׁבֵּחַ לַאֲדוֹן הַכֹּל, לָתֵת גְּדֻלָּה לְיוֹצֵר בְּרֵאשִׁית.
שֶׁלֹּא עָשָׂנוּ כְּגוֹיֵי הָאֲרָצוֹת, וְלֹא שָׂמָנוּ כְּמִשְׁפְּחוֹת הָאֲדָמָה.
שֶׁלֹּא שָׂם חֶלְקֵנוּ כָּהֶם, וְגֹרָלֵנוּ כְּכָל־הֲמוֹנָם.

וַאֲנַחְנוּ כּוֹרְעִים וּמִשְׁתַּחֲוִים וּמוֹדִים לִפְנֵי מֶלֶךְ מַלְכֵי
הַמְּלָכִים, הַקָּדוֹשׁ בָּרוּךְ הוּא.

שֶׁהוּא נוֹטֶה שָׁמַיִם וְיוֹסֵד אָרֶץ, וּמוֹשַׁב יְקָרוֹ בַּשָּׁמַיִם מִמַּעַל
וּשְׁכִינַת עֻזּוֹ בְּגָבְהֵי מְרוֹמִים. הוּא אֱלֹהֵינוּ, אֵין עוֹד, אֱמֶת
מַלְכֵּנוּ, אֶפֶס זוּלָתוֹ, כַּכָּתוּב בְּתוֹרָתוֹ: וְיָדַעְתָּ הַיּוֹם וַהֲשֵׁבֹתָ
אֶל־לְבָבֶךָ, כִּי יְיָ הוּא הָאֱלֹהִים בַּשָּׁמַיִם מִמַּעַל וְעַל הָאָרֶץ
מִתָּחַת, אֵין עוֹד.

עַל־כֵּן נְקַוֶּה לְךָ, יְיָ אֱלֹהֵינוּ, לִרְאוֹת מְהֵרָה בְּתִפְאֶרֶת עֻזֶּךָ.
לְהַעֲבִיר גִּלּוּלִים מִן הָאָרֶץ, וְהָאֱלִילִים כָּרוֹת יִכָּרֵתוּן.
לְתַקֵּן עוֹלָם בְּמַלְכוּת שַׁדַּי. וְכָל־בְּנֵי בָשָׂר יִקְרְאוּ בִשְׁמֶךָ,
לְהַפְנוֹת אֵלֶיךָ כָּל־רִשְׁעֵי אָרֶץ.

יַכִּירוּ וְיֵדְעוּ כָּל־יוֹשְׁבֵי תֵבֵל כִּי לְךָ תִּכְרַע כָּל־בֶּרֶךְ, תִּשָּׁבַע
כָּל־לָשׁוֹן. לְפָנֶיךָ, יְיָ אֱלֹהֵינוּ, יִכְרְעוּ וְיִפֹּלוּ, וְלִכְבוֹד שִׁמְךָ
יְקָר יִתֵּנוּ, וִיקַבְּלוּ כֻלָּם אֶת־עֹל מַלְכוּתֶךָ, וְתִמְלֹךְ עֲלֵיהֶם
מְהֵרָה לְעוֹלָם וָעֶד.

כִּי הַמַּלְכוּת שֶׁלְּךָ הִיא, וּלְעוֹלְמֵי עַד תִּמְלֹךְ בְּכָבוֹד,
כַּכָּתוּב בְּתוֹרָתֶךָ: יְיָ יִמְלֹךְ לְעֹלָם וָעֶד.

We must praise the Master of all, ascribing greatness to the Creator, who has distinguished us among the other nations and families of the earth by giving us a unique portion and destiny.

So we humbly bow down in acknowledgment before the supreme Ruler of rulers, the Holy One of Blessing.

God spread out the heavens and established the earth; Adonai is our God; there is none else. In truth God is our ruler, as it is written: "Know then this day and take it to heart: Adonai is God in the heavens above and on the earth below; there is none else."

Therefore we hope in You, Adonai our God, that we might see soon the glory of Your might, that the false gods will pass away from the earth, and be utterly destroyed, so that the world will be repaired in the image of Your ultimate rule. Then all flesh-and-blood will call upon Your name, for You will have turned toward You all the wicked of the earth.

All those who dwell on earth will recognize that they can bow down to You and that every tongue will pledge faithfulness to You. Before You, Adonai our God, may they bow down and give honor to Your name. May they take upon themselves the responsibility of living by Your rule, and may You rule over them forever.

For Yours is sovereignty, and in glory will You rule for ever, as it has been said in Your Torah: "On that day, Adonai will be one and God's Name will be one."

Aleinu ("It is incumbent upon us") repeats the major themes of the service: the theme of *creation* ("We must praise the Master of all, ascribing greatness to the Creator ..."); the theme of *revelation* ("... who has distinguished us among the other nations ..."); and the theme of *redemption.* This is arguably the most misunderstood verse in Jewish liturgy. Some gentile rulers forbade Jews from singing it in the synagogue, believing that it insulted Christians. Actually the phrase "who has distinguished us" is not ethnic chauvinism. It means that God chose us for a unique task—to teach Torah to the world and to bring the world closer to a belief in the One God.

What are the essential elements of redemption? The Exodus from Egypt is the dress rehearsal for universal redemption. Freedom for one people—the people of Israel—must lead to freedom for all peoples. Redemption means the universal recognition that all are made in the divine image.

The second element of redemption is the weightiest—*letakein olam bemalchut shaddai,* "to repair the world in the image of God's rule." To bring the world closer to how we sense God wants it to be. Our tools for doing this are the *mitzvot.*

But there is another element to redemption—*the eradication of idolatry.* Idolatry is not only worshipping gods of wood and stone. Idolatry means treating as *ultimately important and holy* something that is not ultimately important and holy. The state is a god for some. Work and career are gods for some. Contemporary culture is a god for some. The self is a god for too many. Universal redemption—or as it is often called, the Messianic Age—comes when humanity succeeds in eradicating idolatry. For that reason, *Aleinu* ends with the ancient hope: *Bayom hahu yiheyeh Adonai echad ushemo echad:* "On that [Messianic] day, Adonai will be one and God's Name will be one."

There are other, more tantalizing interpretations of that verse. On that Messianic Day, we will understand that all the names of God are, in fact, only One Name: Adonai. Others disagree. On that Messianic day, they say, we will know that God's Name is Echad, One. We will know that God is the Supernal Unity that binds and bonds all existence.

Meditation

How am I making God One in my life? How am I making God One in the world? How am I bringing about the day when the world will reflect the Divine Unity?

Mourners' Kaddish
Sanctification

יִתְגַּדַּל וְיִתְקַדַּשׁ שְׁמֵהּ רַבָּא בְּעָלְמָא דִּי־בְרָא כִרְעוּתֵהּ,
וְיַמְלִיךְ מַלְכוּתֵהּ בְּחַיֵּיכוֹן וּבְיוֹמֵיכוֹן וּבְחַיֵּי דְכָל־בֵּית
יִשְׂרָאֵל, בַּעֲגָלָא וּבִזְמַן קָרִיב, וְאִמְרוּ: אָמֵן.

יְהֵא שְׁמֵהּ רַבָּא מְבָרַךְ לְעָלַם וּלְעָלְמֵי עָלְמַיָּא!

יִתְבָּרַךְ וְיִשְׁתַּבַּח, וְיִתְפָּאַר וְיִתְרוֹמַם וְיִתְנַשֵּׂא, וְיִתְהַדָּר
וְיִתְעַלֶּה וְיִתְהַלָּל שְׁמֵהּ דְּקוּדְשָׁא, בְּרִיךְ הוּא, לְעֵלָּא מִן־
כָּל־בִּרְכָתָא וְשִׁירָתָא, תֻּשְׁבְּחָתָא וְנֶחֱמָתָא דַּאֲמִירָן בְּעָלְמָא,
וְאִמְרוּ: אָמֵן.

יְהֵא שְׁלָמָא רַבָּא מִן־שְׁמַיָּא וְחַיִּים עָלֵינוּ וְעַל־כָּל־יִשְׂרָאֵל
וְאִמְרוּ: אָמֵן.

עֹשֶׂה שָׁלוֹם בִּמְרוֹמָיו, הוּא יַעֲשֶׂה שָׁלוֹם עָלֵינוּ וְעַל־כָּל־
יִשְׂרָאֵל, וְאִמְרוּ: אָמֵן.

May Your great name be magnified and hallowed, in the world created according to Your will, and may Your reign be quickly established, in our own lives and our own day, and in the life of all of Israel, and let us say: Amen.

May Your great name be blessed for ever and ever!

All praise and glory, splendor, exaltation and honor, radiance and veneration and worship to the Holy One of Blessing, even beyond any earthly prayer or song, any adoration or tribute we can offer, and let us say: Amen.

May there be great peace from the heavens, and life for us and for all of Israel, as we say: Amen.

May the One who makes peace in the high heavens send peace for us and for all of Israel, as we say: Amen.

Finally, there is *Kaddish* ("sanctification"). Kaddish is a prayer in Aramaic, Hebrew's sister language. The opening words of the Christian "Lord's Prayer" were probably adopted from Kaddish.

There are several different versions of Kaddish. Often, it serves as a punctuation point between different sections of the service. But the version of the Kaddish that has most graphically captured the Jewish imagination is the use of Kaddish as a mourners' prayer.

In reality, Kaddish never mentions death. Its origins as a prayer for mourners are buried in Jewish lore. Some say that it was a way to save loved ones from eternal punishment and to ease their entrance into the World to Come. It became a mourners' prayer in the wake of the massacres of Jewish communities by the Crusaders in the Middle Ages while on their way to the Holy Land. Kaddish is a way of saying, even against the chaos of existence and the void of mortality, that there is meaning in life. It is a fervent plea for the coming of God's Kingdom.

I once sat at the bedside of a dying woman who had survived the Holocaust. We spoke about her life in central Europe, about her girlhood in Vienna, about the way that she met her husband. I finally asked if she was afraid of dying. She shook her head, turned to me and asked, "What lasts?"

I answered her, "Every hug, every word, every kiss, every *mitzvah* that you did will survive you. '*Eilu devarim she-ain lahem shiur*,' says our prayer book: 'There are certain things that we do that cannot be measured, for though we eat their fruits in this world, they send forth a ray of light that sustains us even into the next.'"

We have ways of creating our own immortality.

Meditation

What do I have that has been left to me by someone I love? What debts do I have to pay? How do I stand upright against the winds of pain and loss?

To the Heights ... and Beyond

The Shabbat morning service, if approached with *kavvanah*—with sacred intention and awareness and an ear toward hearing both God and hearing ourselves—can take us on a journey. That journey leads us through our fundamental beliefs and needs as Jews, to hearing the wisdom that descends from Sinai, to praying for the ultimate unity of God and the coming of God's Kingdom.

The service is carefully and deliberately orchestrated to take us, ultimately, from the mundane planes of our lives to the heights of Sinai—and beyond.

The bar and bat mitzvah ceremony occurs within this liturgical choreography. This choreography may seem strange or esoteric or irrelevant and beyond your experience. But it is weighted with millennia of Jewish experience and wisdom and hopes. Not the least of these hopes and aspirations is that your child, who is now of the age where he or she can fully appreciate the service, will feel its full force and know, in the depths of his or her youthful soul, what it means to be a Jew who can ascend the mountain of prayers to a summit where every religiously curious Jew has climbed before.

The Need for Community

Bar and bat mitzvah ceremonies ordinarily occur as part of a public Shabbat (or, sometimes, weekday morning) service. Ideally, they should be *part* of that service, not its entire *raison d'être*. But that ideal is far from being a reality. In too many congregations, bar and bat mitzvah ceremonies have hijacked the Shabbat morning service.

This is unsettling. Some synagogues only have Shabbat morning services when there is a bar or bat mitzvah ceremony—creating the impression that *this* experience is the essence of Jewish worship, and that we need a thirteen-year-old and his or her entourage to justify a community's reaching to God. This, in turn, creates the attitude that the Shabbat morning service belongs to the bar or bat mitzvah family, and not to the congregation or to God. In many synagogues, every week a new, temporary congregation magically appears, comprised primarily of the family and friends of the bar or bat mitzvah. Many loyal Friday night worshippers rarely attend Shabbat morning services when there is a bar or bat mitzvah. They say that they feel as if they are intruding into someone else's *simcha*.

Several years ago, I conferred with a family whose son, Jeremy, was about to become bar mitzvah. As I reviewed the honors for the service that were available to the extended family, the father held up his hand. "Rabbi," he said, "there aren't going to be any honors."

"Oh?" I asked. "Why not?"

"Because we're *it*. It's me and my wife, and our son, who is an only child. My wife has no family. My mother is ninety years old and in Florida. I can't bring her up north for this. I'm an only child. We're *it*."

Further discussions revealed that they were relatively new to the community, and they lived in a neighborhood where there were few other Jews. They were also relatively inactive in the synagogue. As a result, they had few Jewish friends. The father asked me, a bit sheepishly, "Maybe we could have the service here in your study?"

I replied, "Don't worry. You'll have a congregation in the sanctuary when your son becomes bar mitzvah."

I went to the synagogue board of trustees, and told them the story. "We say that we are a community," I reminded them. "Now we can prove it. I know that many of you Friday night regulars usually don't come to Shabbat morning services, because the service seems to belong to the bar or bat mitzvah family. I think that we have to end that perception. This is a good time to start. We have to be there for this boy when he becomes bar mitzvah. I need you. And the family needs you."

Weeks later, on the morning when Jeremy became bar mitzvah, about forty people were in the sanctuary: Jeremy's immediate family. Some of his school friends. Our board members and some of their friends as well. The members of the congregation sang the prayers even louder than usual. It was a wonderful moment.

After the service, the father approached me, tears in his eyes. "Who *were* all those people, Rabbi?"

"They were your community, Harry."

He understood.

Making the Service Your Own

Many bar and bat mitzvah families personalize the service to make it more meaningful. In fact, in many Reconstructionist synagogues, families are *expected* to compile readings and poetry to supplement and personally illuminate the liturgy. Sometimes creative readings, prayers, and poetry are added; sometimes parents will speak from their hearts to their child during the ceremony. You should consult your rabbi to find out what your synagogue's policy is in this regard.

Yet here we walk a fine line. We want to deepen the *kavvanah* of the worship experience, but it should not so deeply reflect the personal spiritual needs of a single family that others in the worshipping congregation become onlookers to one family's pageant.

Many congregations permit—and encourage—families to create their own bar and bat mitzvah booklets for the service. With the widespread availability of word processing and desktop publishing, these booklets can be quite attractive. Davka, a Hebrew and Jewish software company, distributes the Hebrew word processors Dagesh and DavkaWriter (Windows format) which make it possible to create your own worship service.

Such bar and bat mitzvah booklets may include:

- A brief history of bar or bat mitzvah. If this is the first bat mitzvah in your family (a phenomenon still common in American Jewish families), then a history of bat mitzvah is crucial here.

- A definition of *mitzvah*, including *mitzvot* that the youth did as part of the process of bar or bat mitzvah.

- An explanation of the worship service.

- The Torah and *haftarah* portions read at the bar or bat mitzvah ceremony, both in Hebrew and in English translation. Introduce both sections with some words on their literary significance. Some people reproduce the Hebrew directly from the *tikkun*, the book that shows how the unvowelled Torah portion appears in the Torah scroll. The standard *tikkun* is *Tikkun LaKorim*, published by KTAV. The *haftarot* are found, in sequence, at the back of the *tikkun*. The English translation can come from the URJ *Torah Commentary* or the Soncino Hertz *Chumash* (see "Go and Learn: Resources for Jewish Parents"). Davka produces a computer disk with the entire Hebrew Bible on it: In conjunction with Hebrew word processors, one can cut and paste the Torah portion into a booklet.

- Your child's *devar Torah*.

- *Tzedakot* (charities) to which you would like people to donate in honor of your child's bar or bat mitzvah.

- A glossary of terms that a worshipper might encounter in the synagogue.

- Personal comments from parents, grandparents, and/or siblings.

What prayers in the liturgy do you find most meaningful? What particular meanings do you associate with them? How would you turn your feelings about bar and bat mitzvah into a prayer? What would you include in a service booklet? How can you help enhance a sense of a worshipping community in your congregation?

C H A P T E R

9

The Changing Jewish Family

My dear, we are living in a time of transition.

—Adam to Eve, overheard outside the Garden of Eden

The Changing Jewish Family

The first literary image of the Jewish family I ever encountered was in the pages of a Jewish book that my parents gave me, Mamie Gamoran's *Hillel's Happy Holidays*, first published by the Union of American Hebrew Congregations in 1939.

Hillel's Happy Holidays was a wonderful book. It introduced us to three children: Hillel, Joseph, and Leah. Their mother shopped for *challah* on Friday afternoon. Their father came home in time for Shabbat. They lit the candles together. They made *kiddush* together. They broke challah together. Life was wonderful. Life was holy.

Since those tranquil days of *Hillel's Happy Holidays*, radically different images of the Jewish family have evolved. Mother now works and might not be able to pick up the challah, let alone bake it at home. Father comes home too late for Shabbat dinner. One parent may not even come home because of divorce. Or there may be a parent who is not Jewish. Or there may be two parents of the same gender. Or the kids are not home for Shabbat dinner because they are doing "other things."

Our Friday night panorama of a family gathered around a table dressed with a white tablecloth as they recite *kiddush* and light Shabbat candles has given way, in many families, to pizza or to take-out Chinese in cardboard containers.

A spiritual crisis exists in many Jewish families. This is the price of many radical changes that have given us a new concept of the family and that, in the process, have given us a new concept of the role of the family in Judaism.

Our Mobility Creates Special Problems

Jews have been mobile since Abraham and Sarah started life in Ur of the Chaldees on the Persian Gulf. They then migrated north to Haran, which is in present-day Syria. Crossing the Fertile Crescent, they went to Canaan (the ancient land of Israel), briefly sojourned in Egypt, and ultimately died and were buried in Hebron, back in Canaan.

Their grandson, Jacob, was no less transient. Born in the land of Israel, he fled from his brother, Esau, back to the family homestead in Haran; came back to the Land; moved to Egypt to be with his beloved son Joseph; died in Egypt; and was buried in the cave of Machpelah, in Hebron in the land of Israel.

Contemporary Jews may be just as mobile, in their own way, as the characters in Genesis. Most American Jews are from "somewhere else." The new American Jewish diaspora gathers in Arizona, Florida, California. Even in non-Sunbelt regions, Jews are moving to areas where Jews never lived before. Outside of the dwindling Jewish communities of Eastern Europe, there are few places in the world where Jews live in the same place that their grandparents did.

Our great-grandparents were often sustained by the *landsman-schaften* (mutual aid societies for immigrants), which helped the needy and buried the dead. In any Jewish cemetery today, you will see the monuments to that period in American Jewish life, the cemetery sections originally bought by these burial societies, painstakingly maintained over the years by networks of cousins' clubs.

Times have changed. Our children will not know what it means to be part of a burial circle or of a cousins' club. Who will inherit the responsibility of maintaining graves so that the family will come to visit and remember? Will the task fall to a son who now lives in Atlanta and a daughter who moved to Los Angeles and a cousin who wound up in Butte, Montana?

The extended family is on the ropes. Many Jews were nourished by memories of Passover seders and breaking their Yom Kippur fasts around a large table at an aunt's house. That aunt now lives in West Palm Beach; one cousin lives in South Bend, Indiana; one child lives in Houston, another in Boston. Once upon a time, transportation to a seder was on foot. Then, it was a subway ride away. Then, a car ride away. It now entails Frequent Flyer mileage.

Family mobility leads to increased distances between the generations. A few years ago, I saw a doll of an old man who had white hair and a white beard and wore a *yarmulke* and *tallit*. The doll was called Grandpa Binyamin. It exists because our children don't have real, live, Grandpa Binyamins anymore. *Bubbe* and *zeyde* once lived in our homes. Living with a grandparent was often an enriching human and Jewish experience. Grandparents are second only to parents in the transmission of values. What happens to Judaism when contact between the generations withers? It, too, can wither and atrophy, and become a lost and amorphous vestige of another era and another time.

Divorce

The divorce rate for the general population in the United States is higher than 50 percent. According to the Barna Research Group, a religious pollster located in Ventura, California, the divorce rate for Jews hovers around 30 percent. Studies show that of all ethnic groups, Jews are most likely after a divorce to remarry, because of the traditional Jewish commitment to the family. Most do so only once, but increasing numbers of American Jews are now on their third marriages. Remarriage creates a whole new constellation of people in a family's life, a constellation that, to me, is most poignant whenever I orchestrate the delicate choreography at a bar or bat mitzvah ceremony, when I have to calculate how to give *aliyot* to four sets of grandparents, some of whom are themselves divorced and remarried.

The late psychotherapist-rabbi Edwin Friedman believed that the actual rite of passage is never *only* the ceremony. The passage takes place throughout the entire year that surrounds the actual celebration. All family relationships seem to go into a state of flux during this period.

Because Jews have a very heavy investment in their children's "performance," there is more parental tension during bar and bat mitzvah than at any other significant moment in the Jewish life cycle. Bar and bat mitzvah parents also must face the expectations of their own parents and families, both for their children and for themselves.

When parents are separated or divorced, this tension gets heightened. Who sits where? Who gets which honor? Who won't stand next to whom? Should the new spouse or girlfriend or boyfriend have an honor? Should there be one party or two? If there are two, which party should the child go to? This can all get very distasteful, especially if the husband or wife gets custody of the synagogue, along with whatever remains of the old network of friends.

Most rabbis can resort to their synagogue's rules about who gets honors. But this doesn't really solve anything, for the rabbi is frankly powerless to solve it. It is the responsibility of the divorced and separated parties to work it out.

Rabbis try hard not to get caught between warring family factions. They establish an implicit (or even, explicit) rule that no one should get hurt at a bar or bat mitzvah, that everyone's dignity and feelings will be respected. Rabbis will remind families that their battles should not eclipse the real focus, which is the bar or bat mitzvah of their beloved son or daughter, grandson or granddaughter.

Rabbis attempt to put the responsibility squarely where it belongs. Years ago, in my first congregation, a couple was involved in a divorce case that had become a local scandal. Now, their son's bar mitzvah ceremony was approaching, the war drums were beating, and I, the rabbi, was in the middle. There was fighting, bickering, yelling: "You can't have an *aliyah*!" "I don't want your parents coming up!"

I finally sat down with them. "You have a choice," I told them, "and the deadline is rapidly approaching for you to make that choice. The choice has nothing to do with who gets which *aliyah*. You can choose how your son will remember his bar mitzvah day. He can remember that your arguing tore his day apart. That traumatic memory will last forever. Or, he can remember that the two of you loved him more than you disliked each other. You choose."

They chose correctly, asking me to construct the service to avoid any difficulty. I divided the *aliyot* so that the estranged parents were on the *bimah* at different times. Our synagogue's usual custom was to call up all the grandparents for a group *aliyah*; instead, they came up in separate pairs. Though it was my usual practice to include the entire family in a circle before the open Ark as a final blessing, in the interests of *shalom* I omitted that custom and blessed the child alone. Few people knew that we had reshaped our usual synagogue traditions for that particular ceremony. The day went without incident—and all breathed a massive sigh of relief.

Here, then, is a basic rule for bar and bat mitzvah etiquette when there has been a separation or divorce: Cool it. Declare a truce. Don't pull your child apart emotionally. And more than anything else, prove to your child that you love him or her more than you now dislike (or distrust or no longer love) each other.

Thawing Out the Family Ice Floes

Some families simply don't get along. There are long-standing feuds between members of families that go back to Vilna in the last century. Many of the same issues that surround divorce and separation also emanate from this general family discord.

When Edwin Friedman looked at the entire phenomenon of bar and bat mitzvah, he began to understand the pressures that many Christians feel around Christmas time. They may become extremely anxious. They may shop for gifts beyond their means. Drinking may become more frequent.

Life-cycle ceremonies may be stress points in a family's life, yet they can also refocus and heal the family.

I remember how one mother in a previous congregation absolutely *dreaded* her son's upcoming bar mitzvah day. She had remarried after divorcing her first husband (the boy's father), who had then died. Her former in-laws had never reconciled themselves to their son's early death. All the family problems that had been submerged over the years were surfacing in the weeks before the bar mitzvah ceremony. "Surfacing" is the wrong word; "exploding" is much closer. The woman's former in-laws were verbally abusive to her, making her life absolutely miserable. When they came up for their *aliyah* at the bar mitzvah, they were virtually paralyzed by their tears. The image of their deceased son in the very visible form of their grandson standing next to them was overwhelming for them. The whole experience was a nightmare for everyone involved.

Months later, I was speaking to the woman on the phone. "Oh, by the way," she said, "you remember my former in-laws, don't you?"

"Yes," I replied tentatively.

"Well, they're over and they send regards."

"They're over at your house? What happened?"

"I don't really know," she said. "But ever since the bar mitzvah, things have been just fine. I decided that I would use the bar mitzvah experience to reshape things. I had the choice of allowing them to continue this stuff, or moving on to a different level."

Family dynamics are like ice floes. At a significant life-cycle moment, they can thaw out and then solidify in a different configuration. Sometimes a bar or bat mitzvah can successfully break up the emotional ice floes and help create new and more healthy ways of being a family.

Jews and Non-Jews: Yours, Mine, and Ours

The 2001 National Jewish Population Survey determined that 31 percent of all Jews who are married are married to non-Jewish spouses. Forty-seven percent of American Jews who married between 1995 and 2000 wed non-Jews. In some places, intermarriage nears 70 percent. Intermarriage is here to stay. Add to this the four thousand people who convert to Judaism every year, and you can well imagine the challenge of a bar or bat mitzvah ceremony when there are significant numbers of non-Jewish family members attending. (See Appendix 1 for suggestions on what to tell non-Jews who come to a bar or bat mitzvah).

The answer to the questions that emerge about intermarriage and the bar or bat mitzvah will largely depend on the branch of Judaism with which you are affiliated.

Orthodox and Conservative Judaism state that the child of a mixed marriage is Jewish only if the mother is Jewish, or if the child has been converted to Judaism according to Jewish law at birth or shortly after birth.

For many years, Reform Judaism has stated that a child is considered Jewish if either of its parents is a Jew and if the child has been raised and educated as a Jew. The movement's Central Conference of American Rabbis reaffirmed this practice in 1983 with its statement on patrilineal descent. Likewise, the Jewish Reconstructionist Federation first officially endorsed patrilineal descent in 1976.

The bar or bat mitzvah ceremony of a child of intermarriage is a powerful moment. As Susan Weidman Schneider wrote in her book, *Intermarriage: The Challenge of Living with Differences Between Jews and Christians*: "After birth, there are few other ceremonial occasions that provide opportunities for the interfaith couple to express how they're raising their children and what their goals are for them." The late sociologist Egon Mayer noted that "bar mitzvah has emerged as the signal Jewish ceremony by which an intermarried family publicly proclaims that their child is being raised as a Jew."

Children of Converts

For the child of a marriage in which a conversion has occurred, bar and bat mitzvah also has great power. The parent who converted to Judaism may consider the bar or bat mitzvah a validation of his or her choice of Judaism. The bar and bat mitzvah celebrates the family's Jewish identity. This is true for all Jews, to be sure, but even more so for a family in which there has been a conversion.

A woman in my last congregation converted to Judaism eighteen years after marriage and a year before her daughter was to become bat mitzvah. "My children," she told me, "can experience their Jewish lives in the right sequence. I haven't done that. After all, my children helped me pick out my Hebrew name!" She continued:

My daughter's bat mitzvah proved that my joining the Jewish people wasn't just something going on in my head. It was real. Rebecca is the first woman on my side of the family to become bat mitzvah. But she was also the first woman to become bat mitzvah in *my husband's* family as well. Although I didn't have to prove anything to my in-laws, it was nice to be able to do so. The sad thing is, my daughter may also be the *only* child to become bat or bar mitzvah in my husband's family in this generation.

What Can a Non-Jew Do in the Service?

All denominational movements in American Judaism try to be as welcoming as possible within their own ideological framework. Still, the extent of a non-Jewish relative's involvement in a bar or bat mitzvah ceremony will depend upon the movement of Judaism with which you are affiliated. Some synagogues will be more or less flexible in how they interpret their movements' standards.

Many Orthodox congregations in the United States do not let intermarried families become members. Conservative Judaism welcomes intermarried families who are living their lives within a Jewish context. Both the Reform and Reconstructionist movements officially encourage their congregations to welcome the intermarried, thus supporting efforts to include intermarried families in synagogue life and to educate the children of intermarriage. It is left to the judgment of the individual Reform and Reconstructionist synagogue how to best fulfill the mandate of outreach.

How would such positions influence a non-Jewish parent's participation at a child's bar or bat mitzvah ceremony?

In Orthodox and Conservative synagogues, a non-Jewish parent would not ascend the *bimah* to say the blessings over the Torah. But beyond this prohibition, some Conservative synagogues let the non-Jewish parent come up to the *bimah* when the bar or bat mitzvah is being blessed by the rabbi, to stand in place for the *shehecheyanu*, or to say a personal prayer for the occasion on the *bimah*. Some encourage the non-Jewish parent to publicly reflect on the bar and bat mitzvah experience at the reception.

Reconstructionist synagogues have a variety of attitudes towards the participation of non-Jews in synagogue ritual. The nature of participation is often similar to Reform synagogues, though most Reconstructionist synagogues do not permit non-Jews to say the blessings over the Torah.

As one might expect in a movement as pluralistic and diverse as Reform, there is a wide variety of opinion on the matter of non-Jewish participation in the liturgy.

Most Reform synagogues believe that it is inappropriate for a non-Jewish spouse to lead the major segments of the service, to publicly recite blessings, or to utter phrases like *asher kideshanu* ("Who has commanded us") or *asher bachar banu* ("Who has chosen us"). Such phrases are in the Torah blessings and in the Friday evening candle blessings, blessings usually performed by parents at a bar or bat mitzvah. There are theological reasons for this decision, since God did not command non-Jews to perform such ritual *mitzvot* nor did God choose them by giving them the Torah.

Some Reform congregations permit a non-Jewish relative to publicly recite a personal prayer or share his or her feelings related to the bar or bat mitzvah ceremony. Others believe that their participation should be limited to specific psalms or responsive readings, preliminary prayers before the "formal" service begins (before *Barechu*), or special prayers that are not found in the regular liturgy, such as the *she-hecheyanu*, thanking God for "keeping us alive, and sustaining us, and allowing us to reach this season."

Many Reform congregations let non-Jewish parents perform certain ritual acts connected to bar and bat mitzvah. The rationale is that the non-Jewish parent's decision to raise the child as a Jew deserves to be honored and recognized by the congregation. Some congregations let non-Jewish mothers light and bless Shabbat candles. They may let non-Jewish parents say the blessing over the Torah, hand the Torah to their child, or open the doors of the Ark during the Torah service. They may let a non-Jew stand as a silent witness next to his or her spouse during the reading of the Torah blessing. Some congregations, believing that the Hebrew Bible is the common spiritual inheritance of all who accept its message, let non-Jewish parents or grandparents read the English translation of the Torah or the *haftarah* portion.

A New Blessing for Non-Jewish Parents

The problem of gentile participation in a bar or bat mitzvah ceremony illustrates a classic tension among Jews. We want to affirm the infinite worth of each individual. We want parents who have nurtured a Jewish child to publicly express their love and their devotion to the God whom we share. On the other hand, when we publicly pray, we want our prayers to have a Jewish legitimacy and a Jewish authenticity.

I have sought to solve this dilemma in the following way. I understand the liturgical climax of the bar and bat mitzvah ceremony to be the Torah reading. Those words have the highest sanctity of any recited during a service. They also symbolize the Jewish people's unique covenantal relationship with God. Therefore, I cannot ask a non-Jewish parent to say *asher bachar banu* ("Who has chosen us") while reciting the blessing over the Torah.

But consider how many non-Jewish parents have supported their child's Jewish nurturance. I think of two good friends in a previous congregation. The father is Jewish; the mother, who was raised as a Methodist in the Midwest, is very sympathetic to Judaism. Although she no longer practices Christianity, she has not converted to Judaism because she fears this would hurt her parents. Years ago, she attended an Introduction to Judaism class that I taught at our synagogue. At the last class, everyone offered a concluding statement. Hers was: "I came into this class mostly to learn about the Jewish past. I leave this class understanding my family's Jewish future."

This couple's family is filled with Jewish commitments. The father, who is active in the synagogue, was president of the Men's Club and chairman of the Adult Education Committee and has become a rather learned Jew.

How did they communicate their family's religious identity to their two daughters? "We taught them that I am Jewish, and Mom is not," the father once told me. "We are a Jewish family. We only have Jewish symbols in our home. We only have Jewish celebrations in our home. We are part of the Jewish community. We have thrown our lot in with the Jewish people."

When Prime Minister Yitzchak Rabin was assassinated, my friends' synagogue held a memorial service in which their daughter read the moving eulogy that had been delivered by Rabin's granddaughter Noa at her grandfather's funeral. This girl has no doubts about who she is. And that is as much her non-Jewish mother's doing as it is her father's.

There are many non-Jewish parents like this girl's mother. They enthusiastically support their children's Jewish education and upbringing. They should be honored. And so, I created the following prayer, which I invite the non-Jewish parent to read after the Jewish parent has given thanks in Hebrew for the gift of Torah:

O God of all humanity:

We lift our voices in gratitude that the Torah has come into the world through the Jewish people.

We lift our voices in gratitude for the ideals it teaches: justice; compassion; devotion; the partnership of mind, heart, and deed.

We lift our voices in gratitude that our son/daughter today takes his/her place among the people of Israel. We pray that he/she will do so with pride and joy. As You called Israel to be a light to the nations, so, too, we pray that our son/daughter will be his/her own ray of light to the world.

The message of the blessing is very clear: "I am proud that my child is a Jew. I am proud that the Torah that he or she reads today is part of the spiritual inheritance of the entire world. I am grateful to have been part of that process."

In my experience, when non-Jewish parents want to participate in their child's bar or bat mitzvah ceremony, they don't really want to weave their way through a transliterated Hebrew blessing. That's not the point. What they *really* want to do is to demonstrate their love and their pride in their child's moment of passage. That pride is holy—and it is worthy of public affirmation.

Many synagogues honor the parents of b'nai mitzvah at the Friday night service before their child's bar or bat mitzvah ceremony. I have created a prayer that would be appropriate for non-Jewish parents to read at such a service:

In the midst of this community, we gather as our child prepares to become a messenger of the Most High, a messenger and bearer of the sacred tradition of the Jewish people.

On the eve of our child's entrance into Jewish maturity as a bar/bat mitzvah:

May he/she always cherish this precious inheritance that comes into his/her hands,

May his/her heart always be filled with joy,

His/her mind with wisdom and insight,

His/her lips with kindness,

And may he/she be a worthy sustainer of the teachings of Torah

That have given light, meaning, and inspiration to all humanity.

Invariably, non-Jewish parents are moved both by the prayer and by feeling appreciated and affirmed, knowing that the synagogue cares about them and their presence in this rite of passage.

I can only believe that when parents of Jewish children feel good about the synagogue, that's good for the synagogue. It is "good for the Jews."

And it is good for God, as well.

In all non-Orthodox movements, the issue of non-Jewish participation in the worship service is under constant discussion. Such discussion is yet another example of the dynamic changes that Judaism must confront. In all cases, if your family situation involves intermarriage, discuss your synagogue's customs with your rabbi. It is an area of great concern and sensitivity, and each rabbi treats it as such.

Dealing with Non-Jews' Sensitivities About Bar and Bat Mitzvah

Ideally, non-Jewish members of the extended family support (or, at least, are neutral) about your raising your son or daughter as a Jew. But this is not always the case. Beyond the issue of participation in the service, there may be other issues related to intermarriage that surface in connection with bar and bat mitzvah.

A Jewish woman in my congregation told me about her non-Jewish mother-in-law: "My daughter's bat mitzvah ceremony is coming up. My husband, as you know, is not Jewish. But he wants our girl to be Jewish and to get a Jewish education. His mother is another story. We invited her to the ceremony, and frankly, I don't know if she'll come. I guess that she's always been angry that her granddaughter wasn't baptized and that she's not being raised as a Catholic. I don't know what to do."

Just as there are sacred moments in Jewish time, from *brit milah* or baby-naming to bar and bat mitzvah to confirmation and beyond, Christianity also has its own sacred moments: baptism, first communion, confirmation, and beyond. We can well imagine a non-Jewish grandparent's pain when a grandchild is not baptized. Such pain might not be anti-Semitism. It may simply reflect a great love of the Christian tradition and of a family's tradition. It may even be something as deep as a fear for the fate of their grandchild's soul within the context of their religious beliefs. For years, how that grandchild is being raised religiously somehow winds up on the back burner. It may surface from time to time, usually during Chanukah and Christmas and at Easter and Passover. But then bar or bat mitzvah comes, and the grandparents confront the issue again. This time it seems irrevocable. There is no question: Their grandchild is a Jew.

What can parents do about these feelings from other members of the family?

- Any bigotry in their comments should not be tolerated. When a family member expresses such sentiments, they should be dealt with firmly and lovingly: "You know, Dad, I'm really surprised to hear you talk that way about the Judaism of my household. You always raised us to be so much more tolerant than that."

- Be extremely clear with your non-Jewish loved ones. Such clarity about the religious identity of your family hopefully started when you got married. You must be able to say, "Our family is Jewish, and our children are Jewish. We never intended to hurt you. We would love to share our joys with you, to the extent that this is possible. But we know that we will always love you, and we know that our son (or daughter) will always deeply love you, also."

- Give them a copy of Appendix 1 in this book, which is designed for non-Jewish guests.

Sometimes anger from non-Jewish family members is not really anger. It is fear, fear of a cultural difference that will "assault" them at the bar or bat mitzvah ceremony and celebration.

You can honor your extended family's ethnicity during the post-ceremony party by selecting music and/or serving food of their ethnic group. Such relatively small gestures can celebrate your family's diversity. It can even help create a bit of *shalom*.

I'll never forget the bat mitzvah celebration of a Vietnamese-Jewish girl in a previous congregation. Her mother had started life as a Buddhist, and she converted to Judaism when she got married.

At the daughter's bat mitzvah ceremony, I spoke about the twin streams that had created her, Jewish and Vietnamese. I reminded her of the plight of the Vietnamese boat people, a cause in which her family had been particularly involved. I reminded her that she was descended from two peoples who had helped shape the moral map of the world in our century. And she understood.

As powerful as the ceremony was, the celebration had its own unique teaching quality. True, certain dishes were missing from the menu—stuffed derma, matzah ball soup, and chopped liver. Instead, and to no one's disappointment, there was veal with black mushroom sauce, Vietnamese meatballs, beef chow fun, chicken and cashew nuts, rice noodles.

Two distinct cultures created a celebration that touched everyone deeply. The family created a party consonant with their self-image of a family that now had one religious identity, but was fed by two ethnic streams.

In the interests of *shalom*, says the Talmud, there are certain things that we do for non-Jews as well as Jews. *Shalom* here does not mean "expediency." It does not even mean "keeping the peace." It means something greater. It means moving the entire cosmos to a higher level.

If you have non-Jewish family members, what can you do to make them more comfortable? How can you help them be involved and participate? Think about the role you would want to have in a bar or bat mitzvah if you were in their place.

After the Thank You Notes
Helping Your Jewish Teenager
Develop Jewish Values

Let young people ... be sure that every deed counts, that every word has power, and that we all can do our share to redeem the world in spite of all its absurdities and frustrations and disappointments.... Let them remember to build a life as if it were a work of art.

—ABRAHAM JOSHUA HESCHEL, ABC INTERVIEW, 1972

After the Thank You Notes

When the non-Jewish father of an upcoming bar mitzvah made an appointment to see me, I assumed that he wanted to discuss the options for his involvement in the ceremony. I was ready for that conversation. What followed, however, was not what I expected.

"Rabbi," said the father, "I want my kid to really love the synagogue. I want my kid to really love being Jewish. I am not Jewish, but I love your people. I really respect what Judaism has taught the world. I'm in the construction business, and my son would be surprised if he heard the stuff that I get from my coworkers because I take off for Yom Kippur. I want my kid to have the right values. I really want this bar mitzvah to help him with that."

For the next hour, we sat and talked—father-to-father. This conversation deeply moved me because it taught a powerful lesson: This non-Jewish father was spiritually and morally invested in his Jewish son's rite of passage. Many parents, Jewish and non-Jewish, are like him. They want bar and bat mitzvah to make a real difference in their children's lives. They want it to be a moment of true passage from one phase of their life to another. What kind of passage can this be? In his classic work, *Childhood and Society*, psychoanalyst Erik Erikson explained that each person goes through eight distinct psycho-social stages. Each stage represents certain inherent tensions in the human personality, and each tension must be resolved if the individual is to enter the next stage of life.

What would Erikson say about bar and bat mitzvah, which represents the passage from school age to adolescence? If young people are too focused on the *skill* of becoming bar and bat mitzvah, if they focus only on performing competently on the *bimah*, then Erikson would relate this to the crisis of every school-age child, to the latent fear in every young child's heart: *"I hope I don't screw this up!"*

Pastoral psychologist Donald Capps says this concern for competence carries its own perils. He has warned that the ritual passage into adolescence can be too formal and too perfectionistic. By equating technique with truth and sacrificing all other values to proficiency, he said, all that remains is empty ceremonialism.

As young people approach bar and bat mitzvah, I tell them (in the presence of their parents), "Please don't hear this as permission to slack off in your Hebrew preparation. If I had the choice between a kid who knows everything cold, but has no real feeling for what it means to become bat mitzvah, or the kid who has really come to love the synagogue, doing *mitzvot*, Jewish learning, but occasionally makes some mistakes in Hebrew, I would prefer the second kid." To parents, I privately say, "Don't let the rite get in the way of the passage."

Now that the ceremony is over, now that the photocopied sheets of Torah and *haftarah* are buried somewhere beneath the basketball magazines, now that the thank you notes are finally written—what now? Where is the true depth of the Jewish passage from childhood to adolescence?

Get Off the Academic Fast Track

I had known the family for years, ever since their children had become bar and bat mitzvah under my tutelage. But when the phone rang, I suddenly knew where this conversation was going even as it began.

"Rabbi," the mother of the teenage boy was saying, "about that essay that my son has to write for confirmation. Does he really have to do it? When you consider the baseball team, and the SAT class, and the honors program..."

Interrupting, I asked the agitated mother, "Why not just get off the merry-go-round? Why not reject all the pressure and the competition?"

"I can't," she answered. "This is the real world. My kid needs all this to get into a good college."

The pressure on our kids to rack up achievement points mounts yearly, forcing them to sacrifice their Jewish involvement on the ephemeral altars of competition. Parents, too, get caught up in this relentless American religion of college admissions. Our young people are taking the SATs earlier and earlier. Parents and kids alike forget that grades are not the same as knowledge, and that knowledge is not the same as wisdom. As Allan Bloom wrote in *The Closing of the American Mind*: "Fathers and mothers have lost the idea that the highest aspiration they might have for their children is for them to be wise. Specialized competence and success are all that they can imagine."

Bar and bat mitzvah can become the time in our young people's lives when we help them set priorities. True, grades are important—because grades are not as important as knowledge and knowledge is not as important as wisdom.

Make Sure Your Child Continues His or Her Jewish Education

Of his Jewish childhood, actor Kirk Douglas recently recalled,

No rational adult would make a business decision based on what they knew when they were 14. You wouldn't decide who to marry based on what you knew about love and relationships when you were 14. But lots of us seem satisfied to dismiss religion based on what we learned at 14, and I was one of those who was that stupid.

Not much has changed since Kirk Douglas was a kid. Saturday morning after Saturday morning, week after week, in synagogues all over America, thirteen-year-olds make beautiful speeches about Jewish responsibility, the value of Jewish learning, and the importance of the synagogue.

Most Jewish American kids become bar and bat mitzvah. But as for after the ceremony, about half of them forget their heartfelt words and wind up missing in action. As Reform leader Rabbi Eric Yoffie has said, "If we had to choose, we would be far better off if the average child had three years of religious school prior to bar or bat mitzvah and three years of school and youth group afterward."

I was recently speaking to a Jewish man who told me that he had no use for "organized Judaism." I asked him his age, and he responded,

"Thirty-three." I then asked him how long it had been since he had done any real Jewish learning. He answered me: "Well, my bar mitzvah, I guess—if you can call that real Jewish learning." Finally, I asked him about his career, and he told me that he was a trial lawyer.

"Imagine being a lawyer now," I cajoled him, "relying only on what you had learned as a young teenager watching reruns of *Perry Mason*."

He laughed and said to me, "You're right. I understand."

Here is the problem: Parents seem less and less interested in making religious demands on their children. But that is precisely your role at this crucial time in their lives. Insist that your children continue their Jewish education into their high school years. To this end, as one of its first innovations, the Reform movement instituted confirmation (which usually occurs in tenth grade)—and it is increasingly found in Conservative synagogues as well. The confirmation class presents Judaism at a sophisticated level, culminating in a group ceremony that is usually held on Shavuot, the festival in late spring that commemorates the giving of the Torah. This is a wonderful experience, building a real sense of connection to the Jewish community and to Jewish learning.

Continuing Jewish education is linked to personal integrity. Your children can intuit whether or not you take the covenantal nature of bar and bat mitzvah seriously. What they learn from you will stay with them the rest of their lives. Ancient rabbis believed that children develop a conscience no later than the thirteenth year. Bar mitzvah or bat mitzvah means, then, one who is "old enough to have a conscience." We must therefore be careful of the messages we send. Every child who reads from a Torah scroll at a bar or bat mitzvah—and then never returns to Jewish education—has learned a lesson in manipulating truth.

Remaining involved with Jewish education also teaches teenagers the value of staying with a task until it is finished. As a professor at an elite women's college said, "For parents to teach students that certain things can be done inadequately or incompletely [e.g., Jewish education and activities] ultimately does damage to the student. They become *comfortable* with mediocrity. There has to be an internalized message: Whatever you do, *do well*." Parents must remember that expectations of excellence in one area of their child's life invariably feed expectations of excellence in all areas.

Dropping out of Jewish education after bar and bat mitzvah mocks all that bar and bat mitzvah stands for—Jewish learning and its power to shape and influence our lives.

No Jewish community that could assimilate while living in freedom survived if it was Jewishly illiterate and uninformed. Such communities, such people are like cut flowers that wither and die. They need their tradition for spiritual sustenance and moral nourishment.

One of the best arguments for high quality Jewish education that I have ever read was written by Mark Jacobson in *Esquire* magazine's now-discontinued "Ethics" column. Jacobson struggled with whether to give his children a Jewish education:

> The notion of someone being "empty-headed" doesn't exist anymore. These days, you watch TV, go to the movies, your head gets filled up. It gets filled up with junk, but junk takes up room like anything else, and it tends to have a nasty half-life. ...
>
> Like any well-intentioned dad, I seek to protect my children from what I consider detrimental. That's why, with increasing urgency, I'm turning to religion. If a mythic value system is going to be involuntarily absorbed by a kid of mine, I'd rather it be a 2,500-year-old mythos, the product of the constant working and reworking of the most creative minds of a society, than a tinny narrative worked up during a twenty-minute meeting in a sleek-lined NBC story conference room.

There is no such thing as a person without a story. There is no such thing as a person without a tribe. We are only obliged to ask: Which story do we want our children to know? Which story do we want them to tell to their children? To which tribe do we want them to belong?

Our children can only choose what they know. They can only explain what they understand. They can only remember what they have learned. They cannot have memories we do not give them. In every teenager's favorite book, J.D. Salinger's *Catcher in the Rye*, Holden Caulfield dreams of catching children as they were being pushed off a cliff. Jewish education seeks to catch our children as they fall over the cliff of assimilation and amnesia. Let us go one step further. The Jewish People is under terrible pressure. Anti-Semitism has begun to creep into the world again—and not just the world in general, but on college campuses. To be forced to intellectually defend the existence of the state of Israel means nothing less than being able to defend the lessons of Jewish history. If we allow our teenagers to leave our homes without that knowledge and values base, they enter the world without the inoculation they need against the ignorance and hatred that they will encounter.

A few years ago, I watched a very disturbing video that featured a dialogue between Jewish students and African American students on an Ivy League college campus. The African American students were berating their Jewish classmates with the discredited anti-Semitic canard: "Don't you know that your ancestors were responsible for the international slave trade?" The Jewish students were nodding in agreement; yes, it was true, they said, and yes, they felt guilty about it.

After the video was over, one of the Jewish parents in the audience asked the presenter, a Hillel rabbi, "How can we prevent this sort of thing?" I will never forget his quick and pointed answer: "Stop sending us ignorant Jewish kids."

Encourage Your Child to Have Jewish Fun: Youth Groups, Camps, and Israel

As important as post-bar and -bat mitzvah Jewish education is, it's not enough. Jewish teenagers need to have fun with each other as well. Informal Jewish education and experiences are as important as formal Jewish education. Encourage your teenager to expand his or her Jewish horizons beyond just religious school. View Jewish education, Jewish youth groups, Jewish camping, and Israel experiences as indispensable to a well-balanced Jewish diet!

Encourage your teenager to join the local Jewish youth group. Encourage your teenager to go to a Jewish summer camp that is run by one of the major synagogue movements—the Union for Reform Judaism camps, Camp Ramah (Conservative), or various Orthodox summer camps. (A sports camp with a lot of Jewish kids is not a Jewish summer camp.) Youth programs and Jewish summer camps are an indispensable way of teaching our kids that Judaism is not only about ritual and intellect, but also about *community*. It turns out that the experiences that our kids have in such programs become building blocks for their sense of what Jewish community and connection can really mean.

Equally indispensable to a Jewish teenager is a trip to Israel. Everyone in the Jewish world seems to be talking about "continuity"— the hope that the Jewish people will continue not only as an ethnic group among many other ethnic groups, but as a distinct spiritual unit with historic ties to a land and a language.

While there is no "quick fix" for the Jewish future, studies repeatedly show that the best thing that we can do for our Jewish teenagers' futures is to give them a meaningful Israel experience. In this time of stress in Israel, where both imagined and real safety issues sit in the center of our souls, this insight remains real. It may even be *more* real. We are a people madly addicted to hope, and we should celebrate the fact that young people are still, despite it all, visiting Israel and attending various high school and college programs there. In the words of the Talmud, the land of Israel is the place where heaven and earth touch. It can be a place that touches the souls of our young people in ways that will stay with them forever.

But *caveat emptor*: A trip to Israel should not be just another teen tour. It should not view Israel as a Jewish theme park. It *should* provide both pre- and post-trip educational and social experiences, because your child needs to know about Israel before the trip, and he or she will need a way to process the experience afterwards. That is why I recommend Israel trips that are sponsored by Jewish youth movements. At their best, they are not simply *tours*. They are *pilgrimages*.

Increasingly, the Jewish community is recognizing the connection between bar and bat mitzvah and Israel, and not simply as a place for a ceremony. Jewish federations have become involved with such programs as Gift of Israel. Families are encouraged to save money annually for trips to Israel to which local federations also contribute money. In lieu of traditional bar and bat mitzvah gifts, some families even ask their guests to contribute to an Israel trip fund for their child in honor of the bar or bat mitzvah.

Sometimes our teenagers ask: "Youth groups, camps, Israel trips: *Do they count?*" How sad that they must pose that question, as if everything in life can be quantified and promote an academic- or career-related goal. What has happened to the sheer joy of living? No wonder so many of our young people are sullen and grim.

I do not like the question, but I do like the answer to it: Yes, Jewish experiences *do* count. Colleges seek well-rounded students who have values and commitments. Not just academics and traditional extracurriculars such as sports, debating team, or playing an instrument matter. Being involved in synagogue youth groups or Jewish camping or Israel trips indicates that a teen cares about higher values. It shows an awareness of the larger society. It shows that the student has gone beyond the self.

Parents tend to have wonderful expectations for their children's lives. They expect that they will finish high school, go to college, start careers, get married, and have children. But these expectations are mostly *secular*. Parents should have *Jewish* hopes and expectations, as well. To borrow an image that I once heard from Conservative Rabbi Daniel Gordis: Your family's Jewish life is comprised of numerous choices and decisions. Each choice or decision is like a small colored dot on a huge canvas. When you look at those dots at close range, they are merely dots. But when you stand at a distance and look at the dots, they become, like an Impressionist painting, something large, beautiful, and coherent.

As a teenager in my synagogue recently said in a class I was teaching: "If Judaism doesn't ask you to make any changes in your life, then it's not really Judaism."

So instead, imagine a Judaism that asks us to make changes in our lives. Moreover, *demand* a Judaism that requires such changes. Anything less is not Judaism.

Teach Your Child About the Power of Jewish Memory

We live in a "referral" culture. Middle-class people *refer* tasks to professionals. If the car is broken, call a mechanic. If the computer won't boot up, call technical support. If someone is troubled, go to a therapist. If you want Judaism for your child, go to the synagogue.

But while organized Jewish education is indispensable, don't completely "farm out" the task to a professional. Consider that the most powerful Jewish experiences are still yours to create.

Memory is the fundamental commandment of Jewish life. It defines who we are and links our past to our present and teaches us how to create the future.

The spiritual life of the family begins when we reclaim our past. If we have forgotten our children's Hebrew names, we must try to remember them. If we have forgotten our parents' Hebrew names, we must try to remember them. If we have forgotten the holy qualities of the great-aunts and -uncles for whom our children were named or for whom we were named, we must try to remember them. If we have forgotten the names of the cities in Europe where our families came from and the names of the great teachers of those cities, we must try to remember them.

I will always remember something that happened to me at the Jewish Museum in New York many years ago. Walking through an exhibit of Czech Judaica that the Nazis had intended to be a permanent record of a dead people, I found myself gazing at a Torah curtain that had once hung over the Holy Ark in the Altneuschul in Prague, the oldest synagogue in Europe. The curtain was from 1608. It was the oldest Torah curtain in Europe. I read the name of the person who had given that Torah curtain to the Altneuschul more than three centuries ago— Natan Bar Yissachar, also known as Karpel Zaks. As I saw that name, my eyes filled with tears and my hands began to shake: My mother's family was from Prague. Her maiden name was Karpel.

But do not think that if you lack an early seventeenth-century Torah curtain from Prague then you lack access to Jewish memory. Each of us is a descendant, and each of us is also an ancestor. Our task is not only to inherit memory, but to also *create* memory. Before you and your child jointly decide that his or her Jewish education has ended, ask your child: "Do you know enough to create Jewish memories for your own children? Do you know enough to hold a seder when Grandpa and Grandma and Daddy and I are gone? Do you know how to teach your children the story of Chanukah? Do you know how to say Kaddish? Do you have some sense of the flow and flavor of Jewish history? Do you know enough to begin to create Jewish memories?"

A woman who was responsible for cleaning out the house of her recently deceased mother once told me, "The sterling silver and the minks meant nothing to me. When I saw the *haggadot* that we used at our seders, with the wine stains of long-forgotten seders on the pages, and with matzah crumbs still in the bindings, I broke down crying."

She had discovered the power of Jewish memory.

Finding the Sanctuary of the Spirit

If God is truly on the guest list at our bar or bat mitzvah ceremony, that divine presence will resound through the years. If God is not on the guest list, then we and our young people will notice. Maybe not right away, but God's absence will be noticed.

On the Friday after a recent Thanksgiving, a young man who was a sophomore in college made an appointment to see me in my office. We had never met before. He had become bar mitzvah at my synagogue years before I had arrived. "Bar mitzvah, for me and my friends," he said, "was a big party and expensive gifts and a lot of questions about 'How much did you make?' I looked back on it and said to myself, 'Where was the religious grandeur and the power?' I rebelled. At college, I've gotten involved with Native Americans. Their spirituality and religious ecstasy is what I've always wanted to find in Judaism.

"I went on the Sacred Run to support the rights of Native Americans. We ran across Canada and across Europe. Somehow we wound up at Auschwitz. My Native American friends said to me, 'This is your tribe's place of overwhelming darkness. Will you lead us in a ceremony at this place?'

"I didn't know what to say. I called my mother collect—from Auschwitz!—and asked her to find the prayer book that I got when I became bar mitzvah. It was somewhere in my room. Then I asked her to read me the transliteration of the Kaddish prayer, so that I could write it down and say it at Auschwitz.

"Rabbi," he said, "I want to come back to my people. I really want to find that spirit again. My Native American friends sent me back to my tribe."

The prophet Isaiah knew what he was doing when he named one of his children *Shear Yashuv* ("A Remnant Will Return"). A remnant will. A remnant has.

Bar mitzvah and bat mitzvah can be the gateway for our young people into their tribe, into their moral wisdom, into their sense of the Eternal.

Together with your teenager, list Jewish values that you would like to become part of his or her moral vocabulary. What are some concrete actions that will bring your teenager to that goal? Write them down here.

APPENDIX 1

What Non-Jews Should Know About the Bar and Bat Mitzvah Service

This appendix restates some of the material found in earlier chapters. It is a model for an explanation of the bar and bat mitzvah that you can send to non-Jewish guests with their invitations.

Jews and Christians look at many things differently. We have a different theology, a different liturgy, a different holiday cycle, and a different life cycle.

But Jews and Christians share certain things, and that sharing is no less profound than the differences. As philosopher Martin Buber once said, "Jews and Christians share a Book and a hope"—a Messianic hope. Jews and Christians share the first five books of the Bible. We both believe in a God that can be approached through prayer and worship. We believe in a God who loves and who is revealed through Scripture and holy interventions in history.

Jews and Christians also share a belief in the power of ritual. Rituals make a group distinctive and transmit identity from generation to generation. They dramatize a religious group's beliefs about the world and about how God interacts with it.

Bar and bat mitzvah means that a thirteen-year-old Jewish child is old enough to perform *mitzvot* (the commandments of Jewish life). It is one of the most venerable and most potent of Jewish symbols and rituals. When a Jewish child becomes bar or bat mitzvah, he or she publicly reads a section from the Torah, the Five Books of Moses. Each week, every congregation in the Jewish world reads the identical passage. In this way, the youth is linked to the entire Jewish people, regardless of where the thirteen-year-old happens to live. The youth also reads a *haftarah*, which is a selection from the weekly section of the prophetic writings—from Isaiah, Amos, Hosea, etc., or from historical books like Judges, Samuel, or Kings.

There is More to the Service Than Meets the Ear

The bar and bat mitzvah ceremony occurs during the Sabbath worship service. The first part of the service ends with the congregation singing *Mi Chamocha* ("Who is like You among the gods that are worshipped?"). It echoes the song that Moses and the Israelites sang at the shores of the Sea of Reeds when the Israelites had been saved from the Egyptians. The second part of the service ends with a prayer for peace for the Jewish people and for the whole world. During the third section of the service, the Torah is read. The *haftarah*, by tradition, must end on a note of *nechemta* (comfort). This portion of the service ends with the implicit hope that all humanity will embrace God's words.

The entire service concludes with two prayers: *Aleinu*, a triumphant plea that the world will *ultimately* recognize that there is only one God, and *Kaddish*, a plaintive mourners' prayer that proclaims that God's Kingdom, the fulfillment of God's hopes for the world, will come someday. Kaddish's form and function are closely related to the Lord's Prayer.

The ultimate message of the service is *the triumph of hope*: hope for freedom, hope for peace, hope that all our words will end on joyful notes, hope for universal redemption.

There Is More to the Torah Scroll Than Meets the Eye

The Torah symbolizes the moment when God met the Jewish people at Sinai and made a covenant with them. It reminds us of God's revelation and of God's intervention in human history.

The Torah also symbolizes all that the Jewish people hold sacred: stories, laws, histories, poetry. When a Jewish child reads from the Torah, he or she is enveloped in its heritage, in its power, in the majesty of Sinai. He or she says to the community: "I am now thirteen years old. I am now ready to fulfill the covenant with God by being responsible for performing *mitzvot*, the obligations of Jewish life."

All Ritual Moments of Becoming
Are More or Less Alike

All religions—all cultures—have their moments of *becoming*. It is a moment when an individual goes from childhood to maturity, a moment of sacred initiation.

Bar and bat mitzvah have certain parallels in Christianity. In the Baptist tradition, *baptism* itself is that moment of becoming. Baptism occurs during young adulthood rather than infancy because only then, Baptists believe, can one freely assent to Christianity.

In most Christian denominations, the closest parallel to bar and bat mitzvah is *confirmation*. Confirmation acknowledges a mature entry into the rights and the embrace of the church. It ratifies the baptismal vows that had been made for the child in infancy, just as bar and bat mitzvah acknowledge the pledge the parents made when their child was an infant that their child would study Torah.

Bar and bat mitzvah is a symbolic way to usher a child into the adult Jewish community, a way for the entire community to say to that no-longer-child, "All we cherish, all we hope to be, the sum total of our visions, we place them in your hands. May God make you ready. May God make you strong."

This material is from *Putting God on the Guest List, 3rd Edition: How to Reclaim the Spiritual Meaning of Your Child's Bar or Bat Mitzvah* by Rabbi Jeffrey K. Salkin, © 2005, published by Jewish Lights Publishing, P.O. Box 237, Woodstock, VT 05091. (802) 457-4000; www.jewishlights.com. The Publisher grants permission to you to copy Appendix 1 for distribution to your guests. All rights to all other parts of this book are still covered by copyright and may not be copied without written permission.

A List of Places for Your Tzedakah

The following is a list of organizations that do worthwhile mitzvot. *It can be used in a number of ways. Your child may choose to give part of his or her bar or bat mitzvah gift money to a particular organization whose work is meaningful to your family. You may choose to put certain organizations on a list that will accompany the bar or bat mitzvah invitations, suggesting that your guests donate to the groups of their choice in honor of the bar or bat mitzvah. Or, your family may volunteer for the organization and enrich the bar and bat mitzvah experience by making it an experiment in living* mitzvot.

Soup Kitchens for the Homeless

Soup kitchens feed the poor and the homeless. Sometimes, they feed entire families. Donate leftovers from your bar or bat mitzvah celebration. Consider how much smoked salmon and salad is thrown out on any Saturday afternoon after a bar and bat mitzvah party, and then consider how many hungry people walk around the streets of even the poshest suburbs. It doesn't have to be that way. To find your local food bank, consult the "Social and Human Services" section of your Yellow Pages.

Some notable food banks:

Interfaith Nutrition Network (INN), 211 Fulton Ave., Hempstead, NY 11550. (516) 486-8506. www.the-inn.org.

Island Harvest, 199 2nd St., Mineola, NY 11501. (516) 294-8528. www.islandharvest.org. Picks up unused food from a caterer or restaurant and distributes it to the needy.

Long Island Cares, Inc., 10 Davids Dr., Hauppauge, NY 11788. (631) 582-FOOD. www.licares.org. Operates the Long Island Regional Food Bank, which distributes huge quantities of donated food to soup kitchens and hunger organizations throughout Long Island.

Rachel's Table, 1160 Dickinson St., Springfield, MA 01108. (413) 733-9165. www.rachelstablespringfield.org. This New

England-based chain of food pantries picks up leftovers from *simchas* and distributes it to the needy.

Hebrew Union College, Brookdale Center, 1 West 4th St., New York, NY 10012. (212) 674-5300. www.huc.edu. A one-night-a-week program to feed the homeless.

Agencies that Help the Home-Bound Jewish Elderly

Many aged live in utter isolation in bleak apartments with multiple locks on their doors. The conditions in which they live are a scandal, and their numbers are larger than most people think. Agencies organized to help these individuals include:

Dorot, 171 West 85th St., New York, NY 10024. (212) 769-2850. www.dorotusa.org. *Dorot* means "generations"—generations of Jews together bringing light into lives that would have been otherwise darkened. Dorot operates a soup kitchen and distributes clothing to home-bound elderly Jews.

Hatzilu Rescue Organization, Inc., 45 Manetto Hill Rd., Plainview, NY 11803. (516) 931-2884. www.hatzilurescue.org. Aids the Jewish poor and elderly of Brooklyn, Queens, and Long Island.

The Ark, 6450 N. California Ave., Chicago, IL 60645. (773) 973-1000. www.arkchicago.org. Offers extensive services to poor Jews, including dental and medical care, employment counseling, a food pantry, and help in navigating the social service bureaucracy.

Project Ezra, 465 Grand St., 4th Floor, New York, NY 10002. (212) 982-4124. www.projectezra.org. Works with the Jewish elders on the Lower East Side of Manhattan. They also offer *mitzvah*-based tours of that historic immigrant neighborhood.

Other Organizations That Do Worthy Things

Abraham Fund Initiatives, 9 East 46th St., New York, NY 10017. (212) 661-7770. www.abrahamfund.org. Promotes coexistence between Jews and Arab citizens of Israel, through dialogue, awareness campaigns and advocacy.

ARMDI: American Red Magen David for Israel, 352 Seventh Ave., Suite 400, New York, NY 10001. (212) 757-1627. www.armdi.org. The sole support arm in the United States for the Magen David, Israel's emergency medical and blood services organization.

American Jewish World Service, 45 West 36th St., 10th Floor, New York, NY 10018. (212) 792-2900. www.ajws.org. Has become the Jewish response to suffering caused by famine, epidemic, or natural disaster. The group has managed projects in Africa, South America, Mexico, and the United States.

Bet Tzedek, 145 S. Fairfax Ave., Suite 200, Los Angeles, CA 90036. (323) 939-0506. www.bettzedek.org. Provides free legal work for poor Jews and non-Jews. Has produced a video, narrated by actress Bea Arthur, that portrays six examples of its work.

The Blue Card, 171 Madison Ave., Suite 1405, New York, NY 10016. (212) 239-2251. www.bluecardfund.org. Finds impoverished Holocaust survivors and provides them with direct financial support.

Chicago Chesed Fund, 7045 N. Ridgeway, Lincolnwood, IL 60712. (847) 679-7799. www.chicagochesedfund.org. Provides assistance for those in need of food, clothing, employment, and other living necessities.

Federations. Your local Jewish federation supports JCCs, Jewish education, nursing homes, youth activities, etc. It should be an essential part of every Jew's *tzedakah* plans.

Foundation for Jewish Camping, Inc. 15 West 36th St., 13th Floor, New York, NY 10018. (646) 278-4500. www.jewishcamp.org. Jewish camping is one of the most powerful ways of building Jewish identity. The Foundation advocates for Jewish camping, encourages growth of Jewish camps, helps camps recruit staff, makes grants to promote programmatic excellence, champions the growth of camp scholarships, and offers information resources to parents, camps, and the Jewish community.

God's Love We Deliver, 166 Avenue of the Americas, New York, NY 10013. (212) 294-8100. www.glwd.org. Prepares and delivers meals for people with AIDS.

HIAS (Hebrew Immigrant Aid Society), 333 Seventh Ave., 16th Floor, New York, NY 10001-5019. (212) 967-4100. www.hias.org. Provides information, support, education, and a broad program of services at all stages of the migration process for refugees and immigrants; advocates for fair and just policies affecting refugees and immigrants; maintains an office in Vienna that can provide immigration information for people living in Europe.

Hillel: The Foundation for Jewish Campus Life, Charles and Lynn Schusterman International Center, Arthur and Rochelle Belfer Building, 800 Eighth St., NW, Washington, DC 20001-3742. (202) 449-6500. www.hillel.org. As its website says, "The largest Jewish campus organization in the world, Hillel: The Foundation for Jewish Campus Life provides opportunities for Jewish students to explore and celebrate their Jewish identity through its global network of over 500 regional centers, campus Foundations and Hillel student organizations. Hillel is working to provoke a renaissance of Jewish life."

Israel Bonds. www.israelbonds.com. This and the UJA are the great international pillars of support for Israel. Israel's capital improvements and infrastructure are largely the result of the strong commitment to Israel Bonds by Jews all over the world. Not just *tzedakah*—it's an investment in Israel's future.

JACS, 135 West 50th St., New York, NY 10020. (212) 632-4600. www.jbfcs.org/jacs. Provides resources for Jewish alcoholics, chemically dependent persons, and their significant others. Sponsors retreats and various spiritual support groups.

Jewish AIDS Network of Chicago, 3150 N. Sheridan Rd., Chicago, IL 60657. (773) 275-2626. Provides services and referrals to those affected by HIV or AIDS.

Jewish Big Sisters, 3150 N. Sheridan, #27B, Chicago, IL 60657. (312) 458-9003. www.jewishbigsisters.org. Volunteer program that provides a supportive environment for Jewish girls.

The Jewish Braille Institute of America, 110 East 30th St., New York, NY 10016. (212) 889-2525. www.jbilibrary.org. Provides books, tapes, special materials for summer camps, college and career counselling, and free *b'nai mitzvah* training to blind and partially sighted Jewish adults. Improves the quality of Jewish life for the estimated 20,000 Jewish blind and 50,000 Jews who are severely visually impaired.

Jewish Foundation for the Righteous, 305 Seventh Ave., 19th Floor, New York, NY 10001-6008. (212) 727-9955. www.jfr.org. As Rabbi Harold Schulweis taught us, many Christians who saved Jews from the Nazis now live in poverty in the United States, Europe, and Israel. Jews must remember them; our history is incomplete without them. The foundation sustains them financially and emotionally, thus bearing witness to eternal gratitude.

Jewish National Fund, 42 East 69th St., New York, NY 10021. (888) JNF-0099. www.jnf.org. Improves and develops the land of Israel, most notably through the planting of trees. Virtually all forested land in the Jewish state is the gift of the JNF. This is one of the most important, and most worthwhile, ways of contributing to the ongoing welfare of Israel.

The Koby Mandell Foundation, Inc., 366 Pearsall Ave., Suite 1, Cedarhurst, NY 11516. (301) 576-6235. www.kobymandell.org. Created in memory of a boy who was murdered by Arab terrorists in 2001, this foundation supports various endeavors that reflect the values of Koby, may his memory be a blessing. Of particular interest is Camp Koby, a camp for children whose parents or siblings have been struck by terror, and the Sports Integration Project, a youth football and softball program that uses participatory sports to integrate Israeli immigrant teenagers with veteran Israelis.

Lifeline for the Old—Yad LaKashish, 14 Shivtei Yisrael St., Jerusalem, Israel 91000. (972-2)-628-7829. www.lifeline.org.il. Created so Jerusalem's elderly would make lovely handicrafts, *challah* covers, *tallitot,* toys, metal *mezuzot,* ceramic items, and clothing, and bind books. Also employs young and old handicapped individuals.

MAZON, 10495 Santa Monica Blvd., Suite 100, Los Angeles, CA 90025. (800) 813-0557. www.mazon.org. Asks Jews to send 3 percent of the cost of a *simcha* to MAZON so we can share our blessing with the needy. MAZON then makes allocations to hunger organizations around the country.

Myriam's Dream, Inc., 907 Four Seasons Dr., Wayne, NJ 07470 www.myriamsdream.org. Continues the inspirational work of the late Myriam Mendilow, who founded Lifeline for the Old in Jerusalem. Gives grants to elder centers and to elderly and disabled people who live in rural areas, small towns, and large cities.

National Institute for Jewish Hospice, 732 University St., North Woodmere, NY 11581. (800) 446-4448. www.nijh.org. The only national Jewish organization providing nonhospital alternatives for the terminally ill. Hospice is a place where people go to die with dignity and appropriate care.

The National Yiddish Book Center, Harry and Jeanette Weinberg Building, 1021 West St., Amherst, MA 01002. (413) 256-4900. www.yiddishbookcenter.org. Yiddish must survive, and more than in vulgar humor or small catch-phrases. By finding, saving, and treasuring Yiddish books, the Book Center redeems a small part of the Jewish past.

The New Israel Fund, 330 Seventh Ave., 11th Floor, New York, NY 10001. (212) 613-4400. www.nif.org. Funds the following programs in Israel: Jewish/Arab relations; pluralism; civil rights and civil liberties; women's rights, especially rape crisis centers; and community action.

North American Conference on Ethiopian Jewry, 255 W. 36th St., Suite 701 New York, NY 10018. (212) 233-5200. www.nacoej.org. Helps Ethiopian Jews who have settled in Israel.

Shelters for Battered Jewish Women
Provide temporary shelter, counseling, and support services to Jewish women who are victims of domestic violence.
Examples include:

Rebbetzin Chana Weinberg, 398 Mt. Wilson Lane, Baltimore, MD 21208. (410) 486-0322. Operates one of fewer than ten Jewish battered women's shelters in North America. Contributions should be made out to Chana Weinberg Tzedakah Fund.

Shalva, P.O. Box 46375 Chicago, IL 60646 (773) 583-4673. www.shalvaonline.org. Founded by Orthodox women who worked in a *mikveh* (ritual bath) and noticed scars on the women they were tending.

Other Organizations

Simon Wiesenthal Center, 1399 S. Roxbury Dr., Los Angeles, CA 90035. (310) 553-9036. www.wiesenthal.com. Has taken a leading role in discovering Nazis in hiding as well as exposing modern hate groups. Ensures that Americans will remember the Holocaust and its lessons.

Jewish Federations of North America, P.O. Box 157, Wall Street Station, New York, NY 10268. (212) 284-6500. www.jewishfederations.org. Serves 156 Jewish federations and 400 independent Jewish communities across North America. It reflects the values of social justice and human rights that define the Jewish people.

Go and Learn: Resources for Parents

The following list comprises what I believe to be the best and most accessible books on Judaism for the lay reader. Any of these would be an excellent way to continue your Jewish learning and can be used to help deepen the bar and bat mitzvah experience.

"I'd like to be able to tell my family some Jewish stories. Where can I learn some?"

Elkins, Dov Peretz, ed. *Jewish Stories from Heaven and Earth: Inspiring Tales to Nourish the Heart and Soul.* Woodstock, VT: Jewish Lights Publishing. Universal stories of kindness, hope, faith and discovery will intrigue the minds and warm the hearts of people from all walks of life.

Feinstein, Ed. *Capturing the Moon: Classic and Modern Jewish Tales.* NJ: Berhman House. One of the best collections of powerful stories available, each one accompanied by a series of questions.

Gellman, Marc. *Does God Have a Big Toe?* New York: Harper and Row. Modern *midrashim* from a contemporary master.

————. *God's Mailbox: More Stories about Stories in the Bible.* New York: Beech Tree Books. More of the same, equally sweet and compelling.

Kushner, Lawrence. *Invisible Lines of Connection: Sacred Stories of the Ordinary.* Woodstock, VT: Jewish Lights Publishing. Finding the holy in everyday encounters.

Schwartz, Howard. *Gabriel's Palace: Jewish Mystical Tales.* New York: Oxford University Press. Powerful, romantic, uplifting, though the mystical references can often be obscure to newcomers to Jewish lore.

"I'd like to think more about what it means to raise Jewish children."

Adelman, Penina, Ali Feldman, and Shulamit Reinharz. *The JGirl's Guide: The Young Jewish Woman's Handbook for Coming of Age.* Woodstock, VT: Jewish Lights Publishing. Written for pre-teen girls, this inspirational, interactive book offers a uniquely Jewish look at adolescence and the time surrounding bat mitzvah.

Diamant, Anita, and Karen Kushner. *How to Be a Jewish Parent: A Practical Handbook for Family Life.* New York: Schocken Books. The title of this book says it all. An interesting, useful guide.

Doades, Joanne. *Parenting Jewish Teens: A Guide for the Perplexed.* Woodstock, VT: Jewish Lights Publishing. Groundbreaking guidebook that will help you navigate the tumultuous journey of parenting a Jewish child into adulthood.

Gordis, Daniel. *Becoming a Jewish Parent: How to Explore Spirituality and Tradition with Your Children.* New York: Three Rivers Press. An excellent blend of theology and practical tips for Jewish parents.

Grishaver, Joel. *Forty Things You Can Do to Save the Jewish People.* Los Angeles: Aleph Design Group. Forty practical suggestions about deepening your Jewish family life. One of the best comprehensive guides to Jewish family life in print.

Mogel, Wendy. *The Blessing of a Skinned Knee: Using Jewish Teachings to Raise Self-Reliant Children.* New York: Penguin Books. An excellent, lyrical description of a Jewish values–based view of parental discipline.

Wolfson, Ron. *God's To-Do List: 103 Ways to Be an Angel and Do God's Work on Earth.* Woodstock, VT: Jewish Lights Publishing. An inspiring gift to uplift your spirit and share with others. Whatever your faith, you can do God's To-Do List.

"Bar and bat mitzvah has raised some important questions about intermarriage and conversion."

Friedland, Ronnie, and Edmund Case, eds. *The Guide to Jewish Interfaith Family Life: An InterfaithFamily.com Handbook.* Woodstock, VT: Jewish Lights Publishing. Created by the editors of the InterfaithFamily.com online magazine, it provides wisdom, practical tips, and encouragement from a Jewish perspective.

King, Andrea. *If I'm Jewish and You're Christian, What Are the Kids? A Parenting Guide for Interfaith Families.* New York: URJ Press. The challenges, pitfalls, and potentials of raising children in an interfaith family. Offers excellent stories about families grappling with the big issues, especially regarding adolescence.

Olitzky, Kerry M. *Introducing My Faith and My Community: The Jewish Outreach Institute Guide for the Christian in a Jewish Interfaith Relationship.* Woodstock, VT: Jewish Lights Publishing. Provides an introduction to both the basics and complexities of Judaism and Jewish life through the lens of an interfaith relationship.

————. with Joan Peterson Littman. *Making a Successful Jewish Interfaith Marriage: The Jewish Outreach Institute Guide to Opportunities,*

Challenges and Resources. Woodstock, VT: Jewish Lights Publishing. From a Jewish perspective, this book guides interfaith couples at any stage of their relationship, and the people who are affected by their relationship, including counselors who work with interfaith couples as well as their families.

Silverstein, Alan. *Preserving Jewishness in Your Family After Intermarriage Has Occurred.* Northvale, NJ: Jason Aronson. A guide to issues surrounding intermarriage and conversion, written by a prominent Conservative rabbi. The material on raising children in interfaith families is particularly helpful.

"I'd like to learn more about the Jewish worship service."

Comins, Mike. *Making Prayer Real: Leading Jewish Spiritual Voices on Why Prayer Is Difficult and What to Do about It.* Woodstock, VT: Jewish Lights Publishing. A candid conversation about the *why* and *how* of prayer: how prayer changes us and how to discern a response from God.

Hoffman, Lawrence A. *The Way Into Jewish Prayer.* Woodstock, VT: Jewish Lights Publishing. One of the most important books about Jewish worship individually and in community.

————, ed. *My People's Prayer Book: Traditional Prayers, Modern Commentaries.* Woodstock, VT: Jewish Lights Publishing. An excellent ten-volume series of commentaries on the traditional Jewish worship service in which teachers and scholars from all movements in the Jewish world add their interpretations of what is going on as we worship.

"The bar or bat mitzvah experience has made me more curious about Bible and Torah."

Artson, Bradley Shavit. *The Bedside Torah: Wisdom, Visions, and Dreams.* New York: McGraw-Hill/Contemporary Books. A collection of excellent sermonettes on the Torah portions. Nowhere near as childlike as the title and cover would prompt the reader to believe.

Cohen, Norman J. *Self, Struggle and Change: Family Conflict Stories in Genesis and Their Healing Insights for Our Lives.* Woodstock, VT: Jewish Lights Publishing. A noted scholar looks at the messages that the stories in Genesis have for all of us. A wonderful resource for parents who want to understand these classic texts.

―――. *The Way Into Torah*. Woodstock, VT: Jewish Lights Publishing. An excellent introduction to the magic of Torah study, in all of its forms, written by one of its contemporary masters.

Eisen, Arnold M. *Taking Hold of Torah: Jewish Commitment and Community in America* (The Helen and Martin Schwartz Lectures in Jewish Studies). Bloomington, IN: Indiana University Press. Eisen's personal and scholarly meditations on each book of the Torah are challenging, yet always inviting.

Eskenazi, Tamara Cohn and Andrea L. Weiss, eds. *The Torah: A Women's Commentary*. New York: URJ Press. Valuable Torah resource for both men and women alike.

Frankel, Ellen. *The Five Books of Miriam: A Woman's Commentary on the Torah*. New York: HarperSanFrancisco. Frankel imagines women's voices, both ancient and contemporary, looking at the various Torah portions. A delight, particularly for bat mitzvah students.

Goldstein, Elyse, ed. *The Women's Torah Commentary: New Insights from Women Rabbis on the 54 Weekly Torah Portions*. Woodstock, VT: Jewish Lights Publishing. Over 50 inspiring rabbis bring their rich perspective—a women's perspective, and especially a feminist per-spective—to bear on the *entire* biblical text.

―――. *The Women's Haftarah Commentary: New Insights from Women Rabbis on the 54 Weekly Haftarah Portions, the 5 Megillot and Special Shabbatot*. Woodstock, VT: Jewish Lights Publishing. More than 80 women rabbis offer readers inspiring insights on the second and third portions of the Hebrew Scripture: the Prophets and Writings.

Lieber, David, and Jules Harlow, eds. *Etz Hayim: Torah and Commentary*. Philadelphia: Jewish Publication Society. With commentary by Chaim Potok and Harold Kushner, it is a masterpiece of modern scholarship and is becoming the standard Torah commentary with-in the Conservative movement.

Plaut, W. Gunther, ed. *The Torah: A Modern Commentary*. New York: Union of American Hebrew Congregations. The first Torah com-mentary produced and published in North America. The articles on each Torah portion and the pages called "Gleanings," containing insights from the tradition, are extremely valuable.

Salkin, Jeffrey K., ed. *The Modern Men's Torah Commentary: New Insights from Jewish Men on the 54 Weekly Torah Portions*. Woodstock, VT: Jewish Lights Publishing. Includes commentaries by some of the most creative and influential rabbis, cantors, journalists, media figures, educators, professors, authors, communal leaders, and musicians in contemporary Jewish life, and represents all denominations in Judaism.

————. *Text Messages: A Torah Commentary for Teens*. Woodstock, VT: Jewish Lights Publishing. A collection of messages on each Torah portion, aimed specifically for teens.

Zornberg, Avivah Gottlieb. *Genesis: The Beginning of Desire*. New York: Image Books. The best contemporary *parasha*-by-*parasha* commentary on Genesis. Zornberg soars from Biblical text to classic rabbinic commentary to linguistics to philosophy to literature without batting an eye. For the intellectually sophisticated Jewish parent who is ready for the Jewish journey of a lifetime.

————. *The Particulars of Rapture: Reflections on Exodus*. New York: Image Books. By the same author, with the same invigorating intellectual and spiritual results.

"I need some clear reference books on Jewish concepts and terminology."

Green, Arthur. *These Are the Words: A Vocabulary of Jewish Spiritual Life*. 2nd ed. Woodstock, VT: Jewish Lights Publishing. A modern glossary of Jewish religious life, from one of the masters of contemporary Jewish thought.

Kertzer, Morris, with Lawrence A. Hoffman. *What Is a Jew?* New York: Touchstone Books. A classic, rewritten by the scholarly nephew of the author. A concise guide to Judaism, written in a helpful question-and-answer format.

Kushner, Harold. *To Life! A Celebration of Jewish Thinking and Being*. New York: Warner Books. One of America's most famous rabbis teaches us his views on Judaism. Lively and lyrical.

Matlins, Stuart M., ed. *The Jewish Lights Spirituality Handbook: A Guide to Understanding, Exploring and Living a Spiritual Life*. Woodstock, VT: Jewish Lights Publishing. Rich, creative material from fifty spiritual leaders on every aspect of today's Jewish spirituality.

Telushkin, Joseph. *Jewish Literacy: The Most Important Things to Know about the Jewish Religion, Its People, and Its History*. New York: William Morrow and Co. The best one-volume introduction to Judaism in recent years. Written with joy, humor, and authenticity. Truly "entry level" and highly recommended.

"I need some good basic books on observing Jewish holidays and life cycle events."

Greenberg, Irving. *The Jewish Way: Living the Holidays*. New York: Touchstone Books. One of the great modern Orthodox scholars and leaders of our time explains the inner dynamics of the holiday cycle. Masterful.

Knobel, Peter. *Gates of the Seasons: A Guide to the Jewish Year*. New York: Central Conference of American Rabbis. An outline of the *mitzvot* of the holiday cycle, written from a Reform perspective.

Maslin, Simeon. *Gates of Mitzvah: A Guide to the Jewish Life Cycle*. New York: Central Conference of American Rabbis. An outline of the *mitzvot* of the life cycle, written from a Reform perspective.

Milgram, Goldie. *Living Jewish Life Cycle: How to Create Meaningful Jewish Rites of Passage at Every Stage of Life*. Woodstock, VT: Jewish Lights Publishing. Guides you in making your Jewish rites come alive with meaning, beauty and with lasting impact on you, your friends and family.

Shapiro, Mark Dov. *Gates of Shabbat: A Guide for Observing Shabbat*. New York: Central Conference of American Rabbis. An entry point for all serious non-Orthodox Jews.

Strassfeld, Sharon and Michael, and Richard Siegel. *The Jewish Catalog*. Three volumes. Philadelphia: Jewish Publication Society. Classic works on modern Jewish observance.

Wolfson, Ron. *Shabbat: The Family Guide to Preparing for and Celebrating the Sabbath; Passover: The Family Guide to Spiritual Celebration;* and *Hanukkah: The Family Guide to Spiritual Celebration;* all part of The Art of Jewish Living Series, a project of the Federation of Jewish Men's Clubs and the University of Judaism (books are all Woodstock, VT: Jewish Lights Publishing). A delightful, rich, multi-layered guide to the Jewish holidays. Families will find numerous resources for their own celebrations.

"I'd like to learn more about modern Jewish theology."

Borowitz, Eugene B., and Frances W. Schwartz. *A Touch of the Sacred: A Theologian's Informal Guide to Jewish Belief*. Woodstock, VT: Jewish Lights Publishing. Borowitz shares with you his rich inner life, which draws from both the rational and mystical Jewish thought that have inspired two generations of rabbis, cantors, and educators.

Cosgrove, Elliot J., ed. *Jewish Theology in Our Time: A New Generation Explores the Foundations and Future of Jewish Belief.* Woodstock, VT: Jewish Lights Publishing. Sets the next stage of Jewish theological thought, bringing together a cross section of interesting new voices from all movements in Judaism.

Feinstein, Edward. *Tough Questions Jews Ask: A Young Adult's Guide to Building a Jewish Life.* 2nd ed. Woodstock, VT: Jewish Lights Publishing. Geared toward those of bar and bat mitzvah age but also great for adults. Covers questions such as, "Why should I believe in God?" and "Why be Jewish?"

Gillman, Neil. *The Way Into Encountering God in Judaism.* Woodstock, VT: Jewish Lights Publishing. Great, accessible outlines of Jewish positions on who God is, what God's nature is, and why we seek to define God.

Gordis, Daniel. *God Was Not in the Fire: The Search for a Spiritual Judaism.* New York: Touchstone Books. How Judaism responds to the quest for meaning, by one of Conservative Judaism's best scholars.

Green, Arthur. *Seek My Face: A Jewish Mystical Theology.* Woodstock, VT: Jewish Lights Publishing. A modern theology that listens to the insights of Jewish mysticism and Chasidism, and yet speaks to the spiritual needs of the contemporary moment.

Hartman, David. *A Heart of Many Rooms: Celebrating the Many Voices within Judaism.* Woodstock, VT: Jewish Lights Publishing. Hartman teaches us, once again, that there are many voices within traditional Jewish teaching and that all Jews, especially Israelis, can profit from paying attention to those voices.

———, and Charlie Buckholtz. *The God Who Hates Lies: Confronting & Rethinking Jewish Tradition.* Woodstock, VT: Jewish Lights Publishing. Probes the deepest questions at the heart of what it means to be a human being and a Jew.

Pearl, Judea and Ruth, eds. *I Am Jewish: Personal Reflections Inspired by the Last Words of Daniel Pearl.* Woodstock, VT: Jewish Lights Publishing. An inspiring collection of many viewpoints—147 contributors from 12 countries—examines what this short statement means to Jewish people from all walks of life, from all around the world, in their own words.

Schulweis, Harold. *For Those Who Can't Believe: Overcoming the Obstacles to Faith.* New York: Harper Perennial. A masterful inquiry into the struggle for faith.

Wolpe, David J. *The Healer of Shattered Hearts: A Jewish View of God.* New York: Penguin Books. A scholar points to where God might be found, with road maps provided by *midrash.*

———. *Why Be Jewish?* New York: Owl Books. A small book, but one filled with riches for those who are searching for meaning in Jewish life today.

"I'm curious about the Jewish mystical search and spirituality. What are some good books to read?"

Green, Arthur. *Ehyeh: A Kabbalah for Tomorrow.* Woodstock, VT: Jewish Lights Publishing. A contemporary exploration of Kabbalah, showing how the ancient Jewish mystical tradition can be retooled to address the needs of our generation.

Kushner, Lawrence. *The Book of Letters.* Woodstock, VT: Jewish Lights Publishing.

———. *The Book of Miracles: A Young Person's Guide to Jewish Spiritual Awareness.* Woodstock, VT: Jewish Lights Publishing.

———. *The Book of Words: Talking Spiritual Life, Living Spiritual Talk.* Woodstock, VT: Jewish Lights Publishing.

———. *Eyes Remade For Wonder: A Lawrence Kushner Reader.* Woodstock, VT: Jewish Lights Publishing.

———. *God Was in This Place and I, i Did Not Know: Finding Self, Spirituality, and Ultimate Meaning.* Woodstock, VT: Jewish Lights Publishing.

———. *Honey from the Rock: An Introduction to Jewish Mysticism.* Special anniversary edition. Woodstock, VT: Jewish Lights Publishing.

———. *I'm God; You're Not: Observations on Organized Religion & Other Disguises of the Ego.* Woodstock, VT: Jewish Lights Publishing. These inspiring insights will warm you during the dark times of your own doubts even as they brighten your quest for meaning, faith, identity and community.

———. *Jewish Spirituality: A Brief Introduction for Christians.* Woodstock, VT: Jewish Lights Publishing.

———. *The River of Light: Jewish Mystical Awareness.* Special anniversary edition. Woodstock, VT: Jewish Lights Publishing.

———. *The Way Into Jewish Mystical Tradition.* Woodstock, VT: Jewish Lights Publishing. A brilliant explanation of the principles of Jewish mystical thinking and their significance and how they relate to our lives. Kushner's books are the best introduction to Jewish spirituality for the lay reader.

Matlins, Stuart M., ed. *The Jewish Lights Spirituality Handbook: A Guide to Understanding, Exploring and Living a Spiritual Life.* Woodstock, VT: Jewish Lights Publishing. Fifty of today's foremost spiritual leaders share their ideas on prayer, meditation, mysticism, Jewish traditions and rituals, life passages, and more.

Matt, Daniel C. *God and the Big Bang: Discovering Harmony Between Science and Spirituality.* Woodstock, VT: Jewish Lights Publishing. Draws on insights of physics and Jewish mysticism to reveal the links between us, God, and the universe.

"What are some good books that will give me and my family some more ideas about *tzedakah* and *mitzvah* projects?"

Artson, Bradley Shavit. *It's a Mitzvah! Step-by-Step to Jewish Living.* West Orange, NJ: Behrman House/Rabbinical Assembly. Deals with the major categories of Jewish action, and offers concrete suggestions for activities. Written from a Conservative viewpoint.

Siegel, Danny. *Gym Shoes and Irises: Personalized Tzedakah* (Books 1 and 2). Spring Valley, NY: The Town House Press.

———. *Mitzvahs.* Pittsboro, NC: The Townhouse Press.

———. *Munbaz II and Other Mitzvah Heroes.* Spring Valley, NY: The Town House Press.

Siegel's books contain more ideas for *tzedakah* than one could possibly do in a lifetime. He turns *mitzvah*-doing into a poetry of the Jewish soul.

Suneby, Liz and Diane Heiman. *The Mitzvah Project Book: Making Mitzvah Part of Your Bar/Bat Mitzvah … and Your Life.* Woodstock, VT: Jewish Lights Publishing. Packed with ideas to help you connect something you love to a mitzvah project or *tikkun olam* initiative that you can be passionate about.

"How do I put together my own service for bar and bat mitzvah?"

As described in Chapter Eight, Davka distributes Dagesh and DavkaWriter, Hebrew word processors, as well as disks with the complete *siddur* and *Tanach.* Davka, 7074 N. Western Ave., Chicago, IL 60645. (800) 621-8227.

Glossary

aliyah (plural, *aliyot*): literally, "going up." The ascent to the *bimah* to say the blessings over the Torah scroll.

amidah: literally, the "standing" prayer. The nineteen prayers that constitute the main body of Jewish liturgy; also known as *tefilah* and the *shemoneh esreh*.

Baruch shepetarani me-onsho shel zeh: blessing traditionally uttered by the father at the occasion of his son becoming bar mitzvah: "Blessed is the One Who has now freed me from responsibility for this one."

bikur cholim: visiting the sick.

bimah: the raised platform in most synagogues where the service is conducted.

birchat hamazon: the Hebrew blessing that is said after the meal.

chesed: loving kindness.

chumash (from *chameish*, "five"): the Pentateuch (Five Books of Moses), or a book containing the Pentateuch.

derashah: a brief exposition of the Torah portion for the week. Sometimes referred to as the *devar Torah*, "a word of Torah."

haftarah: literally, "completion." The reading of the section from the Prophets for a particular Shabbat.

halachah: literally, "the going." Traditional Jewish law.

havdalah: literally, "separation," "distinction." The ceremony that ends Shabbat.

kavvanah: sacred intention, the goal of Jewish prayer and worship.

ketuvim: the third section of the Hebrew Bible (Tanach). Includes Psalms, Proverbs, Job, Song of Songs, Ruth, Lamentations, Ecclesiastes, Esther.

midrash: literally, "the searching out." A postbiblical, rabbinic interpretation of a Biblical verse.

mikra: the Hebrew Bible.

mincha: the afternoon Jewish worship service.

Mishnah: the classic postbiblical code of Jewish law, compiled in Israel circa 200 C.E. by Rabbi Judah Ha-nasi (Judah the Prince).

mitzvah (plural, *mitzvot*): an obligation of Jewish life.

musaf: the "additional" prayer in traditional liturgy. Recalls the ancient sacrificial rites of the Temple (the *musaf* or additional sacrifices), and repeats some themes covered earlier in the liturgy.

neviim: the second section of the Hebrew Bible (*Tanach*). Consists of the prophetic and historical writings.

nichum aveilim: the *mitzvah* of comforting mourners.

parasha: the Torah portion of the week. Also sometimes referred to as the *sedra*.

parochet: the curtain that hung before the Holy of Holies in the ancient Temple in Jerusalem. Now refers to the curtain that hangs before the *aron Hakodesh* (the Ark) in the synagogue.

pidyon shevuim: the *mitzvah* of redeeming captives.

Pirke Avot: literally, "the chapters of the fathers." The ethical maxims of the Mishnah, as quoted in the names of the early Rabbis.

Shulchan Aruch: literally, "the set table." The sixteenth-century code of Jewish law compiled by Joseph Caro.

Talmud: literally, "learning." Commentaries and discussions of the Mishnah, compiled circa 450 C.E..–500 C.E. One Talmud was compiled in Palestine (the Palestinian or Jerusalem Talmud, known as the *Yerushalmi*); the more authoritative one was compiled in Babylonia (the Babylonian Talmud, known as the *Bavli*).

Tanach: acronym for *Torah*, *Neviim* (the Prophets), and *Ketuvim* (the later Writings) that comprise the Hebrew Bible.

tefilah: the major section of Jewish liturgy. The generic term for Jewish worship.

Torah: literally, "teaching" or "direction." Narrowly, the first part of the Hebrew Bible that is read from the scroll; broadly, all Jewish sacred literature and, by implication, all of Judaism.

tzedakah: the *mitzvah* of sacred giving.

Bibliography and Suggestions for Further Reading

Adelman, Penina, Ali Feldman and Shulamit Reinharz. *The JGirl's Guide: The Young Jewish Woman's Handbook for Coming of Age*. Woodstock, Vt.: Jewish Lights, 2005.

Artson, Bradley Shavit. *It's a Mitzvah!: Step-by-Step to Jewish Living*. West Orange, N.J.: Behrman House/Rabbinical Assembly, 1995.

Braunstein, Susan L., and Jenna Weissman Joselit. *Getting Comfortable in America: The American Jewish Home, 1880–1950*. New York: The Jewish Museum, 1990.

Cohen, Alfred S. "Celebration of the Bat Mitzvah," *Journal of Halacha and Contemporary Society* 12 (Fall 1986/Sukkot 5747): 5–16.

Cohen, Arthur A., and Paul Mendes-Flohr, eds. *Contemporary Jewish Religious Thought*. New York: Charles Scribner's Sons, 1987.

Coles, Robert. *The Spiritual Life of Children*. Boston: Houghton Mifflin Co., 1990.

Douglas, Mary. *Natural Symbols: Explorations in Cosmology*. New York: Pantheon, 1982.

Eliade, Mircea. *Cosmos and History: The Myth of the Eternal Return*. New York: Harper and Row, 1954.

____. *Rites and Symbols of Initiation: The Mysteries of Birth and Rebirth*. New York: Harper Torchbooks, 1965.

Epstein, Isadore, trans. *The Babylonian Talmud*. London: Soncino Press, 1958.

Erikson, Erik H. *Childhood and Society*. New York: W.W. Norton, 1950.

Fein, Leonard. *Where Are We? The Inner Life of American Jews*. New York: Harper and Row, 1988.

Feuer, Leon I. "Second Thoughts About Bar-Bat Mitzvah," *Journal of Reform Judaism* 27, no. 1 (Winter 1980): 1–9.

Fishman, Sylvia Barack. *The Way Into the Varieties of Jewishness*. Woodstock, Vt.: Jewish Lights, 2006.

Freedman, H., trans. *The Midrash Rabbah*. London: Soncino Press, 1977.

Friedman, Edwin. *Generation to Generation: Family Process in Church and Synagogue*. New York: Guilford Press, 1985.

Glatzer, Nahum N., ed. *On Jewish Learning*. New York: Schocken Books, 1955.

Goldstein, Albert S. "Let's Bar Bar Mitzvah," *Central Conference of American Rabbis Journal* 3 (October 1953): 19–25.

Hall, Edward T. *Beyond Culture*. Garden City, N.Y.: Anchor Books, 1976.

Heinemann, Joseph. *Literature of the Synagogue*. New York: Behrman House, 1975.

Hertzberg, Arthur. *The Jews in America*. New York: Simon and Schuster, 1989.

Heschel, Abraham Joshua. *Quest for God: Studies in Prayer and Symbolism.* New York: Crossroad, 1954.

Himmelfarb, Milton, ed. *The Condition of Jewish Belief: A Symposium Compiled by the Editors of Commentary Magazine.* Northvale, N.J.: Jason Aronson, 1989.

Hoffman, Lawrence A. *The Art of Public Prayer,* 2nd Ed.: *Not for Clergy Only.* Woodstock, Vt.: SkyLight Paths, 1999.

Jacob, Walter, ed. *American Reform Responsa: Collected Responsa of the Central Conference of American Rabbis, 1889–1983.* New York: Central Conference of American Rabbis, 1983.

___. "Initiation into Judaism," *Religious Education* 74, no. 6 (November–December 1979): 598–563.

Joselit, Jenna Weissman. *The Wonders of America: Reinventing Jewish Culture, 1880–1950.* New York: Hill and Wang, 1994.

Levinson, Daniel J. *The Seasons of a Man's Life.* New York: Ballantine Books, 1978.

Maimonides. *Mishneh Torah.* Warsaw-Vilna Edition, n.d.

Marcus, Ivan G. *Rituals of Childhood: Jewish Acculturation in Medieval Europe.* New Haven: Yale University Press, 1996.

Maslow, Abraham H. *Religions, Values, and Peak-Experiences.* London: Penguin Books, 1970.

Meyer, Michael. *Response to Modernity: A History of the Reform Movement in Judaism.* New York: Oxford University Press, 1988.

Midrash Rabbah (Vilna edition). Jerusalem: 1975.

Neusner, Jacob. *The Enchantments of Judaism.* New York: Basic Books, 1987.

Orlean, Susan. *Saturday Night.* New York: Alfred A. Knopf, 1990.

Pearl, Judea and Ruth. *I Am Jewish: Personal Reflections Inspired by the Last Words of Daniel Pearl.* Woodstock, Vt.: Jewish Lights, 2005.

Pogrebin, Letty Cottin. *Deborah, Golda, and Me: Being Female and Jewish in America.* New York: Crown Publishers, Inc., 1991.

Raphael, Marc Lee. *Profiles in American Judaism: The Reform, Conservative, Orthodox, and Reconstructionist Traditions in Historical Perspective.* San Francisco: Harper and Row, 1984.

Raphael, Ray. *The Men from the Boys: Rites of Passage in Male America.* Lincoln, Neb.: University of Nebraska Press, 1990.

Roth, Cecil. *A History of the Marranos.* New York: Schocken Books, 1974.

Saperstein, Marc. *Jewish Preaching, 1200–1800: An Anthology.* New Haven, Conn.: Yale University Press, 1989.

Schauss, Hyman. *The Lifetime of the Jew.* New York: Union of American Hebrew Congregations, 1950.

Schulweis, Harold. *For Those Who Can't Believe: Overcoming the Obstacles to Faith.* New York: HarperCollins, 1994.

___. *In God's Mirror: Reflections and Essays.* Hoboken, N.J.: KTAV, l990.

Sherwin, Byron L. *In Partnership with God: Contemporary Jewish Law and Ethics.* Syracuse, N.Y.: Syracuse University Press, 1990.

Silver, Daniel Jeremy. *The Story of Scripture: From Oral Tradition to the Written Word.* New York: Basic Books, 1990.

Slonimsky, Henry. *Essays.* Cincinnati: Hebrew Union College Press, 1967.

Snyder, Herman E. "Is Bar-Bat Mitzvah Destroying Attendance at Synagogue Services?" *Journal of Reform Judaism* 27, no. 1 (Winter 1980): 11–14.

Sofrim. Michael Higger edition. New York: Ginsburg, 1937.

Woocher, Jonathan S. *Sacred Survival: The Civil Religion of American Jews.* Bloomington, Ind.: Indiana University Press, 1986.

Zborowski, Mark, and Elizabeth Herzog. *Life Is with People.* New York: International Universities Press, 1952.

About the Art

Robert Lipnick is an American artist living in Davenport, Iowa. His work, considered Midwest Judaica, focuses on the themes of justice, genesis, the home, family, and nature. He has been commissioned by many families to create special artworks in commemoration of meaningful life-cycle events. His ceramics and paintings are found in the collections of major museums and institutions throughout the world.

The images Lipnick uses on this book's cover are familiar to everyday Jewish life: family, Torah, prayer, Israel, love, and peace. The kiddush cup/tablets/mountains and the empty chair found in the cover art have been chosen as ornamentation for the text of the book. Together, they symbolize an invitation to all to celebrate while finding spiritual meaning in bar and bat mitzvah.

About the Hebrew Text

The text of the Hebrew prayers in *Putting God on the Guest List* was created by Joel Hoffman, Excelsior Computer Services, Brooklyn, New York, using "Servicemaker," a program he designed for IBM computers and compatibles. This program provides the user with all of the necessary step-by-step instructions to create a Jewish religious service. It includes the complete Hebrew and English texts for the major prayers, all necessary fonts, outlines, and detailed notes for each type of service.

Congregation Resources

Empowered Judaism: What Independent Minyanim Can Teach Us about Building Vibrant Jewish Communities
By Rabbi Elie Kaunfer; Foreword by Prof. Jonathan D. Sarna
Examines the independent minyan movement and the lessons these grassroots communities can provide. 6 x 9, 224 pp, Quality PB, 978-1-58023-412-2 **$18.99**

Spiritual Boredom: Rediscovering the Wonder of Judaism *By Dr. Erica Brown*
Breaks through the surface of spiritual boredom to find the reservoir of meaning within. 6 x 9, 208 pp, HC, 978-1-58023-405-4 **$21.99**

Building a Successful Volunteer Culture
Finding Meaning in Service in the Jewish Community
By Rabbi Charles Simon; Foreword by Shelley Lindauer; Preface by Dr. Ron Wolfson
Shows you how to develop and maintain the volunteers who are essential to the vitality of your organization and community. 6 x 9, 192 pp, Quality PB, 978-1-58023-408-5 **$16.99**

Inspired Jewish Leadership: Practical Approaches to Building Strong Communities
By Dr. Erica Brown 6 x 9, 256 pp, HC, 978-1-58023-361-3 **$27.99**

Rethinking Synagogues: A New Vocabulary for Congregational Life
By Rabbi Lawrence A. Hoffman, PhD 6 x 9, 240 pp, Quality PB, 978-1-58023-248-7 **$19.99**

The Spirituality of Welcoming: How to Transform Your Congregation into a
Sacred Community *By Dr. Ron Wolfson* 6 x 9, 224 pp, Quality PB, 978-1-58023-244-9 **$19.99**

Children's Books

Around the World in One Shabbat
Jewish People Celebrate the Sabbath Together
By Durga Yael Bernhard
Takes your child on a colorful adventure to share the many ways Jewish people celebrate Shabbat around the world.
11 x 8½, 32 pp, Full-color illus., HC, 978-1-58023-433-7 **$18.99** *For ages 3–6*

What You Will See Inside a Synagogue
By Rabbi Lawrence A. Hoffman, PhD, and Dr. Ron Wolfson; Full-color photos by Bill Aron
A colorful, fun-to-read introduction that explains the ways and whys of Jewish worship and religious life.
8½ x 10½, 32 pp, Full-color photos, Quality PB, 978-1-59473-256-0 **$8.99** *For ages 6 & up*
(A book from SkyLight Paths, Jewish Lights' sister imprint)

Because Nothing Looks Like God
By Lawrence Kushner and Karen Kushner Introduces children to the possibilities of spiritual life. 11 x 8½, 32 pp, Full-color illus., HC, 978-1-58023-092-6 **$17.99** *For ages 4 & up*

The Book of Miracles: A Young Person's Guide to Jewish Spiritual Awareness
Written and illus. by Lawrence Kushner
6 x 9, 96 pp, 2-color illus., HC, 978-1-879045-78-1 **$16.95** *For ages 9–13*

In God's Hands *By Lawrence Kushner and Gary Schmidt* 9 x 12, 32 pp, Full-color illus.,
HC, 978-1-58023-224-1 **$16.99** *For ages 5 & up*

In Our Image: God's First Creatures *By Nancy Sohn Swartz*
9 x 12, 32 pp, Full-color illus., HC, 978-1-879045-99-6 **$16.95** *For ages 4 & up*

The Kids' Fun Book of Jewish Time
By Emily Sper 9 x 7½, 24 pp, Full-color illus., HC, 978-1-58023-311-8 **$16.99** *For ages 3–6*

What Makes Someone a Jew? *By Lauren Seidman*
Reflects the changing face of American Judaism.
10 x 8½, 32 pp, Full-color photos, Quality PB, 978-1-58023-321-7 **$8.99** *For ages 3–6*

Children's Books by Sandy Eisenberg Sasso

Adam & Eve's First Sunset: God's New Day

Engaging new story explores fear and hope, faith and gratitude in ways that will delight kids and adults—inspiring us to bless each of God's days and nights.

9 x 12, 32 pp, Full-color illus., HC, 978-1-58023-177-0 **$17.95** *For ages 4 & up*

Also Available as a Board Book: Adam and Eve's New Day

5 x 5, 24 pp, Full-color illus., Board, 978-1-59473-205-8 **$7.99** *For ages 0–4*

(A book from SkyLight Paths, Jewish Lights' sister imprint)

But God Remembered

Stories of Women from Creation to the Promised Land

Four different stories of women—Lillith, Serach, Bityah, and the Daughters of Z—teach us important values through their faith and actions.

9 x 12, 32 pp, Full-color illus., Quality PB, 978-1-58023-372-9 **$8.99**; HC, 978-1-879045-43-9

$16.95 *For ages 8 & up*

Cain & Abel: Finding the Fruits of Peace

Shows children that we have the power to deal with anger in positive ways. Provides questions for kids and adults to explore together.

9 x 12, 32 pp, Full-color illus., HC, 978-1-58023-123-7 **$16.95** *For ages 5 & up*

God in Between

If you wanted to find God, where would you look? This magical, mythical tale teaches that God can be found where we are: within all of us and the relationships between us. 9 x 12, 32 pp, Full-color illus., HC, 978-1-879045-86-6 **$16.95** *For ages 4 & up*

God's Paintbrush: Special 10th Anniversary Edition

Wonderfully interactive, invites children of all faiths and backgrounds to encounter God through moments in their own lives. Provides questions adult and child can explore together. 11 x 8½, 32 pp, Full-color illus., HC, 978-1-58023-195-4 **$17.95** *For ages 4 & up*

Also Available as a Board Book: I Am God's Paintbrush

5 x 5, 24 pp, Full-color illus., Board, 978-1-59473-265-2 **$7.99** *For ages 0–4*

(A book from SkyLight Paths, Jewish Lights' sister imprint)

Also Available: God's Paintbrush Teacher's Guide

8½ x 11, 32 pp, PB, 978-1-879045-57-6 **$8.95**

God's Paintbrush Celebration Kit

A Spiritual Activity Kit for Teachers and Students of All Faiths, All Backgrounds

8-Student Activity Sheet Pack (40 sheets/5 sessions), 978-1-58023-058-2 **$19.95**

In God's Name

Like an ancient myth in its poetic text and vibrant illustrations, this award-winning modern fable about the search for God's name celebrates the diversity and, at the same time, the unity of all people.

9 x 12, 32 pp, Full-color illus., HC, 978-1-879045-26-2 **$16.99** *For ages 4 & up*

Also Available as a Board Book: What Is God's Name?

5 x 5, 24 pp, Board, Full-color illus., 978-1-893361-10-2 **$7.99** *For ages 0–4*

(A book from SkyLight Paths, Jewish Lights' sister imprint)

Also Available: In God's Name video and study guide

Computer animation, original music, and children's voices. 18 min. **$29.99**

Noah's Wife: The Story of Naamah

When God tells Noah to bring the animals of the world onto the ark, God also calls on Naamah, Noah's wife, to save each plant on Earth. Based on an ancient text.

9 x 12, 32 pp, Full-color illus., HC, 978-1-58023-134-3 **$16.95** *For ages 4 & up*

Also Available as a Board Book: Naamah, Noah's Wife

5 x 5, 24 pp, Full-color illus., Board, 978-1-893361-56-0 **$7.95** *For ages 0–4*

(A book from SkyLight Paths, Jewish Lights' sister imprint)

For Heaven's Sake: Finding God in Unexpected Places

9 x 12, 32 pp, Full-color illus., HC, 978-1-58023-054-4 **$16.95** *For ages 4 & up*

God Said Amen: Finding the Answers to Our Prayers

9 x 12, 32 pp, Full-color illus., HC, 978-1-58023-080-3 **$16.95** *For ages 4 & up*

Social Justice

Confronting Scandal
How Jews Can Respond When Jews Do Bad Things
By Dr. Erica Brown

A framework to transform our sense of shame over reports of Jews committing crime into actions that inspire and sustain a moral culture.

6 x 9, 192 pp, HC, 978-1-58023-440-5 **$24.99**

There Shall Be No Needy
Pursuing Social Justice through Jewish Law and Tradition
By Rabbi Jill Jacobs; Foreword by Rabbi Elliot N. Dorff, PhD; Preface by Simon Greer

Confronts the most pressing issues of twenty-first-century America from a deeply Jewish perspective. 6 x 9, 288 pp, Quality PB, 978-1-58023-425-2 **$16.99**

There Shall Be No Needy Teacher's Guide 8½ x 11, 56 pp, PB, 978-1-58023-429-0 **$8.99**

Conscience
The Duty to Obey and the Duty to Disobey
By Rabbi Harold M. Schulweis

Examines the idea of conscience and the role conscience plays in our relationships to government, law, ethics, religion, human nature, God—and to each other.

6 x 9, 160 pp, Quality PB, 978-1-58023-419-1 **$16.99**; HC, 978-1-58023-375-0 **$19.99**

Judaism and Justice
The Jewish Passion to Repair the World
By Rabbi Sidney Schwarz; Foreword by Ruth Messinger

Explores the relationship between Judaism, social justice and the Jewish identity of American Jews. 6 x 9, 352 pp, Quality PB, 978-1-58023-353-8 **$19.99**

Spirituality/Women's Interest

New Jewish Feminism
Probing the Past, Forging the Future
Edited by Rabbi Elyse Goldstein; Foreword by Anita Diamant

Looks at the growth and accomplishments of Jewish feminism and what they mean for Jewish women today and tomorrow.

6 x 9, 480 pp, Quality PB, 978-1-58023-448-1 **$19.99**; HC, 978-1-58023-359-0 **$24.99**

The Divine Feminine in Biblical Wisdom Literature
Selections Annotated & Explained
Translation & Annotation by Rabbi Rami Shapiro

5½ x 8½, 240 pp, Quality PB, 978-1-59473-109-9 **$16.99**
(A book from SkyLight Paths, Jewish Lights' sister imprint)

The Quotable Jewish Woman
Wisdom, Inspiration & Humor from the Mind & Heart
Edited by Elaine Bernstein Partnow

6 x 9, 496 pp, Quality PB, 978-1-58023-236-4 **$19.99**

The Women's Haftarah Commentary
New Insights from Women Rabbis on the 54 Weekly Haftarah Portions, the 5 Megillot & Special Shabbatot
Edited by Rabbi Elyse Goldstein

Illuminates the historical significance of female portrayals in the Haftarah and the Five Megillot. 6 x 9, 560 pp, Quality PB, 978-1-58023-371-2 **$19.99**

The Women's Torah Commentary
New Insights from Women Rabbis on the 54 Weekly Torah Portions
Edited by Rabbi Elyse Goldstein

Over fifty women rabbis offer inspiring insights on the Torah, in a week-by-week format.

6 x 9, 496 pp, Quality PB, 978-1-58023-370-5 **$19.99**; HC, 978-1-58023-076-6 **$34.95**

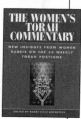

See Passover for *The Women's Passover Companion: Women's Reflections on the Festival of Freedom* and *The Women's Seder Sourcebook: Rituals & Readings for Use at the Passover Seder.*

Meditation

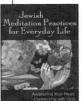

Jewish Meditation Practices for Everyday Life
Awakening Your Heart, Connecting with God
By Rabbi Jeff Roth
Offers a fresh take on meditation that draws on life experience and living life with greater clarity as opposed to the traditional method of rigorous study. 6 x 9, 224 pp, Quality PB Original, 978-1-58023-397-2 **$18.99**

The Handbook of Jewish Meditation Practices
A Guide for Enriching the Sabbath and Other Days of Your Life
By Rabbi David A. Cooper Easy-to-learn meditation techniques.
6 x 9, 208 pp, Quality PB, 978-1-58023-102-2 **$16.95**

Discovering Jewish Meditation: Instruction & Guidance for Learning an Ancient Spiritual Practice *By Nan Fink Gefen* 6 x 9, 208 pp, Quality PB, 978-1-58023-067-4 **$16.95**

Meditation from the Heart of Judaism: Today's Teachers Share Their Practices, Techniques, and Faith *Edited by Avram Davis*
6 x 9, 256 pp, Quality PB, 978-1-58023-049-0 **$16.95**

Ritual/Sacred Practice

The Jewish Dream Book: The Key to Opening the Inner Meaning of Your Dreams *By Vanessa L. Ochs with Elizabeth Ochs; Full-color illus. by Kristina Swarner*
Instructions for how modern people can perform ancient Jewish dream practices and dream interpretations drawn from the Jewish wisdom tradition.
8 x 8, 128 pp, Full-color illus., Deluxe PB w/flaps, 978-1-58023-132-9 **$16.95**

God in Your Body: Kabbalah, Mindfulness and Embodied Spiritual Practice
By Jay Michaelson
The first comprehensive treatment of the body in Jewish spiritual practice and an essential guide to the sacred.
6 x 9, 288 pp, Quality PB, 978-1-58023-304-0 **$18.99**

The Book of Jewish Sacred Practices: CLAL's Guide to Everyday & Holiday Rituals & Blessings *Edited by Rabbi Irwin Kula and Vanessa L. Ochs, PhD*
6 x 9, 368 pp, Quality PB, 978-1-58023-152-7 **$18.95**

Jewish Ritual: A Brief Introduction for Christians
By Rabbi Kerry M. Olitzky and Rabbi Daniel Judson
5½ x 8½, 144 pp, Quality PB, 978-1-58023-210-4 **$14.99**

The Rituals & Practices of a Jewish Life: A Handbook for Personal Spiritual Renewal *Edited by Rabbi Kerry M. Olitzky and Rabbi Daniel Judson*
6 x 9, 272 pp, illus., Quality PB, 978-1-58023-169-5 **$18.95**

The Sacred Art of Lovingkindness: Preparing to Practice
By Rabbi Rami Shapiro 5½ x 8½, 176 pp, Quality PB, 978-1-59473-151-8 **$16.99**
(A book from SkyLight Paths, Jewish Lights' sister imprint)

Science Fiction/Mystery & Detective Fiction

Mystery Midrash: An Anthology of Jewish Mystery & Detective Fiction
Edited by Lawrence W. Raphael; Preface by Joel Siegel
6 x 9, 304 pp, Quality PB, 978-1-58023-055-1 **$16.95**

Criminal Kabbalah: An Intriguing Anthology of Jewish Mystery & Detective Fiction *Edited by Lawrence W. Raphael; Foreword by Laurie R. King*
All-new stories from twelve of today's masters of mystery and detective fiction—sure to delight mystery buffs of all faith traditions.
6 x 9, 256 pp, Quality PB, 978-1-58023-109-1 **$16.95**

Wandering Stars: An Anthology of Jewish Fantasy & Science Fiction
Edited by Jack Dann; Introduction by Isaac Asimov
6 x 9, 272 pp, Quality PB, 978-1-58023-005-6 **$18.99**

More Wandering Stars: An Anthology of Outstanding Stories of Jewish Fantasy and Science Fiction *Edited by Jack Dann; Introduction by Isaac Asimov*
6 x 9, 192 pp, Quality PB, 978-1-58023-063-6 **$16.95**

Inspiration

God of Me: Imagining God throughout Your Lifetime
By Rabbi David Lyon Helps you cut through preconceived ideas of God and dogmas that stifle your creativity when thinking about your personal relationship with God. 6 x 9, 176 pp, Quality PB, 978-1-58023-452-8 **$16.99**

The God Upgrade: Finding Your 21st-Century Spirituality in Judaism's 5,000-Year-Old Tradition *By Rabbi Jamie Korngold; Foreword by Rabbi Harold M. Schulweis* A provocative look at how our changing God concepts have shaped every aspect of Judaism. 6 x 9, 176 pp, Quality PB, 978-1-58023-443-6 **$15.99**

The Seven Questions You're Asked in Heaven: Reviewing and Renewing Your Life on Earth *By Dr. Ron Wolfson* An intriguing and entertaining resource for living a life that matters. 6 x 9, 176 pp, Quality PB, 978-1-58023-407-8 **$16.99**

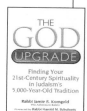

Happiness and the Human Spirit: The Spirituality of Becoming the Best You Can Be *By Rabbi Abraham J. Twerski, MD* Shows you that true happiness is attainable once you stop looking outside yourself for the source. 6 x 9, 176 pp, Quality PB, 978-1-58023-404-7 **$16.99**; HC, 978-1-58023-343-9 **$19.99**

A Formula for Proper Living: Practical Lessons from Life and Torah *By Rabbi Abraham J. Twerski, MD* 6 x 9, 144 pp, HC, 978-1-58023-402-3 **$19.99**

The Bridge to Forgiveness: Stories and Prayers for Finding God and Restoring Wholeness *By Rabbi Karyn D. Kedar* 6 x 9, 176 pp, Quality PB, 978-1-58023-451-1 **$16.99**

The Empty Chair: Finding Hope and Joy—Timeless Wisdom from a Hasidic Master, Rebbe Nachman of Breslov *Adapted by Moshe Mykoff and the Breslov Research Institute* 4 x 6, 128 pp, Deluxe PB w/ flaps, 978-1-879045-67-5 **$9.99**

The Gentle Weapon: Prayers for Everyday and Not-So-Everyday Moments— Timeless Wisdom from the Teachings of the Hasidic Master, Rebbe Nachman of Breslov *Adapted by Moshe Mykoff and S. C. Mizrahi, together with the Breslov Research Institute* 4 x 6, 144 pp, Deluxe PB w/ flaps, 978-1-58023-022-3 **$9.99**

God Whispers: Stories of the Soul, Lessons of the Heart *By Rabbi Karyn D. Kedar* 6 x 9, 176 pp, Quality PB, 978-1-58023-088-9 **$15.95**

God's To-Do List: 103 Ways to Be an Angel and Do God's Work on Earth *By Dr. Ron Wolfson* 6 x 9, 144 pp, Quality PB, 978-1-58023-301-9 **$16.99**

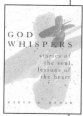

Jewish Stories from Heaven and Earth: Inspiring Tales to Nourish the Heart and Soul *Edited by Rabbi Dov Peretz Elkins* 6 x 9, 304 pp, Quality PB, 978-1-58023-363-7 **$16.99**

Life's Daily Blessings: Inspiring Reflections on Gratitude and Joy for Every Day, Based on Jewish Wisdom *By Rabbi Kerry M. Olitzky* 4½ x 6½, 368 pp, Quality PB, 978-1-58023-396-5 **$16.99**

Restful Reflections: Nighttime Inspiration to Calm the Soul, Based on Jewish Wisdom *By Rabbi Kerry M. Olitzky and Rabbi Lori Forman-Jacobi* 4½ x 6½, 448 pp, Quality PB, 978-1-58023-091-9 **$15.95**

Sacred Intentions: Morning Inspiration to Strengthen the Spirit, Based on Jewish Wisdom *By Rabbi Kerry M. Olitzky and Rabbi Lori Forman-Jacobi* 4½ x 6½, 448 pp, Quality PB, 978-1-58023-061-2 **$16.99**

Kabbalah/Mysticism

Jewish Mysticism and the Spiritual Life: Classical Texts, Contemporary Reflections *Edited by Dr. Lawrence Fine, Dr. Eitan Fishbane and Rabbi Or N. Rose* Inspirational and thought-provoking materials for contemplation, discussion and action. 6 x 9, 256 pp, HC, 978-1-58023-434-4 **$24.99**

Ehyeh: A Kabbalah for Tomorrow *By Rabbi Arthur Green, PhD* 6 x 9, 224 pp, Quality PB, 978-1-58023-213-5 **$18.99**

The Gift of Kabbalah: Discovering the Secrets of Heaven, Renewing Your Life on Earth *By Tamar Frankiel, PhD* 6 x 9, 256 pp, Quality PB, 978-1-58023-141-1 **$16.95**

Seek My Face: A Jewish Mystical Theology *By Rabbi Arthur Green, PhD* 6 x 9, 304 pp, Quality PB, 978-1-58023-130-5 **$19.95**

Zohar: Annotated & Explained *Translation & Annotation by Dr. Daniel C. Matt; Foreword by Andrew Harvey* 5½ x 8½, 176 pp, Quality PB, 978-1-893361-51-5 **$15.99**
(A book from SkyLight Paths, Jewish Lights' sister imprint)

See also *The Way Into Jewish Mystical Tradition* in The Way Into... Series.

Theology/Philosophy

The God Who Hates Lies: Confronting & Rethinking Jewish Tradition
By Dr. David Hartman with Charlie Buckholtz
The world's leading Modern Orthodox Jewish theologian probes the deepest questions at the heart of what it means to be a human being and a Jew.
6 x 9, 208 pp, HC, 978-1-58023-455-9 **$24.99**

Jewish Theology in Our Time: A New Generation Explores the Foundations and Future of Jewish Belief *Edited by Rabbi Elliot J. Cosgrove, PhD; Foreword by Rabbi David J. Wolpe; Preface by Rabbi Carole B. Balin, PhD*
A powerful and challenging examination of what Jews can believe—by a new generation's most dynamic and innovative thinkers.
6 x 9, 240 pp, HC, 978-1-58023-413-9 **$24.99**

Maimonides, Spinoza and Us: Toward an Intellectually Vibrant Judaism
By Rabbi Marc D. Angel, PhD A challenging look at two great Jewish philosophers and what their thinking means to our understanding of God, truth, revelation and reason. 6 x 9, 224 pp, HC, 978-1-58023-411-5 **$24.99**

The Death of Death: Resurrection and Immortality in Jewish Thought
By Rabbi Neil Gillman, PhD 6 x 9, 336 pp, Quality PB, 978-1-58023-081-0 **$18.95**

Doing Jewish Theology: God, Torah & Israel in Modern Judaism *By Rabbi Neil Gillman, PhD*
6 x 9, 304 pp, Quality PB, 978-1-58023-439-9 **$18.99**

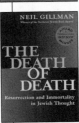

Hasidic Tales: Annotated & Explained *Translation & Annotation by Rabbi Rami Shapiro*
5½ x 8½, 240 pp, Quality PB, 978-1-893361-86-7 **$16.95***

A Heart of Many Rooms: Celebrating the Many Voices within Judaism
By Dr. David Hartman 6 x 9, 352 pp, Quality PB, 978-1-58023-156-5 **$19.95**

The Hebrew Prophets: Selections Annotated & Explained
Translation & Annotation by Rabbi Rami Shapiro; Foreword by Rabbi Zalman M. Schachter-Shalomi
5½ x 8½, 224 pp, Quality PB, 978-1-59473-037-5 **$16.99***

A Jewish Understanding of the New Testament *By Rabbi Samuel Sandmel; Preface by Rabbi David Sandmel* 5½ x 8½, 368 pp, Quality PB, 978-1-59473-048-1 **$19.99***

Jews and Judaism in the 21st Century: Human Responsibility, the Presence of God and the Future of the Covenant *Edited by Rabbi Edward Feinstein; Foreword by Paula E. Hyman*
6 x 9, 192 pp, Quality PB, 978-1-58023-374-3 **$19.99**

A Living Covenant: The Innovative Spirit in Traditional Judaism
By Dr. David Hartman 6 x 9, 368 pp, Quality PB, 978-1-58023-011-7 **$25.00**

Love and Terror in the God Encounter: The Theological Legacy of Rabbi Joseph B. Soloveitchik *By Dr. David Hartman* 6 x 9, 240 pp, Quality PB, 978-1-58023-176-3 **$19.95**

A Touch of the Sacred: A Theologian's Informal Guide to Jewish Belief
By Dr. Eugene B. Borowitz and Frances W. Schwartz
6 x 9, 256 pp, Quality PB, 978-1-58023-416-0 **$16.99**; HC, 978-1-58023-337-8 **$21.99**

Traces of God: Seeing God in Torah, History and Everyday Life *By Rabbi Neil Gillman, PhD*
6 x 9, 240 pp, Quality PB, 978-1-58023-369-9 **$16.99**

Your Word Is Fire: The Hasidic Masters on Contemplative Prayer
Edited and translated by Rabbi Arthur Green, PhD, and Barry W. Holtz
6 x 9, 160 pp, Quality PB, 978-1-879045-25-5 **$15.95**

I Am Jewish
Personal Reflections Inspired by the Last Words of Daniel Pearl
Almost 150 Jews—both famous and not—from all walks of life, from all around the world, write about many aspects of their Judaism.
Edited by Judea and Ruth Pearl 6 x 9, 304 pp, Deluxe PB w/ flaps, 978-1-58023-259-3 **$18.99**
Download a free copy of the *I Am Jewish Teacher's Guide* at www.jewishlights.com.

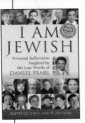

Hannah Senesh: Her Life and Diary, The First Complete Edition
By Hannah Senesh; Foreword by Marge Piercy; Preface by Eitan Senesh; Afterword by Roberta Grossman
6 x 9, 368 pp, b/w photos, Quality PB, 978-1-58023-342-2 **$19.99**

*A book from SkyLight Paths, Jewish Lights' sister imprint

Theology/Philosophy/The Way Into... Series

The Way Into... series offers an accessible and highly usable "guided tour" of the Jewish faith, people, history and beliefs—in total, an introduction to Judaism that will enable you to understand and interact with the sacred texts of the Jewish tradition. Each volume is written by a leading contemporary scholar and teacher, and explores one key aspect of Judaism. *The Way Into...* series enables all readers to achieve a real sense of Jewish cultural literacy through guided study.

The Way Into Encountering God in Judaism
By Rabbi Neil Gillman, PhD

For everyone who wants to understand how Jews have encountered God throughout history and today.

6 x 9, 240 pp, Quality PB, 978-1-58023-199-2 **$18.99**; HC, 978-1-58023-025-4 **$21.95**

Also Available: **The Jewish Approach to God:** A Brief Introduction for Christians
By Rabbi Neil Gillman, PhD

5½ x 8½, 192 pp, Quality PB, 978-1-58023-190-9 **$16.95**

The Way Into Jewish Mystical Tradition
By Rabbi Lawrence Kushner

Allows readers to interact directly with the sacred mystical text of the Jewish tradition. An accessible introduction to the concepts of Jewish mysticism, their religious and spiritual significance and how they relate to life today.

6 x 9, 224 pp, Quality PB, 978-1-58023-200-5 **$18.99**; HC, 978-1-58023-029-2 **$21.95**

The Way Into Jewish Prayer
By Rabbi Lawrence A. Hoffman, PhD

Opens the door to 3,000 years of Jewish prayer, making available all anyone needs to feel at home in the Jewish way of communicating with God.

6 x 9, 208 pp, Quality PB, 978-1-58023-201-2 **$18.99**

Also Available: **The Way Into Jewish Prayer Teacher's Guide**
By Rabbi Jennifer Ossakow Goldsmith

8½ x 11, 42 pp, Quality PB, 978-1-58023-345-3 **$8.99**
Visit our website to download a free copy.

The Way Into Judaism and the Environment
By Jeremy Benstein, PhD

Explores the ways in which Judaism contributes to contemporary social-environmental issues, the extent to which Judaism is part of the problem and how it can be part of the solution.

6 x 9, 288 pp, Quality PB, 978-1-58023-368-2 **$18.99**; HC, 978-1-58023-268-5 **$24.99**

The Way Into *Tikkun Olam* (Repairing the World)
By Rabbi Elliot N. Dorff, PhD

An accessible introduction to the Jewish concept of the individual's responsibility to care for others and repair the world.

6 x 9, 304 pp, Quality PB, 978-1-58023-328-6 **$18.99**; 320 pp, HC, 978-1-58023-269-2 **$24.99**

The Way Into Torah
By Rabbi Norman J. Cohen, PhD

Helps guide in the exploration of the origins and development of Torah, explains why it should be studied and how to do it.

6 x 9, 176 pp, Quality PB, 978-1-58023-198-5 **$16.99**

The Way Into the Varieties of Jewishness
By Sylvia Barack Fishman, PhD

Explores the religious and historical understanding of what it has meant to be Jewish from ancient times to the present controversy over "Who is a Jew?"

6 x 9, 288 pp, Quality PB, 978-1-58023-367-5 **$18.99**; HC, 978-1-58023-030-8 **$24.99**

Spirituality/Prayer

Making Prayer Real: Leading Jewish Spiritual Voices on Why Prayer Is Difficult and What to Do about It *By Rabbi Mike Comins*
A new and different response to the challenges of Jewish prayer, with "best prayer practices" from Jewish spiritual leaders of all denominations.
6 x 9, 320 pp, Quality PB, 978-1-58023-417-7 **$18.99**

Witnesses to the One: The Spiritual History of the *Sh'ma*
By Rabbi Joseph B. Meszler; Foreword by Rabbi Elyse Goldstein
6 x 9, 176 pp, Quality PB, 978-1-58023-400-9 **$16.99**; HC, 978-1-58023-309-5 **$19.99**

My People's Prayer Book Series: Traditional Prayers, Modern Commentaries *Edited by Rabbi Lawrence A. Hoffman, PhD*
Provides diverse and exciting commentary to the traditional liturgy. Will help you find new wisdom in Jewish prayer, and bring liturgy into your life. Each book includes Hebrew text, modern translations and commentaries from all perspectives of the Jewish world.

Vol. 1—The *Sh'ma* and Its Blessings
7 x 10, 168 pp, HC, 978-1-879045-79-8 **$29.99**
Vol. 2—The *Amidah* 7 x 10, 240 pp, HC, 978-1-879045-80-4 **$24.95**
Vol. 3—*P'sukei D'zimrah* (Morning Psalms)
7 x 10, 240 pp, HC, 978-1-879045-81-1 **$29.99**
Vol. 4—*Seder K'riat Hatorah* (The Torah Service)
7 x 10, 264 pp, HC, 978-1-879045-82-8 **$29.99**
Vol. 5—*Birkhot Hashachar* (Morning Blessings)
7 x 10, 240 pp, HC, 978-1-879045-83-5 **$24.95**
Vol. 6—*Tachanun* and Concluding Prayers
7 x 10, 240 pp, HC, 978-1-879045-84-2 **$24.95**
Vol. 7—Shabbat at Home 7 x 10, 240 pp, HC, 978-1-879045-85-9 **$24.95**
Vol. 8—*Kabbalat Shabbat* (Welcoming Shabbat in the Synagogue)
7 x 10, 240 pp, HC, 978-1-58023-121-3 **$24.99**
Vol. 9—Welcoming the Night: *Minchah* and *Ma'ariv* (Afternoon and Evening Prayer) 7 x 10, 272 pp, HC, 978-1-58023-262-3 **$24.99**
Vol. 10—Shabbat Morning: *Shacharit* and *Musaf* (Morning and Additional Services) 7 x 10, 240 pp, HC, 978-1-58023-240-1 **$29.99**

Spirituality/Lawrence Kushner

I'm God; You're Not: Observations on Organized Religion & Other Disguises of the Ego
6 x 9, 256 pp, HC, 978-1-58023-441-2 **$21.99**

The Book of Letters: A Mystical Hebrew Alphabet
Popular HC Edition, 6 x 9, 80 pp, 2-color text, 978-1-879045-00-2 **$24.95**
Collector's Limited Edition, 9 x 12, 80 pp, gold-foil-embossed pages, w/ limited-edition silkscreened print, 978-1-879045-04-0 **$349.00**

The Book of Miracles: A Young Person's Guide to Jewish Spiritual Awareness
6 x 9, 96 pp, 2-color illus., HC, 978-1-879045-78-1 **$16.95** *For ages 9–13*

The Book of Words: Talking Spiritual Life, Living Spiritual Talk
6 x 9, 160 pp, Quality PB, 978-1-58023-020-9 **$18.99**

Eyes Remade for Wonder: A Lawrence Kushner Reader *Introduction by Thomas Moore*
6 x 9, 240 pp, Quality PB, 978-1-58023-042-1 **$18.95**

God Was in This Place & I, i Did Not Know: Finding Self, Spirituality and Ultimate Meaning 6 x 9, 192 pp, Quality PB, 978-1-879045-33-0 **$16.95**

Honey from the Rock: An Introduction to Jewish Mysticism
6 x 9, 176 pp, Quality PB, 978-1-58023-073-5 **$16.95**

Invisible Lines of Connection: Sacred Stories of the Ordinary
5½ x 8½, 160 pp, Quality PB, 978-1-879045-98-9 **$15.95**

Jewish Spirituality: A Brief Introduction for Christians
5½ x 8½, 112 pp, Quality PB, 978-1-58023-150-3 **$12.95**

The River of Light: Jewish Mystical Awareness
6 x 9, 192 pp, Quality PB, 978-1-58023-096-4 **$16.95**

The Way Into Jewish Mystical Tradition
6 x 9, 224 pp, Quality PB, 978-1-58023-200-5 **$18.99**; HC, 978-1-58023-029-2 **$21.95**

Spirituality

Repentance: The Meaning and Practice of *Teshuvah*
By Dr. Louis E. Newman; Foreword by Rabbi Harold M. Schulweis; Preface by Rabbi Karyn D. Kedar
Examines both the practical and philosophical dimensions of *teshuvah*, Judaism's core religious-moral teaching on repentance, and its value for us—Jews and non-Jews alike—today. 6 x 9, 256 pp, HC, 978-1-58023-426-9 **$24.99**

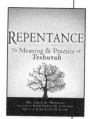

Tanya, the Masterpiece of Hasidic Wisdom
Selections Annotated & Explained
Translation & Annotation by Rabbi Rami Shapiro; Foreword by Rabbi Zalman M. Schachter-Shalomi
Brings the genius of *Tanya*, one of the most powerful books of Jewish wisdom, to anyone seeking to deepen their understanding of the soul.
5½ x 8½, 240 pp, Quality PB, 978-1-59473-275-1 **$16.99**
(A book from SkyLight Paths, Jewish Lights' sister imprint)

Aleph-Bet Yoga: Embodying the Hebrew Letters for Physical and Spiritual Well-Being
By Steven A. Rapp; Foreword by Tamar Frankiel, PhD, and Judy Greenfeld; Preface by Hart Lazer
7 x 10, 128 pp, b/w photos, Quality PB, Lay-flat binding, 978-1-58023-162-6 **$16.95**

A Book of Life: Embracing Judaism as a Spiritual Practice
By Rabbi Michael Strassfeld 6 x 9, 544 pp, Quality PB, 978-1-58023-247-0 **$19.99**

Bringing the Psalms to Life: How to Understand and Use the Book of Psalms
By Rabbi Daniel F. Polish, PhD 6 x 9, 208 pp, Quality PB, 978-1-58023-157-2 **$16.95**

Does the Soul Survive? A Jewish Journey to Belief in Afterlife, Past Lives & Living with Purpose *By Rabbi Elie Kaplan Spitz; Foreword by Brian L. Weiss, MD*
6 x 9, 288 pp, Quality PB, 978-1-58023-165-7 **$16.99**

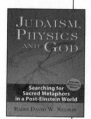

First Steps to a New Jewish Spirit: Reb Zalman's Guide to Recapturing the Intimacy & Ecstasy in Your Relationship with God *By Rabbi Zalman M. Schachter-Shalomi with Donald Gropman* 6 x 9, 144 pp, Quality PB, 978-1-58023-182-4 **$16.95**

Foundations of Sephardic Spirituality: The Inner Life of Jews of the Ottoman Empire
By Rabbi Marc D. Angel, PhD 6 x 9, 224 pp, Quality PB, 978-1-58023-341-5 **$18.99**

God & the Big Bang: Discovering Harmony between Science & Spirituality
By Dr. Daniel C. Matt 6 x 9, 216 pp, Quality PB, 978-1-879045-89-7 **$16.99**

God in Our Relationships: Spirituality between People from the Teachings of Martin Buber *By Rabbi Dennis S. Ross* 5½ x 8½, 160 pp, Quality PB, 978-1-58023-147-3 **$16.95**

The Jewish Lights Spirituality Handbook: A Guide to Understanding, Exploring & Living a Spiritual Life *Edited by Stuart M. Matlins*
What exactly is "Jewish" about spirituality? How do I make it a part of my life? Fifty of today's foremost spiritual leaders share their ideas and experience with us.
6 x 9, 456 pp, Quality PB, 978-1-58023-093-3 **$19.99**

Judaism, Physics and God: Searching for Sacred Metaphors in a Post-Einstein World
By Rabbi David W. Nelson 6 x 9, 352 pp, Quality PB, inc. reader's discussion guide,
978-1-58023-306-4 **$18.99**; HC, 352 pp, 978-1-58023-252-4 **$24.99**

Meaning & Mitzvah: Daily Practices for Reclaiming Judaism through Prayer, God, Torah, Hebrew, Mitzvot and Peoplehood *By Rabbi Goldie Milgram*
7 x 9, 336 pp, Quality PB, 978-1-58023-256-2 **$19.99**

Minding the Temple of the Soul: Balancing Body, Mind, and Spirit through Traditional Jewish Prayer, Movement, and Meditation *By Tamar Frankiel, PhD, and Judy Greenfeld*
7 x 10, 184 pp, Illus., Quality PB, 978-1-879045-64-4 **$18.99**

One God Clapping: The Spiritual Path of a Zen Rabbi *By Rabbi Alan Lew with Sherril Jaffe*
5½ x 8½, 336 pp, Quality PB, 978-1-58023-115-2 **$16.95**

The Soul of the Story: Meetings with Remarkable People
By Rabbi David Zeller 6 x 9, 288 pp, HC, 978-1-58023-272-2 **$21.99**

There Is No Messiah ... and You're It: The Stunning Transformation of Judaism's Most Provocative Idea *By Rabbi Robert N. Levine, DD*
6 x 9, 192 pp, Quality PB, 978-1-58023-255-5 **$16.99**

These Are the Words: A Vocabulary of Jewish Spiritual Life
By Rabbi Arthur Green, PhD 6 x 9, 304 pp, Quality PB, 978-1-58023-107-7 **$18.95**

Holidays/Holy Days

Who by Fire, Who by Water—Un'taneh Tokef
Edited by Rabbi Lawrence A. Hoffman, PhD
Examines the prayer's theology, authorship and poetry through a set of lively essays, all written in accessible language.
6 x 9, 272 pp, HC, 978-1-58023-424-5 **$24.99**

All These Vows—Kol Nidre
Edited by Rabbi Lawrence A. Hoffman, PhD
The most memorable prayer of the Jewish New Year—what it means, why we sing it, and the secret of its magical appeal.
6 x 9, 288 pp, HC, 978-1-58023-430-6 **$24.99**

Rosh Hashanah Readings: Inspiration, Information and Contemplation
Yom Kippur Readings: Inspiration, Information and Contemplation
Edited by Rabbi Dov Peretz Elkins; Section Introductions from Arthur Green's These Are the Words
Rosh Hashanah: 6 x 9, 400 pp, Quality PB, 978-1-58023-437-5 **$19.99**; HC, 978-1-58023-239-5 **$24.99**
Yom Kippur: 6 x 9, 368 pp, Quality PB, 978-1-58023-438-2 **$19.99**; HC, 978-1-58023-271-5 **$24.99**

Jewish Holidays: A Brief Introduction for Christians
By Rabbi Kerry M. Olitzky and Rabbi Daniel Judson
5½ x 8½, 176 pp, Quality PB, 978-1-58023-302-6 **$16.99**

Reclaiming Judaism as a Spiritual Practice: Holy Days and Shabbat
By Rabbi Goldie Milgram 7 x 9, 272 pp, Quality PB, 978-1-58023-205-0 **$19.99**

Shabbat, 2nd Edition: The Family Guide to Preparing for and Celebrating the Sabbath
By Dr. Ron Wolfson 7 x 9, 320 pp, Illus., Quality PB, 978-1-58023-164-0 **$19.99**

Hanukkah, 2nd Edition: The Family Guide to Spiritual Celebration
By Dr. Ron Wolfson 7 x 9, 240 pp, Illus., Quality PB, 978-1-58023-122-0 **$18.95**

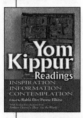

The Jewish Family Fun Book, 2nd Edition
Holiday Projects, Everyday Activities, and Travel Ideas with Jewish Themes
By Danielle Dardashti and Roni Sarig; Illus. by Avi Katz
6 x 9, 304 pp, 70+ b/w illus. & diagrams, Quality PB, 978-1-58023-333-0 **$18.99**

Passover

My People's Passover Haggadah
Traditional Texts, Modern Commentaries
Edited by Rabbi Lawrence A. Hoffman, PhD, and David Arnow, PhD
A diverse and exciting collection of commentaries on the traditional Passover Haggadah—in two volumes!
Vol. 1: 7 x 10, 304 pp, HC, 978-1-58023-354-5 **$24.99**
Vol. 2: 7 x 10, 320 pp, HC, 978-1-58023-346-0 **$24.99**

Freedom Journeys: The Tale of Exodus and Wilderness across Millennia
By Rabbi Arthur O. Waskow and Rabbi Phyllis O. Berman
Explores how the story of Exodus echoes in our own time, calling us to relearn and rethink the Passover story through social-justice, ecological, feminist and interfaith perspectives. 6 x 9, 288 pp, HC, 978-1-58023-445-0 **$24.99**

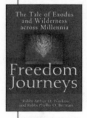

Leading the Passover Journey: The Seder's Meaning Revealed,
the Haggadah's Story Retold *By Rabbi Nathan Laufer*
Uncovers the hidden meaning of the Seder's rituals and customs.
6 x 9, 224 pp, Quality PB, 978-1-58023-399-6 **$18.99**; HC, 978-1-58023-211-1 **$24.99**

Creating Lively Passover Seders, 2nd Edition: A Sourcebook of Engaging Tales,
Texts & Activities *By David Arnow, PhD* 7 x 9, 464 pp, Quality PB, 978-1-58023-444-3 **$24.99**

Passover, 2nd Edition: The Family Guide to Spiritual Celebration
By Dr. Ron Wolfson with Joel Lurie Grishaver 7 x 9, 416 pp, Quality PB, 978-1-58023-174-9 **$19.95**

The Women's Passover Companion: Women's Reflections on the Festival of Freedom
Edited by Rabbi Sharon Cohen Anisfeld, Tara Mohr and Catherine Spector; Foreword by Paula E. Hyman
6 x 9, 352 pp, Quality PB, 978-1-58023-231-9 **$19.99**; HC, 978-1-58023-128-2 **$24.95**

The Women's Seder Sourcebook: Rituals & Readings for Use at the Passover Seder
Edited by Rabbi Sharon Cohen Anisfeld, Tara Mohr and Catherine Spector
6 x 9, 384 pp, Quality PB, 978-1-58023-232-6 **$19.99**

Life Cycle
Marriage/Parenting/Family/Aging

The New Jewish Baby Album: Creating and Celebrating the Beginning of a Spiritual Life—A Jewish Lights Companion
By the Editors at Jewish Lights; Foreword by Anita Diamant; Preface by Rabbi Sandy Eisenberg Sasso
A spiritual keepsake that will be treasured for generations. More than just a memory book, *shows you how—and why it's important*—to create a Jewish home and a Jewish life. 8 x 10, 64 pp, Deluxe Padded HC, Full-color illus., 978-1-58023-138-1 **$19.95**

The Jewish Pregnancy Book: A Resource for the Soul, Body & Mind during Pregnancy, Birth & the First Three Months *By Sandy Falk, MD, and Rabbi Daniel Judson, with Steven A. Rapp* Medical information, prayers and rituals for each stage of pregnancy. 7 x 10, 208 pp, b/w photos, Quality PB, 978-1-58023-178-7 **$16.95**

Celebrating Your New Jewish Daughter: Creating Jewish Ways to Welcome Baby Girls into the Covenant—New and Traditional Ceremonies *By Debra Nussbaum Cohen; Foreword by Rabbi Sandy Eisenberg Sasso* 6 x 9, 272 pp, Quality PB, 978-1-58023-090-2 **$18.95**

The New Jewish Baby Book, 2nd Edition: Names, Ceremonies & Customs—A Guide for Today's Families *By Anita Diamant* 6 x 9, 320 pp, Quality PB, 978-1-58023-251-7 **$19.99**

Parenting as a Spiritual Journey: Deepening Ordinary and Extraordinary Events into Sacred Occasions *By Rabbi Nancy Fuchs-Kreimer, PhD*
6 x 9, 224 pp, Quality PB, 978-1-58023-016-2 **$17.99**

Parenting Jewish Teens: A Guide for the Perplexed
By Joanne Doades Explores the questions and issues that shape the world in which today's Jewish teenagers live and offers constructive advice to parents.
6 x 9, 176 pp, Quality PB, 978-1-58023-305-7 **$16.99**

Judaism for Two: A Spiritual Guide for Strengthening and Celebrating Your Loving Relationship *By Rabbi Nancy Fuchs-Kreimer, PhD, and Rabbi Nancy H. Wiener, DMin; Foreword by Rabbi Elliot N. Dorff, PhD*
Addresses the ways Jewish teachings can enhance and strengthen committed relationships. 6 x 9, 224 pp, Quality PB, 978-1-58023-254-8 **$16.99**

The Creative Jewish Wedding Book, 2nd Edition: A Hands-On Guide to New & Old Traditions, Ceremonies & Celebrations *By Gabrielle Kaplan-Mayer*
9 x 9, 288 pp, b/w photos, Quality PB, 978-1-58023-398-9 **$19.99**

Divorce Is a Mitzvah: A Practical Guide to Finding Wholeness and Holiness When Your Marriage Dies *By Rabbi Perry Netter; Afterword by Rabbi Laura Geller*
6 x 9, 224 pp, Quality PB, 978-1-58023-172-5 **$16.95**

Embracing the Covenant: Converts to Judaism Talk About Why & How
By Rabbi Allan Berkowitz and Patti Moskovitz 6 x 9, 192 pp, Quality PB, 978-1-879045-50-7 **$16.95**

The Guide to Jewish Interfaith Family Life: An InterfaithFamily.com Handbook
Edited by Ronnie Friedland and Edmund Case
6 x 9, 384 pp, Quality PB, 978-1-58023-153-4 **$18.95**

A Heart of Wisdom: Making the Jewish Journey from Midlife through the Elder Years
Edited by Susan Berrin; Foreword by Rabbi Harold Kushner
6 x 9, 384 pp, Quality PB, 978-1-58023-051-3 **$18.95**

Introducing My Faith and My Community: The Jewish Outreach Institute Guide for the Christian in a Jewish Interfaith Relationship
By Rabbi Kerry M. Olitzky 6 x 9, 176 pp, Quality PB, 978-1-58023-192-3 **$16.99**

Making a Successful Jewish Interfaith Marriage: The Jewish Outreach Institute Guide to Opportunities, Challenges and Resources *By Rabbi Kerry M. Olitzky with Joan Peterson Littman*
6 x 9, 176 pp, Quality PB, 978-1-58023-170-1 **$16.95**

A Man's Responsibility: A Jewish Guide to Being a Son, a Partner in Marriage, a Father and a Community Leader *By Rabbi Joseph B. Meszler*
6 x 9, 192 pp, Quality PB, 978-1-58023-435-1 **$16.99**; HC, 978-1-58023-362-0 **$21.99**

So That Your Values Live On: Ethical Wills and How to Prepare Them
Edited by Rabbi Jack Riemer and Rabbi Nathaniel Stampfer
6 x 9, 272 pp, Quality PB, 978-1-879045-34-7 **$18.99**

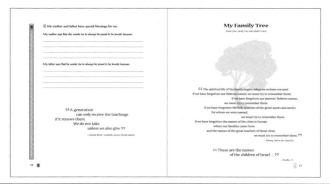

Bar/Bat Mitzvah

The JGirl's Guide: The Young Jewish Woman's Handbook for Coming of Age
By Penina Adelman, Ali Feldman, and Shulamit Reinharz
This inspirational, interactive guidebook helps pre-teen Jewish girls address the many issues surrounding coming of age. 6 x 9, 240 pp, Quality PB, 978-1-58023-215-9 **$14.99**
   Also Available: **The JGirl's Teacher's and Parent's Guide**
   8½ x 11, 56 pp, PB, 978-1-58023-225-8 **$8.99**

Bar/Bat Mitzvah Basics: A Practical Family Guide to Coming of Age Together
Edited by Cantor Helen Leneman 6 x 9, 240 pp, Quality PB, 978-1-58023-151-0 **$18.95**

The Bar/Bat Mitzvah Memory Book, 2nd Edition: An Album for Treasuring the Spiritual Celebration *By Rabbi Jeffrey K. Salkin and Nina Salkin*
8 x 10, 48 pp, Deluxe HC, 2-color text, ribbon marker, 978-1-58023-263-0 **$19.99**

For Kids—Putting God on Your Guest List, 2nd Edition: How to Claim the Spiritual Meaning of Your Bar or Bat Mitzvah *By Rabbi Jeffrey K. Salkin*
6 x 9, 144 pp, Quality PB, 978-1-58023-308-8 **$15.99** *For ages 11–13*

Putting God on the Guest List, 3rd Edition: How to Reclaim the Spiritual Meaning of Your Child's Bar or Bat Mitzvah *By Rabbi Jeffrey K. Salkin*
6 x 9, 224 pp, Quality PB, 978-1-58023-222-7 **$16.99**; HC, 978-1-58023-260-9 **$24.99**
   Also Available: **Putting God on the Guest List Teacher's Guide**
   8½ x 11, 48 pp, PB, 978-1-58023-226-5 **$8.99**

Tough Questions Jews Ask: A Young Adult's Guide to Building a Jewish Life
By Rabbi Edward Feinstein 6 x 9, 160 pp, Quality PB, 978-1-58023-139-8 **$14.99** *For ages 12 & up*
   Also Available: **Tough Questions Jews Ask Teacher's Guide**
   8½ x 11, 72 pp, PB, 978-1-58023-187-9 **$8.95**

Bible Study/Midrash

The Modern Men's Torah Commentary: New Insights from Jewish Men on the 54 Weekly Torah Portions *Edited by Rabbi Jeffrey K. Salkin*
A major contribution to modern biblical commentary. Addresses the most important concerns of *modern* men by opening them up to the life of Torah.
6 x 9, 368 pp, HC, 978-1-58023-395-8 **$24.99**

The Genesis of Leadership: What the Bible Teaches Us about Vision, Values and Leading Change *By Rabbi Nathan Laufer; Foreword by Senator Joseph I. Lieberman*
Unlike other books on leadership, this one is rooted in the stories of the Bible.
6 x 9, 288 pp, Quality PB, 978-1-58023-352-1 **$18.99**; HC, 978-1-58023-241-8 **$24.99**

Hineini in Our Lives: Learning How to Respond to Others through 14 Biblical Texts and Personal Stories *By Norman J. Cohen* 6 x 9, 240 pp, Quality PB, 978-1-58023-274-6 **$16.99**

Moses and the Journey to Leadership: Timeless Lessons of Effective Management from the Bible and Today's Leaders *By Dr. Norman J. Cohen*
6 x 9, 240 pp, Quality PB, 978-1-58023-351-4 **$18.99**; HC, 978-1-58023-227-2 **$21.99**

Self, Struggle & Change: Family Conflict Stories in Genesis and Their Healing Insights for Our Lives *By Norman J. Cohen* 6 x 9, 224 pp, Quality PB, 978-1-879045-66-8 **$18.99**

The Triumph of Eve & Other Subversive Bible Tales *By Matt Biers-Ariel*
5½ x 8½, 192 pp, Quality PB, 978-1-59473-176-1 **$14.99**; HC, 978-1-59473-040-5 **$19.99**
(A book from SkyLight Paths, Jewish Lights' sister imprint)

The Wisdom of Judaism: An Introduction to the Values of the Talmud
By Rabbi Dov Peretz Elkins
Explores the essence of Judaism. 6 x 9, 192 pp, Quality PB, 978-1-58023-327-9 **$16.99**
   Also Available: **The Wisdom of Judaism Teacher's Guide**
   8½ x 11, 18 pp, PB, 978-1-58023-350-7 **$8.99**

Or phone, fax, mail or e-mail to: **JEWISH LIGHTS Publishing**
Sunset Farm Offices, Route 4 • P.O. Box 237 • Woodstock, Vermont 05091
Tel: (802) 457-4000 • Fax: (802) 457-4004 • www.jewishlights.com
Credit card orders: (800) 962-4544 (8:30AM–5:30PM ET Monday–Friday)
Generous discounts on quantity orders. SATISFACTION GUARANTEED. Prices subject to change.

About Jewish Lights

People of all faiths and backgrounds yearn for books that attract, engage, educate, and spiritually inspire.

Our principal goal is to stimulate thought and help all people learn about who the Jewish People are, where they come from, and what the future can be made to hold. While people of our diverse Jewish heritage are the primary audience, our books speak to people in the Christian world as well and will broaden their understanding of Judaism and the roots of their own faith.

We bring to you authors who are at the forefront of spiritual thought and experience. While each has something different to say, they all say it in a voice that you can hear.

Our books are designed to welcome you and then to engage, stimulate, and inspire. We judge our success not only by whether or not our books are beautiful and commercially successful, but by whether or not they make a difference in your life.

For your information and convenience, at the back of this book we have provided a list of other Jewish Lights books you might find interesting and useful. They cover all the categories of your life:

Bar/Bat Mitzvah	Life Cycle
Bible Study / Midrash	Meditation
Children's Books	Men's Interest
Congregation Resources	Parenting
Current Events / History	Prayer / Ritual / Sacred Practice
Ecology / Environment	Social Justice
Fiction: Mystery, Science Fiction	Spirituality
Grief / Healing	Theology / Philosophy
Holidays / Holy Days	Travel
Inspiration	12-Step
Kabbalah / Mysticism / Enneagram	Women's Interest

Stuart M. Matlins, Publisher

Or phone, fax, mail or e-mail to: **JEWISH LIGHTS Publishing**
Sunset Farm Offices, Route 4 • P.O. Box 237 • Woodstock, Vermont 05091
Tel: (802) 457-4000 • Fax: (802) 457-4004 • www.jewishlights.com
Credit card orders: **(800) 962-4544** (8:30AM–5:30PM ET Monday–Friday)
Generous discounts on quantity orders. SATISFACTION GUARANTEED. Prices subject to change.

For more information about each book, visit our website at www.jewishlights.com